W9-ADB-876

THE PRINTED
WORD

THE PRINTED
WORD

Professional Word Processing
with Microsoft® Word
on the Apple® Macintosh™

David A. Kater
Richard L. Kater

MICROSOFT.
PRESS

Burgess

Z
52.5
.M52
K37
1985

C.1

PUBLISHED BY
Microsoft Press
A Division of Microsoft Corporation
10700 Northup Way, Box 97200, Bellevue, Washington 98009

Copyright © 1985 by David A. Kater, Richard L. Kater
All rights reserved. No part of the contents of this book may be reproduced or transmitted in any form or by any means without the written permission of the publisher.

Library of Congress Cataloging in Publication Data
Kater, David A.
The printed word.
Includes index.
1. Word processing.   2. Microsoft Word (Computer program)
3. Macintosh (Computer)—Programming.   I. Kater, Richard L.
II. Title.
Z52.5.M52K37   1985   652'.5   85-13860
ISBN 0-914845-53-5

Printed and bound in the United States of America.

1 2 3 4 5 6 7 8 9 FGFG 8 9 0 9 8 7 6 5

Distributed to the book trade in the United States by Harper and Row.

Distributed to the book trade in Canada by General Publishing Company, Ltd.

Distributed to the book trade outside the United States and Canada
by Penguin Books Ltd.

Penguin Books Ltd., Harmondsworth, Middlesex, England
Penguin Books Australia Ltd., Ringwood, Victoria, Australia
Penguin Books N. Z. Ltd., 182-190 Wairau Road, Auckland 10, New Zealand

British Cataloging in Publication Data available

PostScript™ is a trademark of Adobe Systems, Incorporated. Linotron® 202 is a registered trademark of Allied Corporation. FONTastic™ is a trademark of Altsys Corporation. Animation Toolkit™ and Font Blaster™ are trademarks of Ann Arbor Softworks, Incorporated. Apple® is a registered trademark and AppleTalk™, Image-Writer™, LaserWriter™, MacDraw™, MacPaint™, and MacWrite™ are trademarks of, and Macintosh™ is a trademark licensed to, Apple Computer, Incorporated. Fluent Fonts™ is a trademark of Casady Company. Blue Mac™ is a trademark of Cogitate, Incorporated. ProPrint™ is a trademark of Creighton Development, Incorporated. Epson FX-80™, FX-100™, LQ-1500™, MX-80™, MX-100™, RX-80™, and RX-100™ are trademarks of Epson America, Incorporated. IBM® and Selectric® are registered trademarks of International Business Machines Corporation. Smart Cable™ is a trademark of I. Q. Technologies. ProWriter™ is a trademark of C. Itoh Digital Products, Incorporated. Microsoft® and Multiplan® are registered trademarks and Mac-Enhancer™ is a trademark of Microsoft Corporation. Mac the Knife™ is a trademark of Miles Computing, Incorporated. NEC 2010 Spinwriter® is a registered trademark of NEC Corporation. Kaypro® is a registered trademark of Non-Linear Systems, Incorporated. Letterpro 20™ and Sprint 11™ are trademarks of Qume Corporation. Epstart™ is a trademark of SoftStyle, Incorporated. Diablo® is a registered trademark of XEROX Corporation.

To Taff, who was there
when the paper was blank.

Contents

Acknowledgments

If anyone should ask what we consider to be the most important qualifications of a publisher, we won't have to think about it. The answer is quite clear: Salley Oberlin, Tracy Smith, Ron Lamb, Joyce Cox, Barry Preppernau, Dave Rygmyr, Lia Matteson, Karen de Robinson, Debbie Kem, Stephanie Ideta, Marianne Moon, Lee Thomas, Lesley Link-Moore, and others who form a highly competent, exacting, and professional team of warm, friendly, helpful, and cooperative individuals. Writing this book with their help and guidance has been a very rewarding learning experience.

We are indebted to so many people for efforts and contributions far beyond our expectations, that it would be difficult to know where to stop. But there is no question where to start. Our editor, Ron Lamb, took our rough manuscript and transformed it into a cohesive entity. With incredible dedication, determination, and patience, he guided us through a process of rethinking, reorganizing, and rewriting. He not only reshaped the book, but, in the process, reshaped the authors. We are, most sincerely, grateful.

We were told that we could rely on Barry Preppernau, Manager, Technical Review, for technical support. We did, and he came through with timely answers, and did a thorough job of testing every shred of manuscript.

To Equipment Interface Technician Dave Rygmyr and Managing Editor Joyce Cox, we offer special thanks for a completed printing project when we needed it most.

Salley Oberlin, Editorial Director, was the active force that coordinated the total effort and pulled this book through to completion, with excellence.

Tracy Smith, Director of Acquisitions, was our first contact with Microsoft Press. She made the initial connection between our experience and this book, and she followed the progress all the way, mostly with needed encouragement.

Thanks also to Art Department Supervisor Nick Gregoric, who did the illustrations; Graphic Artist Gloria Sommer, who did the pasteup; and Typographer John D. Berry, who typeset the book.

To each of the people at Microsoft Press who contributed to this book, we can say with respect and enthusiasm, we expected the best when we first approached your company; we didn't realize what the best is until we worked with you; and we are proud to have been part of the team that produced this book.

Susan J. Thomas designed and implemented several of the printing projects in Section Three, including the newsletter and brochure. And she was invaluable in pulling us down the final stretch.

Susan Heaton and Russell Schnapp did outstanding jobs roughwriting the chapters on form letters and business forms, respectively.

Rick Boarman applied his knowledge of Word and especially of the Macintosh to keep us accurate in the early stages.

And our thanks to the EduKater staff: Ramona, Griselda, Joe, Maureen, and Tina, who kept us organized throughout the project.

David A. Kater
Richard L. Kater
San Diego, California

Introduction

In the past, the most powerful word-processing programs were also the most difficult to learn. But, with Microsoft Word for the Macintosh, that's no longer the case. Simple to learn and easy to use, Microsoft Word is the most powerful word-processing program available for the Macintosh today.

Learning Word, of course, is only the first step. The final step is creating an end product; and the end product in most cases is the printed word.

This book covers all aspects of using Word. If you're just learning about computers and word processors, you'll find all the basic information you need to use Word on the Macintosh. And, if you're already familiar with word processing, you'll learn new techniques and useful tricks for creating projects you may not have realized possible.

About This Book

Starting with the basics and finishing with professional printing projects, here's what you'll find in this book:

Section One:
Writing with Word

The four chapters in Section One introduce you to Microsoft Word. Chapter 1 is a general introduction; Chapters 2 and 3 take you step-by-step from turning on your computer through the actual typing, modifying, formatting, and printing of a sample document. These tutorial chapters will help you learn the basic features of Word so that you can confidently create your own documents. The last chapter in this section, Chapter 4, offers useful tips for saving time when using Word.

Section Two:
Printing with Word

Word is the first major application for the Macintosh that accommodates several printers other than the familiar Apple ImageWriter. In Section Two, we introduce some of the printers that operate with the Mac and show you how to set them up. We also explain the Macintosh printing process and explore the type possibilities opened up by this new technology.

Section Three:
Professional Printing
Projects

In Section Three, we show you how to apply what you learned in the first two sections to produce five professional printing projects: a form letter, a report, a newsletter, a business form, and a brochure. No matter what you plan to do with Word, you'll likely find something of use in each project.

What You Need

To get the maximum benefit from this book, you'll need a Macintosh (you can use either a 128K or the new, faster 512K Macintosh), a copy of Microsoft Word for the Mac, and at least two extra disks for storing the sample documents you'll create. A second, external disk drive is a virtual necessity, and you'll need a printer. You can print most of the sample documents on an ImageWriter, but occasionally we include a project for which we use a LaserWriter or fully formed character (often called a letter-quality) printer to produce the final product.

Now that you know what you'll need, turn to Chapter 1 to learn why Word is the most advanced word-processing program available for the Macintosh.

SECTION ONE

WRITING WITH WORD

1 Why Word?

The next time you are in a business office, look at the equipment being used to prepare letters, reports, and other documents. It's likely that typewriters have been swept into a back corner in favor of word processors—computers assigned the task of producing text. Just a quick look around should be enough to convince you that electronic word processing is fast becoming an accepted part of the business communication world.

One of the major reasons for this acceptance is that electronic word processing frees you from the limitations of a typewriter, allowing you to concentrate on creating and polishing your text. You can make corrections, move text from one place to another, or reshape the appearance of your document—while you are typing or a week later. And you can do all this on the screen, before you print anything on paper.

Word processors are loaded with useful features. But having a lot of features can make learning to use a word processor a tedious chore. Each additional feature usually means another sequence of keystrokes to memorize. Apple, with its creation of the Macintosh, has simplified the process of learning to use a word processor in several ways.

The Macintosh Difference

The three most important differences between the Mac and other computers are its use of pull-down menus, the fact that the programs designed for it all work in similar ways, and its graphics-oriented screen display.

Pull-Down Menus

With the Macintosh, you do not have to learn specialized codes to activate commands. Instead, you use a pointing device called a mouse to choose each command from a list of options called a menu. For instance, to boldface a word, you just mark the word by pointing to it using the mouse, then choose the boldface command from a menu of character style commands. The process of using the mouse to choose commands from a menu is so simple and natural that you will probably remember most of what you learn after only one session.

Uniform Software Design

Another subtle, but powerful feature of learning on the Mac is the consistency of design between programs written for the Mac. Once you learn how to select text in one program, for instance, you don't have to relearn the process for each new program.

Graphic Orientation

One of the Mac's most intriguing factors is its graphics-oriented display. The characters are displayed on the screen immediately, just as they will appear in the printout. This visual feedback lets you know whether to proceed or stop and correct what you see on the Mac screen before printing. You can also pull pictures from graphics programs, such as MacPaint and Chart, and display them on your word-processing screen.

Even more impressive is the way the Macintosh can reproduce this graphics screen image on a variety of printers, including the Laser-Writer and ImageWriter. This visual fidelity between screen images and their printed counterparts, depicted in Figure 1-1, is sometimes described with the phrase "what you see is what you get."

Advantages of Word

Until Microsoft introduced Word, the only word-processing program available for the Macintosh was MacWrite. MacWrite is a good showcase for the Macintosh design, because it uses the pull-down menus, graphics-oriented screen, and a selection of different type sizes and styles. But MacWrite lacks many of the advanced features required in serious word processing: multiple-column printing, footnotes, form-letter printing, and the ability to work with letter-quality printers.

Microsoft Word adds the power of a professional word-processing program to the Mac. You will discover the real depth of this power as you read through the rest of this book and experiment with the program on your own. As a preliminary introduction in this chapter, we picked some of the features that make Word so powerful. We will develop and discuss applications for many of these and other features in Section Three of this book.

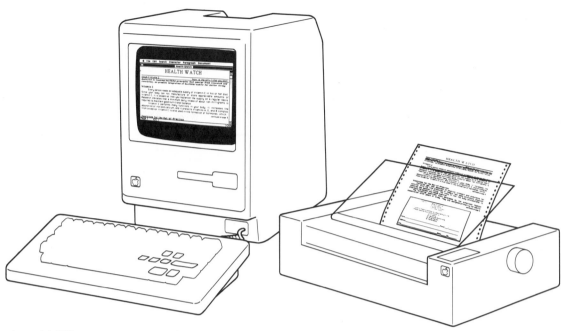

Figure 1-1. What you see
is what you get

**Formatting of Characters
and Paragraphs**

Word's formatting features demonstrate its quality and power. While
all word-processing programs provide some formatting, Word provides more than any other.

You can select commands representing the four distinctly different
types of formatting: character, paragraph, page, and document. By
using these menus, you can control, in detail, nearly any aspect of the
appearance of your document, from page numbering to the type style
of a selected word, or even a single character. As an example of the
kinds of options available, most word processors only allow you to left-
align tabular material. Some word processors also let you set tabs so
that you can align decimal numbers on the decimal points. Word allows you to align text and numbers to the left or right, to center them,
or to align tabular material on the decimal.

**Opening More than
One Window**

One of Word's unprecedented features is its ability to display as many
as four separate windows on the screen at one time. Figure 1-2 shows
how someone might use four different windows to create a newsletter,
with an outline in one window, a project plan in another, notes in another, and the newsletter itself in the fourth.

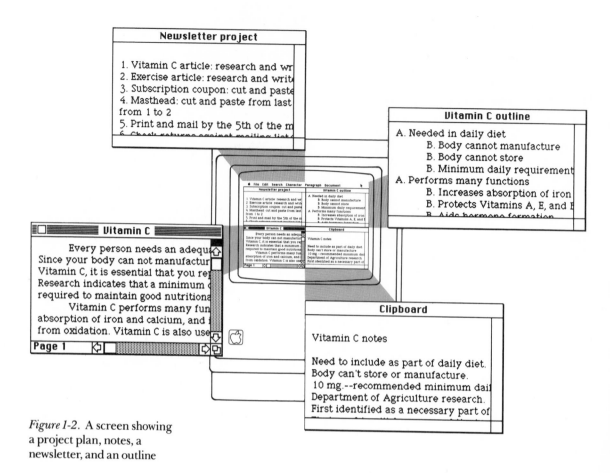

Figure 1-2. A screen showing a project plan, notes, a newsletter, and an outline

Word's windowing capability means that, when writing a report, you can display your document, notes, and outline in separate windows on the screen, rather than having papers scattered all over your desk. You can easily transfer blocks of text from the notes to the document. More than that, you can split a window in half to view two different parts of the same document at the same time. For example, if you are writing a summary at the end of your document, you can refer back to other portions of the document to see how you worded the original text.

Storing Repetitious Text

A characteristic that distinguishes Word as a sophisticated word processor is its ability to handle certain key applications. For example, someone who prepares legal documents or technical specifications will consistently reuse standardized blocks of text. Word has a feature called a glossary that enables you to store text blocks and recall them by using codes that you assign.

Formatting for Multiple-Column and Wide Formats

If you are producing a newsletter or other publication, you'll be glad to know that Word can format documents in multiple columns if you need them. Using multiple columns, you can even print text and graphics so they appear on the same line.

If you want to print your document sideways on the paper to accommodate, for example, a wide form or a financial spreadsheet, Word can tell a printer to print sideways.

Printing Letter-Quality Documents

If you have been hesitant about buying a Macintosh because you need typewriter-quality printing, you may put aside your hesitation when you learn that Word opens the door to many widely used letter-quality printers.

A Few Regrets

Are we enthusiastic about Microsoft Word for the Macintosh? You bet. But no word processor can provide all things for all people, and Word is no exception to that rule. We miss some of the features we've become accustomed to on other word-processing programs.

For instance, although the IBM PC version of Word lets you store formats for several different kinds of paragraphs in a file called a style sheet, Word on the Macintosh does not. In Chapter 4, we suggest a method for approximating a style sheet for the Mac version of Word. And, we miss being able to call up a record of keystrokes or commands, called a macro, that can do a lot of routine actions, such as moving paragraphs. Word can record text characters, but it does not remember where you've been or which commands you've used.

Also, Word allows only four discrete page sizes, which limits your ability to set page lengths and makes a task such as printing a single 6-inch mailing label unnecessarily complicated.

Although we miss these features, we feel more than compensated by the powerful features Word does have. The Mac/Word combination clearly sets a new standard for state-of-the-art microcomputer word processing. We have the pleasure of probing its abilities with you throughout the rest of this book, beginning with the next three chapters, which should help you develop the necessary basic tools to explore further.

2 Getting down to basics

What, more preliminaries? Don't despair. After a few necessary preparations, you will soon be doing creative things on that Macintosh. We'll take you quickly through setting up and turning on your Mac, take a look at the Mac environment, then we'll show you step-by-step how to make a copy of your Word Master disk.

Getting Started

With your Word Master disk at your side and your computer on your desk in front of you, you're ready to roll. First, turn on the power switch, located at the back of the Mac just above the power-cable plug.

Flip the switch.

The Macintosh beeps and the screen lights up to display a gray background, a black arrow, and a representation of a disk with a flashing question mark on it. The arrow, called the mouse pointer, or just the pointer, marks your place on the screen and shows you where the next action will occur. You can move the pointer by sliding the mouse around. Go ahead and try it; you can't hurt anything.

Inserting the Disk

The flashing question mark on the disk symbol on your screen is there to remind you that you need to insert a disk into the disk drive. Before you insert the Word Master disk, you should take a simple but important precaution. To avoid accidentally removing needed information from your only copy of the Word Master disk, you should "write protect" the disk before using it. This is a simple operation. You just slide the little black plastic write-protect tab to the write-protect position. When the tab is in the write-protect position, you can see through the square hole.

The write-protect tab controls the disk drive's ability to record, or write, information onto the disk. When the tab is in the write-protect position, the drive can neither write information onto the disk nor erase anything. It can only read or copy information that is already on the disk, which is all you want to do for now.

One more thing before you insert the disk. You need to break the licensing-agreement seal that covers one corner of the metal protective shutter so that the shutter is free to slide back and forth. (By breaking the licensing-agreement seal, you're indicating acceptance of the contractual conditions for using the program. If you are interested in such things, you will find these contractual conditions on the inside back cover of the manual.)

Carefully break the seal.

You can use your thumbnail to cut the seal, or you can hold the disk firmly by the edges in one hand and slide the shutter open with the other hand. Be careful not to squeeze the two halves of the plastic housing or shutter together and be careful not to touch the exposed surface of the disk while the shutter is open. Even a fingerprint on the delicate surface of the disk can cause the drive to mis-read the information stored there.

Now, insert the Word Master disk.

You should insert the disk, shutter first, with the label up. Use your finger to push the disk into the drive until the disk pops into position.

As soon as the disk is in the drive, you'll hear the drive start up and you'll see the following sequence on the screen: a representation of a Macintosh with a smiling face, a "Welcome to Macintosh" sign, and, until the disk drive stops, a tiny wristwatch. The watch indicates that you have to wait while the computer does some work. You will see the watch frequently as you use the Mac and Word. When the watch changes to the pointer you saw earlier, it means that the computer is now waiting for you to tell it what to do next. In the meantime, the screen has changed and now displays what is called the desktop.

Exploring the Desktop

The Macintosh screen display was designed to represent the area on and around a desk in an office. You can use the items you see on this electronic desktop to do tasks similar to those you would do while sitting at a real desk. For example, you can move documents around, you can label them, you can put them into file folders, and you can even toss them into the trash.

Icons: Visual Symbols

Each item on the desktop is represented by a small picture called an icon. The picture labeled Word Master is an icon for the disk you've just inserted. The picture of a trash can in the lower right corner is an icon, too. Trash is the place you put documents and files that you no longer need.

Ordering from the Menus

The white band across the top of the screen is called the menu bar. Starting at the far left, the menu bar contains an Apple symbol and the words File, Edit, View, and Special. As the word "menu" suggests, each of these items offers you a list of commands you can choose. You use the commands to give your orders to the Mac. With them, you can perform many different kinds of operations—including some you probably haven't even thought of yet.

The menu bar you see now belongs to the initial desktop. Word has its own menu bar, which you'll explore when you get into the Word program.

Using the Pointer

As we mentioned earlier, there is one other item visible on this very neat and orderly desktop: the pointer. The pointer has a very important purpose: You use it as an extension of your hands. Since you can't pick up items from this electronic desktop, you use the mouse to move the pointer to the location where you want an action carried out. You can use the pointer now to see what the Word disk contains by moving the mouse around until the pointer is on the Word disk icon and pressing and quickly releasing the mouse button twice in rapid succession. Pressing and quickly releasing the button is called clicking; pressing and releasing the button twice is called double-clicking.

Position the pointer on the Word Master disk icon and double-click.

When you double-click on the Word Master disk icon, an outline moves across the screen and opens out into a large rectangle. This rectangle, called a disk directory window, has a striped bar, called the title bar, across the top, containing the words Word Master. Much of the rest of the window is filled with icons that represent the contents of the Word Master disk. Let's look at a few.

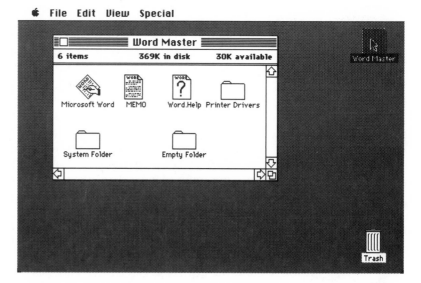

The icon labeled Microsoft Word that looks like a hand writing on a piece of paper with the word WORD at the top represents the Word program.

The icon labeled MEMO that looks like a dog-eared piece of paper with the word WORD at the top represents a sample Word document that Microsoft included on the disk to give you something to practice on as you follow along with the manual.

The icons labeled Printer Drivers, System Folder, and Empty Folder look like file folders and are, in fact, called folders. Folders can hold documents, files, or nothing, as is the case with the folder labeled Empty Folder. The System Folder contains the instructions that tell the Macintosh how to perform certain basic operations. In fact, you won't even get to the desktop without inserting a disk that contains this information.

The icon labeled Word.Help that looks like another dog-eared piece of paper with the word WORD at the top is the Help file, which contains information to help you learn about Word.

Backing Up the Master Disk

Normally, this is the point at which you would double-click the Word program icon to open Word and start creating a document. But first, you should make at least one copy of Word to work with, so you reduce the risk of damaging your only copy of the master disk. (Let's face it: As reliable as computers are, there is always the chance of an occasional power failure, or spilled cup of coffee, or some other disaster.) Don't store your master disk too far away, though; Microsoft's copy-protection safeguard requires you to insert the master disk briefly each time you open Word. After that, you can store the master and let your copies bear the wear and tear of your creative word processing. The first step is to prepare the disk onto which you plan to copy the program. The steps are slightly different for those using only the internal disk drive than for those using both the internal and an external drive. We'll go through the procedure for two-drive users first. Single-drive users should follow along; seeing how much easier it is to work with two drives might convince you to buy that second drive.

Backing Up with Two Drives

To make a backup copy of the master disk, you'll need a blank 3½-inch single-sided micro floppy disk, the only kind the Mac uses. They are usually sold in boxes of 10.

Insert a blank disk in the empty drive.

Make sure the write-protect tab on the blank disk is in the unprotected position before you insert it in the empty drive. It doesn't matter which drive contains Word and which contains the blank disk.

The drive whirs briefly, then the screen displays a new kind of window, called a dialog box, that contains the message, This disk is unreadable: Do you want to initialize it?

The Macintosh uses dialog boxes frequently to ask you for information and give you information. Don't panic at the word "unreadable." Blank disks are supposed to be unreadable. The dialog box is telling you it can't read the disk you've just inserted because the disk hasn't been initialized, or prepared to store information. Below the message are two round-cornered rectangles, called buttons. One contains the word Initialize and the other contains the word Eject. You want to initialize the new disk.

Click the Initialize button.

The Mac hums to life, leaving magnetic marks on the disk that it will use to locate where it can store and retrieve data. When initialization is complete, another dialog box appears, asking you to name this new disk. You can use any name. The name we've chosen to use is Word Working Master. A flashing vertical bar, which represents the insertion point, marks the place where the letters you type will appear.

Type *Word Working Master* in the dialog box, then click the OK button.

If you happen to make a mistake while typing, just use the Backspace key to erase your error, then retype.

When you've finished, a new disk icon labeled Word Working Master appears in the upper right corner of the screen, just below the Word Master disk icon.

Copying a Disk with Two Drives   Now you're ready to actually copy the Word Master disk onto the Word Working Master disk. Those of you who have used your Macs with other application programs may have already used the Disk Copy program provided by Apple on the system disk that comes with the machine. However, the Word Master disk won't allow itself to be copied with this program. You have to use the dragging technique, which we'll do now.

Select the Word Master disk icon and drag it to the Word Working Master disk icon.

To do this, you first place the pointer over the Word Master icon. Now press and hold down the mouse button while sliding the mouse until an outline of the Word Master icon is superimposed on the Word Working Master icon. Pressing and holding the mouse button while you move the pointer is called dragging. When the pointer is positioned over the Word Working Master icon, the icon turns black, indicating that it is now selected. Just release the mouse button to start the copy process.

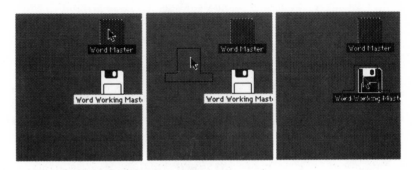

A dialog box appears, asking, Completely replace contents of "Word Working Master" (external drive) with contents of "Word Master" (internal drive)?

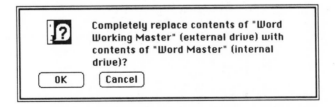

The purpose of this dialog box is to make you stop and ask yourself if you really want to wipe out any data that might be on the second disk (called the destination disk) and replace it with the data on the first disk (called the source disk), since this is what copying a disk does to any information currently on the destination disk. Two buttons are displayed below the message: OK and Cancel. You want to go ahead and replace what's on the second disk (nothing) with what's on the first disk (Word).

Click the OK button.

Another dialog box appears, this time showing the number of files remaining to be copied from the master disk to the working copy disk. Sit back and relax—it takes a while.

Preparing a Data Disk with Two Drives

Most applications software, including Word, is supplied on a disk containing the Macintosh operating system. Such a disk is called a system disk. Having a program on a system disk means you need to insert only one disk to start the Mac and make the program available, but this convenience has one major disadvantage: The operating system takes up a lot of disk storage space. A sophisticated program such as Word also takes up a lot of space, which doesn't leave much space for data storage. The way around this problem is to use a separate disk, called a data disk, for storing data.

So what exactly is a data disk? It's a disk that contains neither the operating system nor an application program. A data disk can't be used to start a work session when the computer is first turned on, since the Mac needs instructions from the operating system to get itself going. The only thing it's good for is storing data—the letters, reports, and prize-winning novels you are going to create with Word. For a two-drive system, the typical arrangement is to put the disk containing the operating system and Word in the internal disk drive and a data disk in the external drive, though, in fact, the opposite arrangement works just as well. Single-drive users can also benefit from using data disks, but must be prepared to do a lot of disk swapping.

Let's prepare a data disk now, so you can use it to store the document you'll create in Chapter 3. First, you need to eject one of the disks from one of the drives.

Select the disk you want to eject by clicking its icon in the upper right corner of the desktop.

When you click on an icon, you're selecting it, and it becomes highlighted. Selecting an icon tells the Mac that's where you want the next action to take place. This is how you work with an object on the desktop: First you select it, then you tell the Mac what to do with it. How do you tell the Mac to eject the disk?

Pull down the File menu and choose the Eject command.

To do this, position the pointer over the word File in the menu bar, then press and hold down the mouse button. A list, or menu, of command names seems to unroll from under the menu bar. You have just "pulled down" a menu. Without releasing the mouse button, move the pointer down the menu until it's over the word Eject. The command becomes highlighted. Now release the mouse button.

The disk drive goes back to work for a second or two and then the disk pops out of the drive opening.

Carefully remove the disk and insert a blank disk.

Just as when you inserted the blank disk earlier, a dialog box asks if you want to initialize the new disk.

Click the Initialize button.

Type *Word Data* as a name.

Click the OK button.

That's all there is to it. You can eject the disks, label them, and turn off the computer, or you can turn straight to Chapter 3, where we start creating a document.

Backing Up with One Drive

Are you single-drive users feeling that we've been testing your patience by spending all that time with the two-drive users? That's exactly what we were doing. But we did it for a good reason: If you're going to use Word with only one drive, you need patience. Lots of it. Let's go through the backing-up process again and we think you'll see what we mean.

First, before you can make a backup copy of the Word Master disk, you have to eject it, so you can initialize a blank disk.

Choose Eject from the File menu.

Insert a blank disk.

Click the Initialize button.

Type *Word Working Master.*

Click the OK button.

A new disk icon appears, labeled Word Working Master. Now you're ready to copy the master disk onto the Word Working Master.

Select the Word Master disk icon and drag it to the Word Working Master disk icon.

Click the OK button.

The Word Working Master disk automatically pops out of the drive opening and a dialog box appears, requesting, Please insert the disk: Word Master.

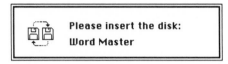

Insert the Word Master disk.

Almost immediately, the Word Master disk pops out again and a dialog box appears, requesting, Please insert the disk: Word Working Master.

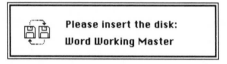

Swap disks.

The same sequence is repeated ten times. The reason for the Mac's fickleness is the limited amount of storage space in its memory. The 128K Mac can read in only a small amount of the data from the Word Master disk at a time before its memory is full and it needs to write some of that data to the Word Working Master disk. Each time it finishes reading, it asks for the working copy and each time it finishes writing, it asks for the original master. On the 512K Macintosh the process is the same, but it doesn't take nearly as many swaps.

Once the disk-swapping is done, put a label on your Word Working Master. At this point, you could prepare a data disk. but that requires still more disk-swapping. We won't require you to use a data disk in Chapter 3, so if you want, you can put off this chore for a while.

If you're serious about word processing (and we assume you are, if you're using Word), you'll want to add a second disk drive to your system. So, from now on, we'll only talk about two-drive systems.

3 Creating the first draft

Now, we invite you to participate in a working session with Word. You will develop a sample business document and, in the process, practice each of the major word-processing activities: typing, editing, formatting, printing, and saving a document. This working session will help allay the starting-up qualms of newcomers and give them a solid foundation for using the program. For those who only need a refresher, it will provide a review.

The Startup Process

To get started, gather your Word Working Master disk and your Word data disk, and be sure your Word Master disk is handy.

Turn on the computer.
Insert the working master disk in the internal drive.
Insert the Word data disk in the external drive.

If the directory window is not displayed, open it.

Double-click on the working master icon.

Without further ado, find the Word program icon inside the working master window.

Double-click on the Word icon.

There is one final step before you get on with the program. Microsoft Word will not operate until it verifies that you also have a Word Master disk. An alert box says, Please insert the disk: Word Master.

Since it ejects the Word Working Master disk at the same time, you'll find it easy to comply.

Insert the Word Master disk.

After a brief whirring of drives, the Word Master disk is ejected and another alert box requests the Word Working Master.

Insert the Word Working Master.

You've satisfied internal system requirements, and you're cleared to run with the working master disk until you turn off the machine.

The Word Window

You now see the window shown in Figure 3-1. This window, called a document window, has a number of new features: a flashing vertical line, a diamond, and a frame across the top and bottom and down the right side. Take a moment to familiarize yourself with the different parts of the Word document window.

The bar across the top of the window with the word "Untitled" in the middle of it is called the title bar.

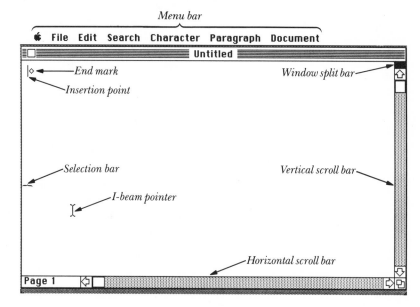

Figure 3-1. A Word document window

The bar along the right edge of the screen is called the vertical scroll bar. This bar is used to move up or down through a long document, bringing other parts of the document into view. The bar along the bottom edge of the window is called the horizontal scroll bar. It enables you to move text from side to side. (Word can handle documents much wider than the screen, up to 22 inches.) Moving up and down or from side to side is called scrolling. We'll discuss and use scrolling a little later in the chapter, when we have a document to scroll through.

The black box near the upper right corner is called a window split bar. It can be used to split the screen vertically into two separate windows, so you can see two different parts of the same document at the same time. This inconspicuous bar can be very useful, as you'll learn in Chapter 4.

Even less conspicuous is the selection bar, an unmarked area along the left edge of the screen. The selection bar is so named because you can use it to quickly select a line, a paragraph, or the whole document. There is nothing on the screen to mark its presence, but you can tell that you're in the selection bar when the pointer changes to an arrow pointing to the right.

If you try moving the mouse now, you can see that it is controlling the I-beam. The pointer takes this I-beam shape when you're working with text. When you move it into a scroll bar at the right or bottom of the window, it changes to an arrow pointing left. And when you move it into the selection bar at the left of the window, it becomes an arrow, this time pointing right.

Along the top of the screen, above the title bar, is the omnipresent menu bar. You'll be better equipped to explore the uses of menu items and other Word window features once you have text to work with. So, let's get right down to it and type some text. On your Word disk, there is a sample memo describing how to prepare a house for sale. You could use this sample memo on the Word disk as sample text, but since we think it is important for you to learn about Word by doing the typing yourself, we have put together a similar document, shown in Figure 3-2, with some pointers on shopping for a house. The information in our house-buying guide is practical advice from real estate experts, so after you type in this document, you may even want to save it for your next house-hunting excursion.

Bay Shore Mortgage
1001 Ocean View Blvd.
Morena, California
(725) 045-1200

SHOPPING FOR A NEW HOME

Buying a house is the biggest investment many people will ever make; a mistake may not only cost you a lot of money in unexpected repairs but can also shatter dreams of a warm and happy home. Here are some tips for avoiding this fate.

Shopping Tips

Always go house hunting during the day, so you can get a good look at the house. Bring a house-hunting notebook to record your impressions of view, layout, and style. Include price, name of owner, location, square footage, number of bedrooms and baths, and any special features. You may want to bring a tape measure to check wall space, windows, etc.

Be sure to get a list of items that will come with the home. Also ask for any permits on any work done on the house.

Get Help From Professionals

Deal only with reputable real estate firms. Ask family and friends whom they would recommend. Check credentials and references fully.

Other professionals can help you make sound decisions throughout the home-buying process:

- Lender
- Home inspector
- Termite inspector

- Attorney
- Appraiser
- Experts in heating, plumbing, and electrical systems

1

continued

Figure 3-2. A sample document

Location

Select the location of your home carefully. Location not only affects property value, but it shapes the lifestyle of your family.

Drive through the neighborhood. Is this the kind of neighborhood you'd be happy in? Are the houses well kept? Visit the neighborhood at various times of the day, if possible. Don't be afraid to stop a few of the neighbors to ask appropriate questions.

Check with the local planning department on building restrictions and proposed changes for the area. Find out if the district is strictly residential or open to commercial development.

Are bus lines and major transportation lines conveniently located? How far is it to work, shops, medical, and recreational facilities? Keep in mind that buildings and utilities that are convenient a few blocks away may prove to be a nuisance if they are too close.

Visit the local schools, even if you don't have children. The quality of the schools can affect property values.

Find out the location of the nearest police and fire stations. Ask the police department about the local crime rate.

Exterior

Check the grounds to see if they are well landscaped. If the house is below the street level, is there adequate drainage? Are the pool, shed, fences, and other structures in good repair? Check walkways and driveways for safety and maintenance requirements.

Note the orientation of the house with respect to the sun. A house that gets plenty of sun may cost less to heat.

Check the roof and gutters for signs of wear and cracks. Does the roof shape provide adequate water runoff?

Check the exterior walls. What kind of maintenance will they require?

Is the carport or garage space adequate for your needs?

2

continued

Figure 3-2 (continued)

Interior

Does the layout of the house allow easy room-to-room circulation? Are conflicting uses properly separated? Is there easy access to bathrooms and kitchen?

Check exposed wood for signs of termites and under sinks and counters for signs of rodents and other pests.

Test doors and windows to see that they open and close freely and make sure they provide ample ventilation and light.

Note the storage facilities. Do cupboards, closets, shelving, and counters provide sufficient storage for all your treasures?

Examine ceilings and walls for cracks and signs of water damage.

Look at floor coverings. Is the kitchen floor covered with a durable surface? If possible, check under rugs to observe the condition of the floors.

Utilities

Heating, plumbing, and electrical systems are particularly difficult to examine because they are located mostly within walls and under floors. If you have any doubts, hire a professional to inspect them.

Examine the heating and cooling systems. Can all parts of the house be maintained at a comfortable temperature? Ask to see electrical bills.

Check the condition of pipes and drains in the basement, kitchen, and bathrooms. Turn on faucets and flush toilets to check for reduced water flow, rusty water, and noisy pipes.

Inspect electrical outlets and any exposed wires. Frayed or cracked wiring may indicate that the wiring in general is bad. Note the number and placement of outlets.

Courtesy Bay Shore Mortgage. If we can be of further assistance, please call.

3

Figure 3-2 (continued)

Typing Text

Text is entered in front of the flashing vertical line, called the insertion point. This symbol also marks the place where you can make changes to the document. Right now, the insertion point is flashing next to a diamond. The diamond identifies the end of the document and is called the end mark. As you type, the insertion point and the end mark will remain together until you click a new insertion point within your text.

Try to see if you can enter the following text fast enough to outrun the computer. Don't worry about errors; just plunk those keys as fast as you can. You'll find that Microsoft Word handles keyboard input from the fastest typists without losing so much as a character. Sometimes you may type several strokes and not see the characters on the screen immediately. Each of those strokes is recorded in a section of computer memory called the input buffer that's used for temporary storage, while the computer is attending to other processing, usually at the end of a line. Just keep typing the text, and Word will catch up with you.

At the end of each line, notice how words automatically move to the beginning of the next line. This feature, called word wrap, is not unique to Microsoft Word, but it certainly is a very handy feature, courtesy of electronic word processing. This saves you the bother of estimating how much text will fit and putting a carriage return at the end of every line. You press the Return key only where you want to start a new line, regardless of where you are on the current line, such as at the end of a paragraph. For the following practice session and elsewhere in this book when you're asked to type in text, press the Return key only when you see the word [Return].

Now, type the following:

SHOPPING FOR A NEW HOME [Return]

Buying a house is the biggest investment many people will ever make; a mistake may not only cost the buyer a lot of money in repairs but can also shatter dreams of a warm and a happy home. Here are some tips for avoiding this fate. [Return]

Did you notice that the margins for your paragraph are preset? You will learn how to adjust margin indents, tabs, and first-line indents later in this chapter.

Simple Editing

Now what about those typing errors? Microsoft Word has several ways to handle corrections. If you make an error as you type, you can stop typing right there and erase one character at a time with the Backspace key. However, you can also just continue typing and leave errors for later, so you can concentrate on the flow of your writing. One of the great joys of writing with a word processor is that it allows you to get those important thoughts down while they are hot, then go back later to clean up typos and polish your work.

Inserting Text

Let's go back and rework the text right now. You can start with a little mouse and pointer practice. Remember, the pointer's shape depends on where it is on the screen. Within the Word window, it is an I-beam. If you move it into the text and click the mouse, the insertion point jumps to the new location. It's important to remember that, no matter what you do with the I-beam, the insertion point stays put until you click the mouse.

Now, let's try inserting some text, just one word to start. Let's insert the word *unexpected* in front of *repairs*.

Move your I-beam to the left edge of the first *r* in the word *repairs*.

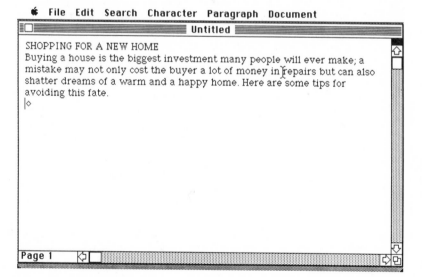

Click the mouse button.

Clicking changes the location of the insertion point, moving it to the left of the *r*. Now you get to see why we call it the insertion point.

Type the word *unexpected* (be sure to include a space after the word).

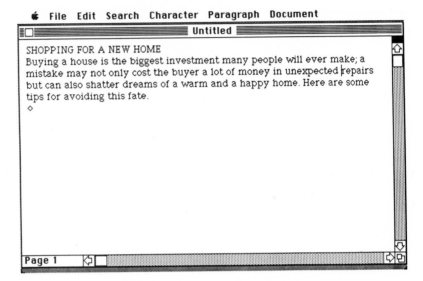

As you type, the letters are automatically inserted to the left of the *r*. Notice that they do not replace, or overtype, current existing text. Word won't let you overtype. To make room for the inserted word, existing text conveniently moves to the right and even word wraps to the next line, if necessary.

Just as on the initial desktop, when using Word, it is necessary to make a selection before taking an action. To see how this works, you can select and replace two words. To select text, you hold down the mouse button, and move the I-beam across the text that you want to select, then release the button. The text you select in this way is highlighted—that is, it appears in reverse (white letters on a black background).

Move the I-beam to the *t* in *the buyer*.

Drag the mouse to highlight *the buyer*.

The two words, *the buyer*, should be enclosed in a black box. If they are not, try again.

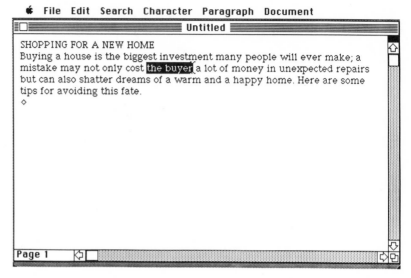

Type the word *you*.

As you press the first letter, the selected words *the buyer* are deleted, and the new insertion point appears in their place. The rest of the text automatically moves to the right as you add each character. Notice also that, once you have selected a portion of text, you can move the I-beam to the far corners of the screen without affecting the selected portion of text, as long as you don't click the mouse button.

🍎 **File   Edit   Search   Character   Paragraph   Document**

≣≣≣≣≣≣≣≣≣≣≣≣≣≣≣≣≣≣ **Untitled** ≣≣≣≣≣≣≣≣≣≣≣≣

SHOPPING FOR A NEW HOME
Buying a house is the biggest investment many people will ever make; a mistake may not only cost you| a lot of money in unexpected repairs but can also shatter dreams of a warm and a happy home. Here are some tips for avoiding this fate.
◇

Page 1

Correcting Corrections

What if you make a mistake while trying to correct an error? Let's try it and see.

> Click the insertion point at the left edge of the word *fate*, the last word in the paragraph.
>
> Type in *tragic* (include a space after *tragic*).

Now, suppose that on seeing this change, you decide that it looked better before the correction. What can you do? The Undo command in the Edit menu enables you to cancel your last action. In this case, your last action was typing text.

> Pull down the Edit menu, and choose Undo Typing.

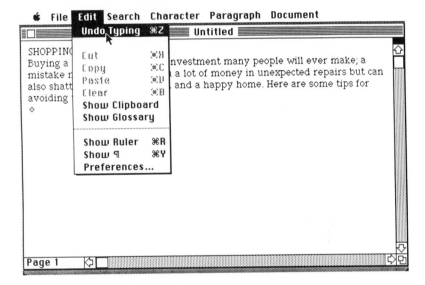

The questionable insert disappears. Now, what was your latest action?

> Pull down the Edit menu.

Undo Typing has changed to Redo Typing. You don't want your fate to be tragic, but if you did, you could choose Redo Typing and it would replace the canceled text. You can continue to remove and replace that same text until you type something else or choose another command. Any time you need to correct an action, choose Undo before you do anything else. Even one click on the mouse before you choose Undo, and Word forgets your last action. Undo won't undo it for you.

Deleting and Selecting

Deleting is just as easy as inserting. The character to the left of the insertion point is deleted each time you tap the Backspace key. You can delete characters as you type new text, or you can reposition the insertion point to delete existing text. If you delete a character by accident, just type it right back in again.

> Click the I-beam just to the left of the word *happy*.
>
> Press Backspace twice.

One backspace deletes the space, the second deletes the *a*.

To delete larger blocks of text, you can drag the I-beam over a section of text to highlight it. If you drag the I-beam vertically, Word selects a line of text at a time. Once a block of text is selected, pressing Backspace deletes the entire block. If you should unintentionally delete a block of text, immediately choose Undo Cut from the Edit menu to retrieve it.

Returning to the End of the Document

Before you can practice more advanced deleting techniques, you need to type in more text. An easy way to put the insertion point next to the end mark is to click your I-beam anywhere in the space below and to the right of the end mark. Try it.

> Locate the I-beam anywhere beyond the end mark and click.
>
> Type in at the end of your text:
>
> *Shopping Tips* [Return]
>
> *Always go house hunting during the day, so you can get a good look at the house. Bring a house-hunting notebook to record your impressions of view, layout, and style. Include price, name of owner, location, square footage, number of bedrooms and baths, and any special features. You may want to bring a tape measure to check wall space, windows, etc.* [Return]
>
> *Be sure to get a list of items that will come with the home. Also, ask for permits on any work done on the house.* [Return]
>
> *Get Help From Professionals* [Return]
>
> *Deal only with reputable real estate firms. Ask family and friends whom they would recommend. Check credentials and references fully.* [Return]
>
> *Other professionals can help you make sound decisions throughout the home-buying process:* [Return]
>
> *Lender Attorney* [Return]
>
> *Home inspector Appraiser* [Return]
>
> *Termite inspector Experts in heating, plumbing, and electrical systems* [Return]

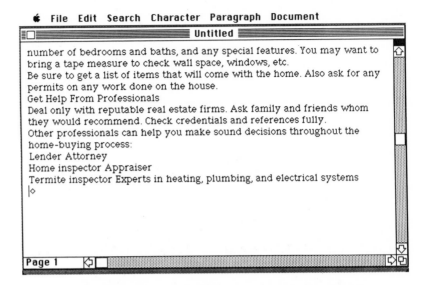

There, that gives you the beginning of an instruction sheet for potential home buyers and a little more text to work with.

Scrolling Through the Document

Something else has happened as you've been typing. Your text is now too long for the screen. You need a time-out to get further acquainted with scrolling. No matter how large your document grows, you can scroll it around so you can see any part of it through the window, as depicted in Figure 3-3.

The window displays only part of a document, but scrolling moves the document so any part can be displayed. Let's start scrolling by using the vertical scroll bar, which frames the right side of the window.

Click your pointer in the arrow at the bottom of the vertical scroll bar.

The arrow points downward and clicking appears to move the window down one line on the document. Of course, the window can't move; rather, the document scrolls upward. If you hold the mouse button down with the pointer in that arrow, you can quickly scroll to the bottom of the document. Now try the same process with the arrow pointing up, located at the top of the scroll bar.

Since this is not a long document, it takes only an instant to scroll to either top or bottom. With a document of several pages, that process would get tedious. So, you'd use another feature in the scroll bar. Between the two arrows in the scroll bar is a small square, called a scroll box, which you can use for rapid scrolling to any position in a long document. To simulate a longer document for practicing purposes,

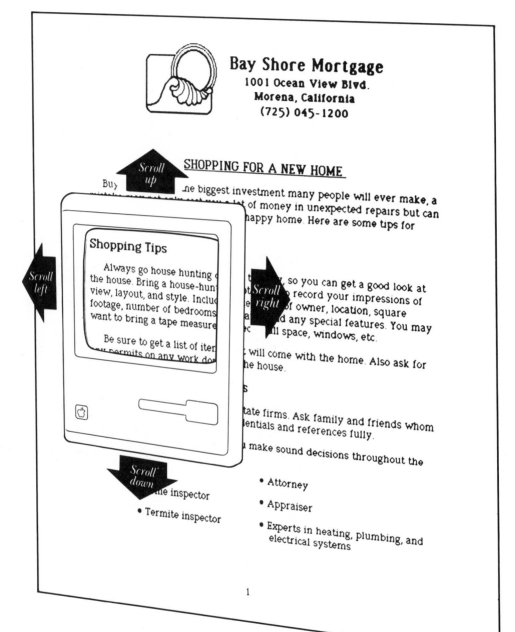

Figure 3-3. Scrolling moves the document past the window.

you can shrink the window. In the bottom right corner is another square with the image of a small square overlapping a larger one. This is called the size box. You can drag it to adjust the size of the window, horizontally to change the horizontal dimension, vertically to change the vertical dimension, or diagonally to change both.

> Move your pointer to the size box and drag it diagonally up and to the left as far as it will go.

You just discovered Word's minimum window size. But that is a little too small. You'll have a better perspective if the window is a bit larger.

> Drag the size box to about the middle of the screen.

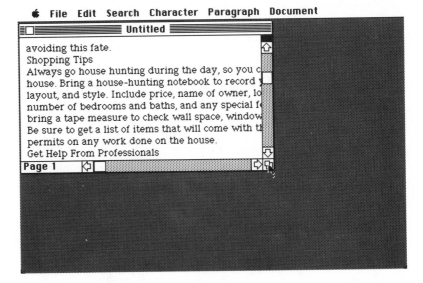

Now, you can scroll to the bottom of the document.

> With your pointer in the vertical scroll box, drag the scroll box to the bottom of the scroll bar.
>
> After the text scrolls to the bottom, drag the scroll box to the top of the scroll bar.

Can you see what an advantage this would be on a 40-page document?

Now move your pointer to the horizontal scroll bar. Try clicking the right arrow, then the left arrow, and move the horizontal scroll box around, as you did to check out the vertical bar. Press and hold the right arrow until the scroll box stops, so you can see that Word scrolls horizontally.

While your window is reduced in size, you can get familiar with another useful feature.

Move your pointer to the title bar at the top of your window.
Press the mouse button and drag the title bar downward.

You relocated the entire window. Now experiment with the window and scrolling features you just learned until you are satisfied that you understand them. When you are done, return the window to its full-screen size.

Double-click on the title bar.

Advanced Deleting and Selecting

Now you have all the tools you need to correct the sample text you typed. This is the time to put them to work, and correct any remaining errors. If your text is free of typos, it is still a good idea to review these techniques and be sure you understand how to use them.

You use the Backspace key to delete short segments of text, but you can also choose the Cut or Clear commands from the Edit menu. If you choose Cut, the text you delete is transferred to the Clipboard, where it can be retrieved by choosing Paste. You will practice using the Clipboard later in this chapter. If you choose Clear, the deleted text is not saved to the Clipboard; it is simply erased from the document. If you choose Clear or Cut in error, use Undo Cut to retrieve your text.

It's important to remember that you must first select text, then delete it. And Word makes it easy to select text. For example, to select a single word, just double-click anywhere on that word.

Double-click on the word *reputable* in the third paragraph.
Choose Clear from the Edit menu.

There, real estate firms are no longer reputable. Of course, you are interested only in ones that are, so, before doing anything else, replace *reputable*.

Choose Undo Cut from the Edit menu.

Another way you can select a word is by pressing the Shift and Backspace keys.

Move the I-beam to the space after the word *hunting* in the second paragraph, click, then press Shift and Backspace.

You learned earlier how to select a block of text by dragging; here's another way.

Move your I-beam to the left of the word *Buying* in the first sentence and click.

Make sure the pointer shape is an I-beam when you click, not a right-facing arrow.

Move the I-beam to the end of the first sentence, just to the right of the period.

Hold down Shift and click.

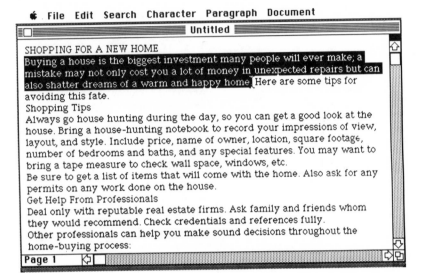

Shift-click highlights all the text between the insertion point and the I-beam—in this case, the first sentence. Now, delete this sentence.

Press Backspace.

Are you impressed? Before you get carried away with all this power, replace the deleted sentence.

Choose Undo Cut from the Edit menu.

The selection bar adds even more options to your selection methods. Step right up to the selection bar by moving your pointer to the left margin until it turns into an arrow. Remember, you can always tell when the pointer is in the selection bar, because it points to the right.

Move the pointer into the selection bar and click once.

You have selected an entire line of text. But you can select more than one line at a time.

> Move the pointer to a different position and double-click.

This time you selected a whole paragraph. Now let's select the entire document.

> Leave the pointer in the selection bar, hold down Command, and click.

Of course, you cancel any selection by clicking anywhere in the text. There are also more selective selection methods. For example, you can select a complete sentence using Command and click.

> Move the I-beam to the word *during* in the second paragraph, press Command, and click to select the whole sentence.

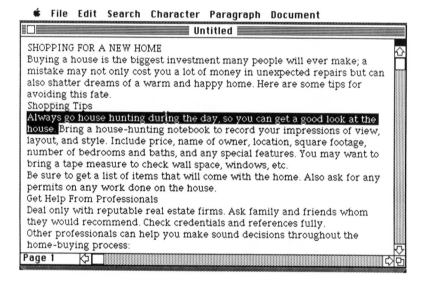

> Click again to remove the highlight.

Saving Files

Typing text into this electronic marvel can give you a false sense of security. It's easy to think that, once typed into the computer, your document is forever secure. Not so. A sudden loss or fluctuation in power, and all your changes during this session can be lost, unless you have the foresight to record your document on a disk. So, it is very important to save your additions and revisions periodically as you work. Saving to a disk is straightforward.

Choose the Save command from the File menu.

The first time you save a new document, whether you choose Save or Save As..., Word displays the Save Current Document As dialog box. Once your first save has established the file, choosing Save again no longer displays the dialog box. Your revised text is simply saved, and you can continue typing or editing.

```
┌─────────────────────────────────────────────────────┐
│ Save Current Document as:      Word Working Master    │
│ ┌─────────────────────────┐   ┌───────┐  ┌───────┐  │
│ ││                        │   │ Save  │  │ Eject │  │
│ └─────────────────────────┘   └───────┘  └───────┘  │
│ ☐ Text Only  ☐ Make Backup    ┌───────┐  ┌───────┐  │
│                               │Cancel │  │ Drive │  │
│                               └───────┘  └───────┘  │
└─────────────────────────────────────────────────────┘
```

Notice the insertion point blinking in the Save Current Document As text box.

Type in the name *Sample Document.*

This dialog box gives you four options: Save, Eject, Cancel, and Drive. You can choose any of these commands by clicking the pointer on the appropriate button. The default button, the one marked by a heavy border, is Save.

The words Word Working Master are displayed above the four buttons, indicating that the disk in the internal drive is active. But you want to save Sample Document on the Word data disk in the external drive, so you want to change the active drive.

Click the Drive button.

The external drive is now active, and the label changes to Word Data. If you click on Drive again, the internal drive will become active again. We call this a toggle action. Try it a few times, but make sure the Word Data label is displayed when you are finished, then save your document.

Click the Save button.

The file is saved on the disk in the active drive. Now, you can continue editing. But don't forget to save your document frequently.

This is a good time for you to type the rest of the sample document. The final document will be three pages long. If you don't want to take the time for that much typing, just type some paragraphs under each of the next two subheadings, *Exterior* and *Location*. That will make your document more than one page long, which will allow you to see how Word breaks a document into pages, or paginates. And be sure to type the final sentence, which we'll use for character formatting.

Click the insertion point in front of the end mark and type the following:

Exterior [Return]

Check the grounds to see if they are well landscaped. If the house is below the street level, is there adequate drainage? Are the pool, shed, fences, and other structures in good repair? Check walkways and driveways for safety and maintenance requirements. [Return]

Note the orientation of the house with respect to the sun. A house that gets plenty of sun may cost less to heat. [Return]

Check the roof and gutters for signs of wear and cracks. Does the roof shape provide adequate water runoff? [Return]

Check the exterior walls. What kind of maintenance will they require? [Return]

Is the carport or garage space adequate for your needs? [Return]

Location [Return]

Select the location of your home carefully. Location not only affects property value, but it shapes the lifestyle of your family. [Return]

Drive through the neighborhood. Is this the kind of neighborhood you'd be happy in? Are the houses well kept? Visit the neighborhood at various times of the day, if possible. Don't be afraid to stop a few of the neighbors to ask appropriate questions. [Return]

Check with the local planning department on building restrictions and proposed changes for the area. Find out if the district is strictly residential or open to commercial development. [Return]

Are bus lines and major transportation lines conveniently located? How far is it to work, shops, medical, and recreational facilities? Keep in mind that buildings and utilities that are convenient a few blocks away may prove to be a nuisance if they are too close. [Return]

Visit the local schools, even if you don't have children. The quality of the schools can affect property values. [Return]

Find out the location of the nearest police and fire stations. Ask the police department about the local crime rate. [Return]

Interior [Return]

Does the layout of the house allow easy room-to-room circulation? Are conflicting uses properly separated? Is there easy access to bathrooms and kitchen? [Return]

Check exposed wood for signs of termites and under sinks and counters for signs of rodents and other pests. [Return]

Test doors and windows to see that they open and close freely and make sure they provide ample ventilation and light. [Return]

Note the storage facilities. Do cupboards, closets, shelving, and counters provide sufficient storage for all your treasures? [Return]

Examine ceilings and walls for cracks and signs of water damage. [Return]

Look at floor coverings. Is the kitchen floor covered with a durable surface? If possible, check under rugs to observe the condition of the floors. [Return]

Utilities [Return]

Heating, plumbing, and electrical systems are particularly difficult to examine because they are located mostly within walls and under floors. If you have any doubts, hire a professional to inspect them. [Return]

Examine the heating and cooling systems. Can all parts of the house be maintained at a comfortable temperature? Ask to see electrical bills. [Return]

Check the condition of pipes and drains in the basement, kitchen, and bathrooms. Turn on faucets and flush toilets to check for reduced water flow, rusty water, and noisy pipes. [Return]

Inspect electrical outlets and any exposed wires. Frayed or cracked wiring may indicate that the wiring in general is bad. Note the number and placement of outlets. [Return] [Return]

Courtesy Bay Shore Mortgage. If we can be of further assistance, please call. [Return]

Rearranging Text

When you reread your work with a more critical eye, you often see better ways to phrase things, and better ways to organize the document. With a word processor, you can rearrange without retyping. One of Word's most useful features is the ability to move blocks of text around. The sample document sections you have just entered (*Exterior, Location, Interior,* and *Utilities*) would be more logically oriented starting with *Location,* then *Exterior, Interior,* and *Utilities.* Even if you don't think this rearrangement will improve the document, think of it as an opportunity to try out a clever move and follow along anyway.

The standard way to move text is to select it, then choose Cut or Copy from the Edit menu to put it onto the Clipboard, and then choose Paste from the Edit menu to insert it into a new location.

Select the text that starts with *Exterior* and ends with *for your needs?*.

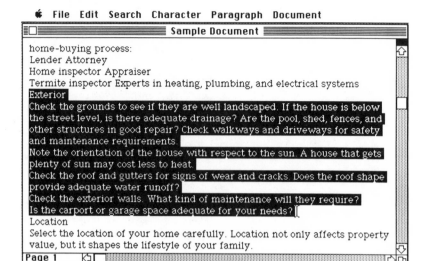

Choose Cut from the Edit menu.

If you use Copy instead, the selection will be copied onto the Clipboard, but the original will remain in the text. Since you want to relocate the text, use Cut. Now take a peek at the Clipboard to make sure the deleted text is there.

Choose Show Clipboard from the Edit menu.

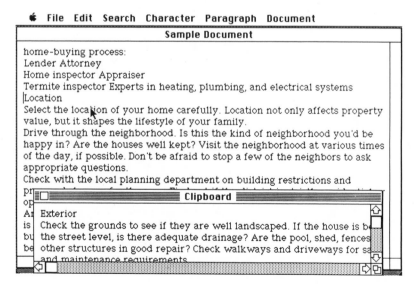

Great. All systems are "go." The insertion point is in position where your paragraph originated, and the deleted text is safely stored on the Clipboard.

Click the Clipboard close box to remove it from the screen.

Click the I-beam at the left edge of the *I* in *Interior*.

Choose Paste from the Edit menu.

It's done. By the time you finish reading this sentence, your newly moved *Exterior* section should be in place. And that's all there is to re-arranging text.

Combining Graphics with Text

At this point, you've done a good bit of typing and learned some of Word's basic editing techniques. Now, you are ready to try out some of the more interesting features. This is a good time to take a short break from word processing and pull some graphics into your document. You'll need a graphics program, such as MacPaint, to create a graphic. If you have a graphics program, quit Word and open a file in that other application.

Pull down the File menu and choose Save.

Choose Quit from the File menu.

After some whirring of drives, you are back on the initial desktop.

Click on the Word Working Master disk icon.

Choose Eject from the File menu.

Insert your graphics application disk and open the application.

We won't take you through a detailed tutorial on using graphics applications. Instead, we'll show you the logo and letterhead we developed for this home-buyers' guide using MacPaint. Copy it as closely as you can, or you can try to create your own version. The object of this exercise is to develop a graphic letterhead, about the size of our sample, that you can paste into your Word document. Your model is the Bay Shore Mortgage letterhead that is shown in Figure 3-4, on the following page.

Figure 3-4. Graphic design for home-buyers' guide

Bay Shore Mortgage
1001 Ocean View Blvd.
Morena, California
(725) 045-1200

The first line, Bay Shore Mortgage, is typed in 18-point bold New York. The other lines are 12-point bold New York. When your letterhead design is completed, select the marquee rectangle and drag the mouse to create a rectangle barely enclosing the design. Then pull down the Edit menu and choose Copy. You can choose Cut if you wish, but it is better to leave the original intact until the final document is complete. Your letterhead is now copied to the Clipboard. Before quitting the graphics program, you might want to save the letterhead file on your Word data disk.

That's all you need from the graphics program. You can quit it, eject the disk, then start up Word again.

Choose Quit from the File menu.

Choose Eject from the File menu.

Insert the Word Working Master disk.

Double-click on the sample document icon.

You may have to swap disks a few times while the system transfers the contents of the Clipboard to your Word disk. When the sample document is back on the screen, you need to add a little space at the top so your letterhead won't run into the text.

Press Return, then click the I-beam at the top of the page.

Your document is now ready to receive the letterhead.

Pull down the Edit menu and choose Paste.

The letterhead is inserted at the top of the page.

That's how easy it is to add graphics to a Word document. But that is only the beginning. Word has a number of other features to help you control graphics. You will use some of these features to create the projects in Section Three of this book. The rest of this chapter is devoted to formatting and printing the sample document.

Adding Formatting

You now have on your screen the basic text for a public service guide. However, it is a long way from being a finished document. You can begin to dress it up with some formatting.

Paragraph Indent

For a simple introduction to paragraph formatting, you can indent the first line of the first paragraph, starting with *Buying a house.*

Select the first paragraph.

Remember, you double-click in the selection bar to the left of the paragraph to select it.

Choose Formats... from the Paragraph menu.

The Paragraph Formats dialog box appears, giving you a lot of options for creating special paragraph formats. At this point, you are just going to indent the first line of the selected paragraph. The Left Indent text box is highlighted; you're not going to change the left margin, so you need to move the highlight to the First Line text box.

Double-click in the First Line text box.

Type .25.

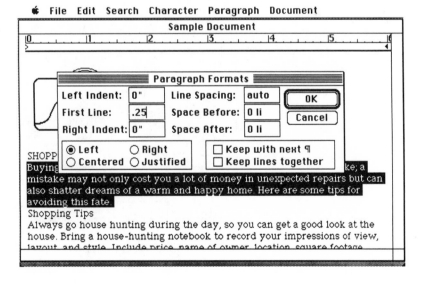

You don't need to type a zero before the decimal point or the inches symbol (″) after the number: Word will add them for you when you execute the command by clicking OK.

Notice that Left Indent and Right Indent are both set at zero. Word assumes you're using standard letter-sized (8½ by 11 inches) paper and automatically sets the left and right page margins at 1¼ inches each. The left and right indent settings in the Paragraph menu enable you to add additional indents for any paragraph or series of paragraphs. The default settings of zero in the indent boxes mean the text width is six inches. This is reflected in the ruler at the top of the screen, which is numbered in inches. The left indent marker is set at 0 inches, and the right indent marker is set at 6 inches, which means the text will be printed from 1¼ to 7¼ inches from the left edge of the paper. (To change the margins for the entire document, you change the preset margins in the Page Setup dialog box.) The other text boxes in the Paragraph Formats dialog box can be left as they are; we will discuss them as you need to use them.

Now, click the OK button.

Your selected paragraph is properly indented.

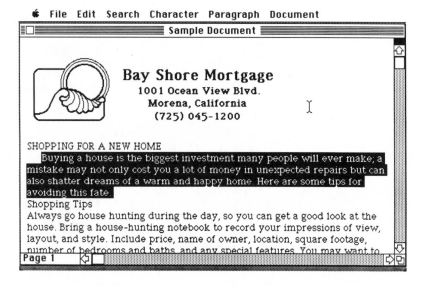

What's good for the first paragraph is dandy for every other paragraph in your document, so you can select the rest of the document.

Move the I-beam to the left edge of *Always* in the second paragraph and drag it downward until the text starts scrolling.

Continue to hold down the mouse button until you get to the end mark; then release the button.

You should see the I-beam over the word Page in the bottom horizontal scroll bar as the highlighted text scrolls upward. It will continue scrolling until you release the mouse button or until the end mark reaches the top of the screen. By selecting the rest of the document, you'll indent the subheadings along with the paragraphs, but that will be corrected easily when you format those subheadings.

Choose Formats... from the Paragraph menu, double-click in the First Line text box, type *.25*, then click OK.

Paragraph Spacing

Now go back to the Paragraph menu for another formatting feature to dress up your document: inserting a space between paragraphs. Before inserting space between paragraphs, it's helpful to see where your paragraphs end. To do this, you need to make the paragraph and space symbols visible on your screen.

Choose Show ¶ from the Edit menu.

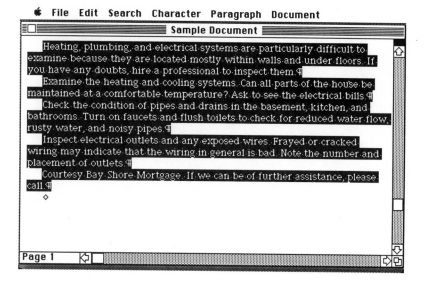

There, now you can see a paragraph symbol every place where you pressed Return while you were typing. You can also see a dot every place you used the space bar.

To insert extra space between every paragraph, you need to select the entire document.

> Move your pointer to the selection bar, hold down Command, and click.
>
> Choose Formats… from the Paragraph menu.
>
> Click an insertion point just to the right of the *0* in the Space After text box.
>
> Press Backspace, then type *1* and click the OK button.

After every paragraph symbol, there is now a blank line.

Margins and Tabs

Word has several features that give you a lot of flexibility in setting margins and tabs. An easy way to make quick changes to a paragraph is to display the ruler.

> Choose Show Ruler from the Edit menu.

A quick look at the ruler will show you that the scale markings are in $\frac{1}{8}$-inch increments. But there are hidden increments, too. You can discover them quite simply. Just below the scaled ruler line is a blank bar with an arrow-shaped symbol at each end.

> Click your pointer anywhere in the blank bar below the scaled ruler line.

There. You have created a tab arrow.

> Drag the tab arrow horizontally, very, very slowly.

You should be able to see the arrow taking two distinct steps for every tick on the ruler. When you are through, remove the tab arrow.

> Drag the tab arrow down into the text area and release.

It disappears.

So, you have determined that the ruler is calibrated in $\frac{1}{16}$-inch increments. In other words, when you use the ruler, you can set tabs and indents to the nearest $\frac{1}{16}$ inch. If you need greater precision, use the dialog boxes that are displayed when you choose Formats or Tabs from the Paragraph menu. Any numbers entered in these two dialog boxes are rounded to the nearest $\frac{1}{100}$ inch and the ruler marks are positioned to the nearest $\frac{1}{72}$ inch (the width of one pixel, one of the dots that make up the screen image). However, although you have greater precision using the Formats and Tabs dialog boxes, you can set only one indent or tab at a time using them. Whether you type the tabs and indents in a dialog box or set them on the ruler using the mouse, they always appear on the ruler, which is displayed when you choose the Formats... or Tabs... command. We'll have you use both the ruler and the dialog boxes, so you're familiar with both methods. First, let's use the ruler.

Select the three lines just above the *Location* heading in your document, starting with *Lender* and ending with *systems*.

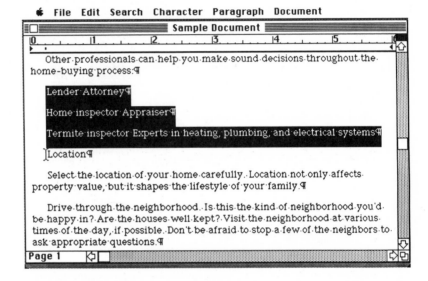

You have already had a little preliminary practice dragging tab arrows. Dragging the triangular indent marker at the far right of the ruler is just as simple. The left indent marker is another story. If you place your pointer near the tip of the left indent marker, you will probably find yourself dragging another tab arrow. Remember, tab arrows are easy to delete from the ruler if they get in the way. Just drag them down into the text area, and they will disappear when you release the mouse button.

A two-step process is needed to place the left indent marker and the first-line indent marker at the same place. The first-line indent marker resides to the right of the left indent marker. It is the little black square under the ¼-inch mark on the ruler. Drag it into position first, and then drag the left indent triangle.

Place your pointer on the black square, and drag the square between the sixth and seventh marks on the ruler.

That places the first-line indent at $^{13}/_{16}$ or .8125 inch. If you want reassurance that you found the right spot, display the Paragraph Formats dialog box (choose Formats... from the Paragraph menu); the First Line text box reads 0.81″.

Drag the triangular left indent marker to the same position.

Now, the Left Indent text box reads 0.81″, but the First Line box reads 0″. The number in the First Line box is always relative to the position of the left indent. If you move the first-line indent marker to the left, you will see negative numbers in the First Line box. Experiment as much as you wish, then leave the first-line indent marker in the same place as the left indent marker.

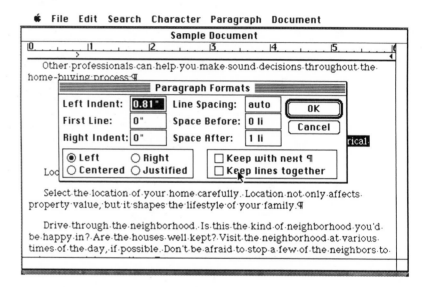

Click the OK button.

This list of professionals to consult doesn't look much like a list yet, so let's use the Tabs... command to format it for two columns.

Choose Tabs... from the Paragraph menu.

The Tabs dialog box gives you a choice of four types of tab alignment: left, center, right, and decimal. You want to set a left-alignment tab. Left is the default alignment, so you don't need to select Left. All you need to do is either type a *3* in the Position text box or click your pointer under the 3 in the ruler.

In the Position text box, type a *3* (for 3 inches).

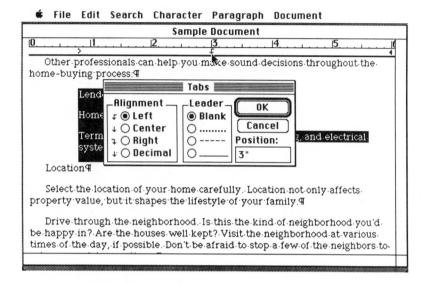

Click the OK button.

In a normal Word session, you would probably simply click in the ruler to set tabs, but we have shown you how to do this using the Paragraph Tabs option because we think it is important for you to understand the interaction between the ruler and dialog boxes. Using the dialog box, you can set only one tab at a time; using the ruler, you can set several at once.

One final adjustment remains. The last of the three lines of text you selected is a special case, since it is longer than the other two lines. Changing the left indent has created a two-line paragraph, which you are going to format with a hanging indent, so-called because the first line "hangs" into the margin to the left of the rest of the paragraph. You can do this by leaving the first-line indent marker where it is at position .81″ and the tab marker at 3.0″, and positioning the left indent marker at 3.19″, or 3³⁄₁₆ inches.

Double-click in the selection bar to select the paragraph starting with *Termite*.

The first-line indent marker is a white square in the middle of the triangular left indent marker when the two symbols are in the same position on the ruler. Before you can move the left indent marker, you have to move the first-line indent marker.

Drag the first-line indent marker halfway across the ruler or to any other position that's out of the way.

Drag the left indent marker 1½ ticks to the right of the 3-inch mark.

Drag the first-line indent marker back to where it was, at .81 inch (between the sixth and seventh ticks).

To verify that the Left Indent text box in the Format Paragraph dialog box now reads *3.19* and the First Line text box reads *−2.37*, you can choose Formats from the Paragraph menu. Now, you can use the new indent and tab settings to restructure these three lines so that they make more sense.

Your Macintosh keyboard provides a special set of characters, courtesy of the Option key. Most of these characters are symbols for scientific and mathematical notation; a few are for legal or financial applications. When you press Option-8, you get a solid dot, called a bullet, that can be used to call attention to a section of text.

Click your insertion point at the left edge of the *L* in *Lender.*

Press Option-8 and type a space.

Click the I-beam at the right edge of the *r* in *Lender.*

Press Tab, then press Option-8.

The next two lines follow the same pattern of tab settings and bullets.

Click your insertion point at the left edge of the *H* in *Home.*
Press Option-8, then type a space.
Click the I-beam at the right edge of the *r* in *inspector.*
Press Tab, then press Option-8.
Click your insertion point at the left edge of the *T* in *Termite.*
Press Option-8, then type a space.
Click the I-beam at the right edge of the *r* in *inspector.*
Press Tab, then press Option-8.

Now, you can see why we asked you to place the left indent marker at 3.19″ for the third paragraph. We experimented and found that to be a good position by dragging the left indent marker in the ruler until the word *electrical* was roughly under the *E* of *Experts.*

Next, you are going to take a look at the Character menu for a preview of font options, which we'll discuss more fully in Chapter 8.

Type Fonts and Styles

Incorporating different type fonts and styles into your documents is a creative part of using Word on the Macintosh that is not generally available on other microcomputers. Now that you are familiar with selecting text and pulling down menus, the process of changing type will be very simple. Start by selecting the main heading, *SHOPPING FOR A NEW HOME.*

Move your pointer to the selection bar and select the first line of text.

Pull down the Character menu and choose the Formats...
command.

Notice that the preset font is New York, and the font size is 12 points. (A point is a printer's unit of measurement that equals approximately $\frac{1}{72}$ inch. A font size is generally the height in points from the bottoms of letters that extend downward the farthest—such as p and y—to the tops of the tallest letters.)

All the text you have typed so far will be printed in 12-point New York, unless you make changes. Your first change will be to increase the font size from 12 to 14 points. So, click on 14 in the Font Size list box, just to the right of the Font Name list box.

In the Character Formats dialog box, choose 14 in the Font Size list box.

Notice that 14 is now displayed in the text box to the right of the list box. Now add emphasis to the heading with boldface and underlining.

In the Style box of the Character Formats dialog box, click the Bold check box and the Underline check box.

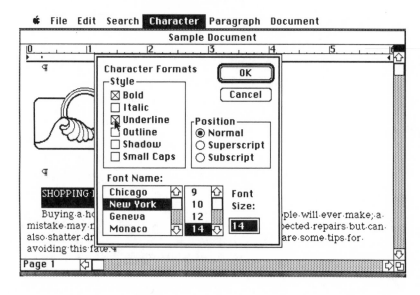

Click the OK button.

That's it. Now your title has more impact. Once you become familiar with the type fonts and understand something about type from our discussion in Chapter 8, you will quickly be able to dress up your documents with appropriate type styles. For now, you can make a slight variation to the subheadings.

Select the line that says *Shopping Tips*.
In the Character Formats dialog box, choose 14 and Bold.
Click the OK button.

You also need to correct this heading's indent position. Do you remember starting with paragraph two and scrolling through the entire document to set first-line indents? Now you get to correct the indents for the headings.

In the ruler, drag the first-line indent marker back to the zero position.

Follow the same process with the subsequent subheadings: *Get Help from Professionals, Location, Exterior, Interior,* and *Utilities.*

Your guide for home buyers is beginning to take on a professional look. But you need to take one more trip to the Character menu. The last paragraph in the document needs a special look.

Scroll to the end of the document, and select the final two sentences, starting with *Courtesy*.
Choose Formats from the Character menu.
Choose Geneva and 10 in the Character Formats dialog box.
Click OK to change the format.

Page Numbering

No discussion of word processing a business document would be complete without a look at how to number pages, and Word offers an easy way of numbering your pages automatically.

Choose Division Layout from the Document menu.
Click the Auto Page Numbering check box.

The default values below Auto Page Numbering will position the page number at the top right corner of the page, but we think centering the page numbers at the bottom of the page is more appropriate for your home-buyers' guide.

⚫ File   Edit   Search   Character   Paragraph   Document

```
Division Layout                                    ┌─── OK ───┐
┌─Break──────  ┌─Page Number Format─┐              ┌─ Cancel ─┐
│ ○ Continuous │ ◉ Numeric           │
│ ○ Column     │ ○ Roman (upper)     │             ┌─Footnotes Appear─┐
│ ◉ Page       │ ○ Roman (lower)     │             │ ◉ On Same Page    │
│ ○ Odd        │ ○ Alphabetic (upper)│             │ ○ At End of Division│
│ ○ Even       │ ○ Alphabetic (lower)│

⊠ Auto Page Numbering:                  Running Head Position:
    From Top:  [0.75"]                      From Top:    [0.75"]
    From Left: [7.25"]                      From Bottom: [0.75"]

Start Page Numbers At: [     ]              Number of Columns:  [1]
                                           Column Spacing:     [0.5"]
```

Page 1

> In the From Top text box, enter *10.2*.
>
> In the From Left text box, enter *4*.
>
> Click OK.

When you print the document, the page numbers will appear in the bottom margin, 4 inches from the left edge and 0.8 inch from the bottom of each page. You cannot print page numbers everywhere on the page. They are restricted to the top and bottom margins. With the top and bottom margins set at 1 inch, acceptable values in the From Top text box are limited to about .6 through .99 and 10.01 to about 10.97.

You need to move back to the top of the first page in order to make the next formatting adjustment: centering the letterhead and the main heading.

> Scroll to the top of the document.
>
> Click once on the letterhead.

The rectangle you see with small boxes in the lower corners and in the center of the bottom line is Word's way of showing that you have selected a graphics section. This rectangle is quite versatile. With your pointer on either vertical line of the rectangle, you can drag the figure from side to side. By placing the pointer in one of the three small black squares at the bottom of the rectangle, you can stretch or shrink the figure to the left or right, or up and down. Appendix D of the Word manual describes the various ways you can stretch and move graphic figures. For now, simply center the letterhead.

Choose Centered from the Paragraph menu.

Now center the main heading the same way.

Select the main heading, starting with *Shopping*.
Choose Centered from the Paragraph menu.

Now, you are ready for the fine-tuning in preparation for printing. The logo in Figure 3-4 has a definite influence on that preparation, since it contains a circle. If it is printed in the default Tall mode, the circle will print out as an oval. The logo must be printed in Tall Adjusted mode for the circle to actually look like a circle. Even though your logo may not contain a circle, this is a good exercise to demonstrate the difference.

Choose Page Setup from the File menu.
In the Page Setup dialog box, click the Tall Adjusted radio button.

Click the OK button.

After you click OK, you can watch the line endings shorten as the change ripples through your text. Since Tall Adjusted printing affects text as well as graphics, all the line lengths must be adjusted by Word.

Next, you need to check for proper spacing. You earlier inserted one line space after each paragraph, and that is what you should see. The only paragraph symbols that should be on separate lines all by themselves are the one after the letterhead and the one before the last line of the document. If you see any others, you should delete them. To delete any extra paragraph symbols, click the I-beam to the right of the symbol and press Backspace.

Your final check is to determine where page endings will be, so you can make necessary adjustments before printing.

Choose Repaginate from the Document menu.

Again, you see a ripple move through your document. You should be able to see a small equal sign in the left margin above the letterhead. That indicates the beginning of a page. Now, scroll slowly through the document to find the next page marker. If your spacing is the same as ours, the next equal sign is just to the left of the word *Location*. That's just where you want it. Your second page will start with a subheading. The next equal sign is below the word *Interior*. Not good. That puts a subheading at the end of page 2, with its headless text on page 3. But this is easy to fix. You can force a page break ahead of the heading.

Click the I-beam at the left edge of the *I* in *Interior*.
Press Shift and Enter.
Choose Repaginate from the Document menu.

A dotted line appears to mark the new page break, and an equal sign in the margin next to the word *Interior* marks the heading as the first line on page 3.

Scrolling down to the end of the document, you find the last line comfortably in place above a double dotted line and the end mark. Congratulations: The sample document is ready to print.

Easy Printing

The final step in word processing is printing the document. This is another phase where Microsoft Word and the Macintosh really shine. With Microsoft Word, you can create documents with multiple combinations of text styles, mixed with graphics. And Word is designed to reproduce documents on a variety of printers.

Make sure the printer is ready before taking this final step. Load the paper, and set the top of the page just above the top of the printer's ribbon. Make sure the printer is on and the cable is securely connecting the computer and printer. The next step is to inform the Mac just which printer you have connected. Microsoft Word assumes you have an ImageWriter (Apple's first Macintosh-compatible printer) unless you tell it otherwise. If you are using a different printer, choose Printer Setup from the File menu. The Mac displays a dialog box with several printer options.

If you're not using an ImageWriter printer, choose Printer Setup from the File menu, then choose the name of your printer from the list box.

Click the OK button.

For a more detailed discussion of the Printer dialog box and its options, see Chapter 6. With these preliminaries out of the way, you are ready to print the document.

Choose Print... from the File menu.

The program displays the Print dialog box.

```
┌──────────────────────────────────────────────────────────────────┐
│ Quality:      ○ High      ◉ Standard   ○ Draft     ┌──────────┐  │
│ Page Range:   ◉ All       ○ From: ▯    To: ▯        │   OK     │  │
│ Copies:       ▯1▯                                   └──────────┘  │
│ Paper Feed:   ◉ Continuous  ○ Cut Sheet      ▶      ┌──────────┐  │
│                                                     │  Cancel  │  │
│                                                     └──────────┘  │
└──────────────────────────────────────────────────────────────────┘
```

Your screen display should show the same preset options as the preceding illustration. If it doesn't, choose the correct settings, and, when all looks well, execute the Print... command.

Click the OK button.

Listen to your computer prepare the document for printing, and watch your printer zing into action. To cancel printing at any time, hold down the Command key and press the period [.] key. Your printout should look like the document shown earlier in Figure 3-2.

There, you have gone from blank screen to edited text and hardcopy printout in a few easy pages. But why stop now? The document is still on the screen, and, if you are using the ImageWriter printer, there are two more printing quality options to try. You'll never have a better chance to get a good comparison.

Pull down the File menu again and choose the Print... command.

This time, pick Draft and click OK.

Draft-quality printing, shown in Figure 3-5, is much faster than the other two options. It ignores all graphics, such as your letterhead, and the various fonts and styles displayed on the screen, and prints out in one mode only, using an elite type font that is stored in the printer memory. Draft quality is designed to display the exact location of words and paragraphs on the page. This gives you a quick approximation of how your document will look so you can make adjustments before the final printing.

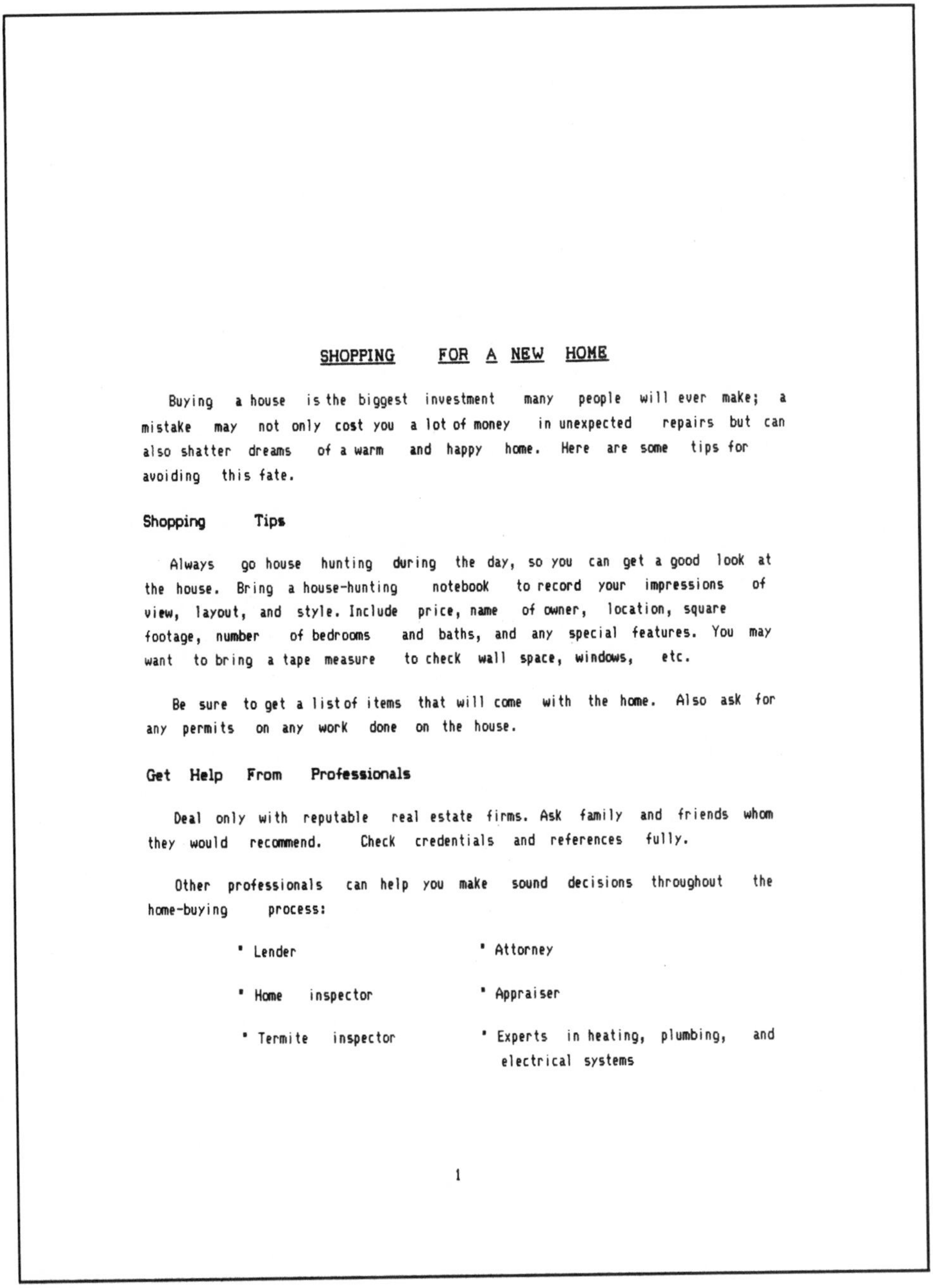

SHOPPING   FOR A NEW HOME

Buying a house is the biggest investment   many   people will ever make; a
mistake may not only cost you a lot of money in unexpected   repairs but can
also shatter dreams of a warm and happy home. Here are some tips for
avoiding   this fate.

Shopping   Tips

Always   go house hunting   during   the day, so you can get a good look at
the house. Bring a house-hunting   notebook   to record your impressions   of
view, layout, and style. Include   price, name of owner, location, square
footage, number   of bedrooms   and baths, and any special features. You may
want to bring a tape measure   to check wall space, windows,   etc.

Be sure to get a list of items that will come with the home. Also ask for
any permits on any work done on the house.

Get Help From   Professionals

Deal only with reputable   real estate firms. Ask family and friends whom
they would recommend.   Check credentials and references   fully.

Other professionals   can help you make   sound   decisions throughout   the
home-buying   process:

* Lender   * Attorney

* Home inspector   * Appraiser

* Termite inspector * Experts in heating, plumbing, and
                        electrical systems

1

Figure 3-5. The first page of
the sample document printed
in draft quality

Now, repeat the process, but choose High quality printing. Your document should look like the one shown in Figure 3-6.

Click High in the Print dialog box.

High quality is certainly the slowest print mode, taking four passes for each line of text. It produces excellent quality text, but the graphics are printed in standard quality because of the way graphics are treated by the Mac. So, you may prefer to print your documents with graphics in Standard mode. We will discuss the differences between the three print modes at length in Chapter 7.

Moving Between Documents

What more could you want from a word-processing session? Well, after you've created a few more documents, you might want to move from one to another without going back to the initial desktop. Word has a couple of handy commands in the File menu for doing just that. Maybe you'd like to create another document right now so you can see how easy it is to go from one document to another. First, close the sample document.

Choose Close from the File menu.

The document disappears, leaving a field of gray where the text area had been. Now, open a new, untitled file. You don't need to create a document, if you don't want to. This is just to show you how to open and close documents.

Choose New from the File menu.

Go ahead and close this new file, even if you haven't done any typing in it, and open the sample document again.

Choose Close from the File menu.
Choose Open... from the File menu.
In the Select a Document dialog box, click Sample Document in the list box, then click the Open button.

Sample Document reappears and you're ready to run again.

Bay Shore Mortgage
1001 Ocean View Blvd.
Morena, California
(725) 045-1200

SHOPPING FOR A NEW HOME

Buying a house is the biggest investment many people will ever make; a mistake may not only cost you a lot of money in unexpected repairs but can also shatter dreams of a warm and happy home. Here are some tips for avoiding this fate.

Shopping Tips

Always go house hunting during the day, so you can get a good look at the house. Bring a house-hunting notebook to record your impressions of view, layout, and style. Include price, name of owner, location, square footage, number of bedrooms and baths, and any special features. You may want to bring a tape measure to check wall space, windows, etc.

Be sure to get a list of items that will come with the home. Also ask for any permits on any work done on the house.

Get Help From Professionals

Deal only with reputable real estate firms. Ask family and friends whom they would recommend. Check credentials and references fully.

Other professionals can help you make sound decisions throughout the home-buying process:

- Lender
- Home inspector
- Termite inspector
- Attorney
- Appraiser
- Experts in heating, plumbing, and electrical systems

1

Figure 3-6. The first page of the sample document printed in high quality

Ending the Session

All good things come to an end, including working with Word. When you finish a word-processing session, you should choose the Quit command instead of just turning off your Mac.

Choose Quit from the File menu.

If you have made any changes to your document since the last save, Word displays a dialog box that asks, Save changes before quitting?

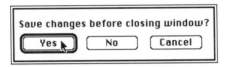

If you have made changes, be sure to click the Save button. Otherwise, all your changes since the last save will be lost.

The computer exits Word and returns to the initial desktop. Select both the working master and data disk icons by clicking on each one while holding down the Shift key or by dragging diagonally across both. Then eject both disks.

Choose Eject in the File menu.

After a moment's pause, both disks will be ejected. Then turn off the Macintosh.

Flip the switch.

There, you've now successfully completed your first practice session with Word.

Learning Strategy

As we explained in Chapter 1, Chapters 2 and 3 are for the novice, to make it easy for you to get started with Macintosh and Word. You have come to the end of Chapter 3, but you have not come to the end of Word. There remains a great deal for you to learn. However, you are no longer a novice. You now have a foundation that you can build on.

You also have an excellent manual that came with your Word program. So, at this point, we will adjust our method of instruction. You have learned how to use the mouse, to use menus, to select portions of text, to edit, to save, and to print. If you have any uncertainty about any of these basic techniques, take a little time right now to review the material you have covered. From this point forward, our instructions will be less detailed.

You have learned enough about Word that you are now equipped to proceed with your own documents. It is quite possible that you won't need to learn many more techniques. On the other hand, with the foundation you now have and with the Word manual as a helpful reference, you should be able to master the information in the rest of this book and work through your own, possibly more complex, projects.

You will find a wealth of Word techniques as you read through the remaining chapters. First, we try to point out ways to get the maximum benefits from your Word program, such as keyboard shortcuts, ways to organize your disks and files, and useful techniques for accomplishing a wide variety of special tasks. Second, while teaching you about printers and processes, we also try to stimulate and challenge you with ways you can use Word and with some of the exciting enhancements that are available now or will be soon. Third, we encourage you to experiment on your own. As you read through our discussions and examples, let them stimulate your imagination and curiosity. Combine your findings with ours, using this book as a guide for your own voyage of discovery.

4 Time-saving tips

Now that you're no longer a novice at using Word, you might be wondering what more there is to learn. Plenty, if you want to use Word at its fastest and most efficient. As you probably already realize, word processing can be a particularly effective way to handle written communication because it can save you time. And the more familiar you are with your word-processing program, the more time it can save.

In this chapter, we'll pass along some time-saving tips for using Word on the Macintosh that we feel are particularly helpful, based on our years of experience with a number of word-processing systems. We'll teach you shortcuts for creating and editing text, we'll discuss quick and easy ways to format and print documents, and we'll explore more efficient ways of using files. We hope these tips will stimulate you to think carefully about ways to optimize the time you spend with Word. Since you'll probably spend most of your time with Word creating and editing documents, that's where we'll start looking at ways to save time.

Time-Saving Tips for Creating and Editing Documents

In this section, we'll show you some of the time-saving features Word offers, and we'll also show you a few ways of using those features that will save you still more time. First, we'll give you some tips on using the keyboard.

Keyboard Shortcuts

Using the mouse simplifies learning Word, because all you need to do is point and click. But when your hands are on the keyboard, as they often are in the keyboard-intensive operation of word processing, the simple act of reaching for the mouse can be a distraction. That, certainly, was a major consideration for the designers of Microsoft Word, because they incorporated a keyboard command for nearly every mouse operation.

Issuing Commands

In Chapter 3, when you pulled down a menu, you may have noticed that many of the command names were followed by a cloverleaf symbol (⌘) and a letter. This cloverleaf symbol represents the Command key, the key to the left of the Spacebar with the cloverleaf symbol on it. When you press the Command key and the letter key indicated on the menu, you activate the corresponding command.

Using the keyboard to issue commands this way can save you considerable time by not having to reach for the mouse and pull down a menu. In addition to the Command key combinations in the menus, there are other combinations that are not displayed. Figure 4-1 lists all of the Command key combinations for commands in all of the menus.

Moving the Insertion Point, Scrolling, and Selecting Text

Despite the recent popularity of the mouse, many microcomputer keyboards still use four directional arrow keys to position a place marker called a cursor. For those of you who miss that time-honored tradition, Word has the answer. Instead of using the mouse, you can move the insertion point (the Mac equivalent of a cursor), scroll to a different part of your document, or select blocks of text by holding down the Option and Command keys and pressing one or more character keys. The character keys used in these moving, scrolling, and selecting operations are a group of 11 keys in three rows on the right side of the keyboard. They aren't visually set off in any special way on the keyboard and the characters on them give no hint as to the action they perform, so memorizing which key is used to perform a particular action may take some time. But once you've gotten used to using the keyboard to move, scroll, and select, you'll probably enjoy the freedom of not constantly having to reach for the mouse, especially when all you want to do is move the insertion point a short distance. For example, if you

Menu	Command	Key Sequence
File	New	Command-N
	Open	Command-O
	Close	Command-W
	Save	Command-S
	Print	Command-P
	Quit	Command-Q
Edit	Undo	Command-Z
	Cut	Command-X
	Copy	Command-C
	Paste	Command-V
	Clear	Command-B
	Show Ruler	Command-R
	Show ¶	Command-Y
Search	Find	Command-F
	Change	Command-H
	Go To	Command-G
Character	Plain	Command-Shift-Spacebar
	Bold	Command-Shift-B
	Italic	Command-Shift-I
	Underline	Command-Shift-U
	Shadow	Command-Shift-S
	Outline	Command-Shift-D
	Small Caps	Command-Shift-K
	Superscript	Command-Shift-Equal Sign
	Subscript	Command-Shift-Hyphen
	Formats	Command-D
Paragraph	Normal	Command-Shift-P
	Left	Command-Shift-L
	Center	Command-Shift-C
	Right	Command-Shift-R
	Justified	Command-Shift-J
	Open Space	Command-Shift-O
	Formats	Command-M
	Tabs	Command-T
Document	Footnote	Command-E
	Repaginate	Command-J

Figure 4-1. Command key combinations and the commands each activates

Figure 4-2. Moving the insertion point and scrolling with the Option and Command keys

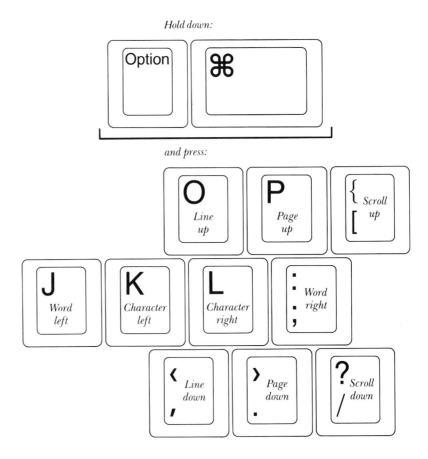

want to move the insertion point up one line, you hold down the Option and Command keys while you press the O key. Figure 4-2 shows how to move the insertion point and scroll by holding down the Option and Command keys and pressing the character key assigned to the action you want.

You can move the insertion point in other ways by holding down the Option and Command keys, pressing the quote key (″), then pressing the appropriate character key shown in Figure 4-3. For example, to move the insertion point to the top of the screen, hold down the Option and Command keys while you press the quote key, then the O key.

You can also use these key sequences to select blocks of text. First, select a starting insertion point using the Option and Command, or Option, Command, and quote key combinations. Then hold down the Shift key and move to the end of your block of text using the appropriate key combination. Word highlights all text between the two insertion points.

Figure 4-3. Moving the
insertion point and scrolling
with the Option, Command,
and quote keys

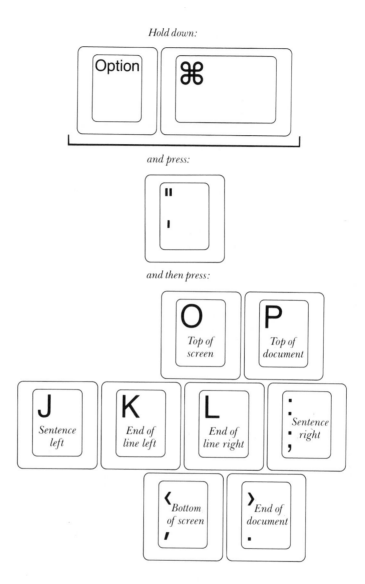

Working with Dialog Boxes

You can also use the keyboard instead of the mouse to perform most
of the actions required when working with dialog boxes. For example,
you can move the insertion point from one typing field to the next
with the Tab key. You can also select the default button (the one with
the heavy black border) by pressing either the Enter key or the Return
key, or cancel the start of a command by pressing the Command key
and the period (.) key. You can select a button by pressing the starting
letter, such as N for Next, P for Previous, Y for Yes, or N for No.

Moving and Copying Text

Using the Cut or Copy command and then the Paste command for moving and copying blocks of text is a four-step process: You select the text you want to cut or copy, you choose the Cut or Copy command, you select the place where you want the text pasted, and then you choose the Paste command. But you can get the same result in three steps using the Option and Shift-Option keys. Figure 4-4 demonstrates how Victorian poet and lyricist W. S. Gilbert might have saved himself some time writing "The Yarn of the Nancy Bell" if he had

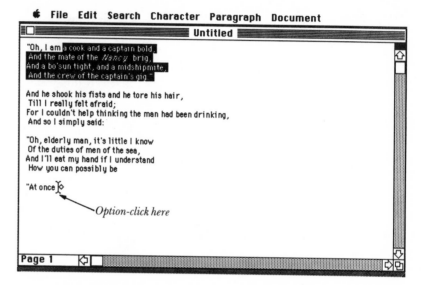

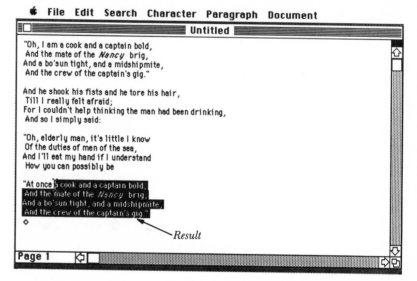

Figure 4-4. Copying text with Option and click

had a Mac and used Option-click. To start, select the text you want to copy. Using the mouse, move the I-beam to a new location. Now hold down the Option key and click the mouse button. Presto. The high-lighted text is instantly copied to the new location.

To move the highlighted text, instead of copying it, follow the same procedure, using Shift-Option-click instead of Option-click.

These two techniques are probably the most convenient for moving words and phrases around as you are creating the initial draft. The only drawback is that these techniques work only within one docu-ment window, since you must be able to scroll from the highlighted source to the new location.

Duplicating Formats

If you use the same character or paragraph formats repeatedly in the same document, you can duplicate those formats without having to choose the same format command again and again. Word offers two different ways to do this: the Option-Command key combination and Command-A (also known as the Again key).

To use the Option-Command key combination, first select the block of text you want to format. If you want to duplicate a character format, hold down the Option and Command keys and click on a character that has the desired format. If you want to duplicate a paragraph for-mat, hold down the Option and Command keys and click in the selec-tion bar beside the paragraph that has the format you want to copy. The highlighted text is immediately transformed to the format of the character or paragraph you clicked, as shown in Figure 4-5.

The Option-Command key combination works best for duplicating a format in one other block of text. But if you want to copy formatting to several blocks of text, there is a better way. If you use Option-Com-mand to copy a format to several blocks of text that aren't adjacent, it could take you a long time because you have to select one block, press Option-Command and click, then move to the next block and repeat the process. In cases such as this, it's quicker to use Command-A.

To duplicate a format using Command-A, select the first block you want to format and choose the format command you want to use. Move to the next block, select it, and press Command-A. The format-ting is instantly duplicated in the second block. Then move to the next block, select it, and press Command-A again. You can do this as many times as you want, as long as you don't type or edit between uses of Command-A. Command-A always repeats your last typing or editing action. You could, if you wanted to, repeat a word, a phrase, or a para-graph again and again using Command-A.

Figure 4-5. Duplicating a format with the Option and Command keys

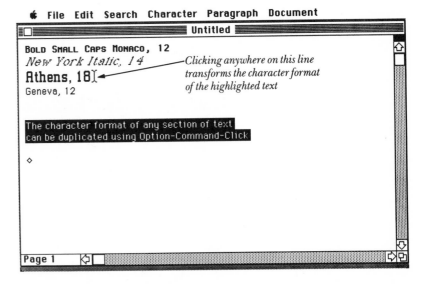

Clicking anywhere on this line transforms the character format of the highlighted text

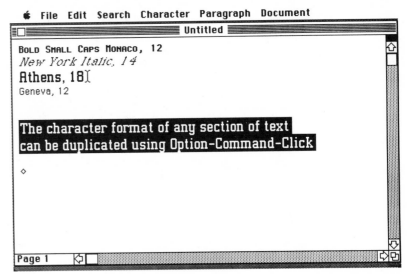

Word Does Windows

Keyboard shortcuts aren't the only time-savers Word offers for creating a document. Word's ability to divide the screen into as many as four windows can save you time by allowing you to see several documents at once rather than going from one to another. You can open up to four different windows, each containing a different document, on your screen by choosing the Open command from the File menu (or by pressing Command-O). Or you can open more than one window for the same document so that you can see different parts of the document at the same time (any editing you do in one window is immediately reflected in the others).

You can have the document you are writing in one window, your outline in another, notes and quotes in a third, and a glossary or index in the fourth. With this setup, you can copy and paste excerpts from notes and quotes directly into the document. You can refer to the outline to refresh your memory or you can update it if you suddenly get inspired to take a new direction. If you introduce a new concept or term, you can add it immediately to the index or glossary. All of this can be done easily, electronically, and without shuffling a single scrap of paper on your desk.

Working with More than One Window

Word positions each new window you open so that the title bar of the previous window is still visible. If you open four windows, you can rearrange the position and size of each so that all four are visible at the same time or the active window fills the entire screen. Using the size box in the lower right corner of each window, you can reduce or expand its size. With your pointer in its title bar, you can drag a window up, down, or sideways. For example, if you have more than one window open, you can use the size box to reduce each window so that it occupies approximately one quarter of the screen, and then move each window to a different corner. Then double-click in the title bar of the active window. It instantly expands to fill the screen. When you want to view or work in a different window, double-click the title bar of the active window to shrink it to its previous size.

Splitting Document Windows

How many times have you had to stop writing in the middle of a document and leaf back to an earlier page to see if you'd already mentioned a topic or to verify what you wrote? Word's ability to split windows allows you to observe what you wrote on the previous page or several pages back at the same time you are creating new text.

The little black bar in the upper right corner of each window is called the split bar. If you drag the split bar down the scroll bar toward the middle of the window, a double line splits the window into two independent sections, with each section becoming, in effect, a separate window that you can scroll separately. When you want to close the lower window, drag the split bar back to the top of the scroll bar where you found it.

One caution: If you have four document windows on your screen and try to split one of them, you will see an alert box with the message, Too many windows are open.

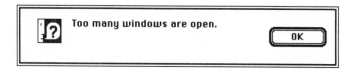

However, there are some windows you can open even if you already have four document windows on the screen. Word allows you to show the Glossary and the Scrapbook (but not the Clipboard) no matter how many windows are open.

Creating and Using Glossaries

Another way to increase your productivity while creating a document is to teach the computer long words or phrases that you use frequently, and then let the computer type them for you. You do this by using a special file, called a glossary. Use glossaries for words or phrases that you have trouble typing or tend to misspell, for words that occur frequently in your business documents, or simply for your return address. A glossary can also store graphics.

When you create a glossary entry, you give it a simple code name. Then, when you want to use that entry, you type the code name and press Command-Backspace. Once you've created a glossary entry, it's available for you to use in any subsequent document until you delete it. The size of a glossary is limited only by available disk space.

To set up a glossary entry, you first type the text you want to use as an entry. It doesn't matter where you type it, since you can delete it once it's stored in a glossary. Format it, if you want, then select it. Cut or copy it to the Clipboard, then choose Show Glossary from the Edit menu. A window titled Glossary appears. In this window, type the code name you want to use for the entry in the Name of Glossary text box and choose Paste from the Edit menu (or press Command-V). Your entry appears below the text box and the name appears in the list box on the right. For example, as an entry, you might type in the following address:

Henry Gondorf, President
408 Washington Street, Suite A
Lancaster, MO 38293

You could give this address the code name *hg*.

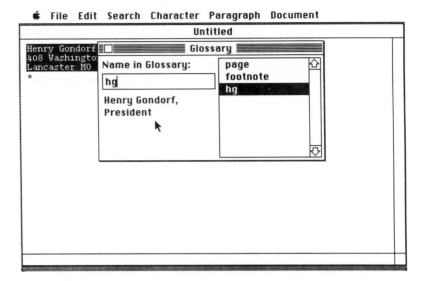

Then, the next time you wanted to use this address in your text, you'd just type *hg*, followed immediately by Command-Backspace. Word would replace your two-letter code with the entire three lines.

Glossaries have possibilities far beyond common phrases and addresses. To store a graphic from another application (a drawing from MacPaint, a financial table from Multiplan, a pie chart from Microsoft Chart), cut or copy it to the Clipboard in the other application, open Word, choose Show Glossary, type a name, and then choose Paste. Since they store graphics from another application, glossaries can provide ready access to a letterhead, a series of cartoon characters to lighten up your memos, or a chart plotting the monthly trend of your company overhead.

Consider the possible use of several glossary files. You might fill one with legalistic terminology for use in proposals, technical specifications, purchase agreements, or contracts. You could use another for clients' names and addresses. If you are working with technical reports, a glossary full of mathematical formulas or troublesome terms could be a great time-saver. For example, it's much faster to type *ptp* instead of *3,3,4,5,7-pentamethyl-4,6,7-triethyl-5-propyldecane.*

You can save glossary entries in a file titled Standard Glossary, the name that automatically appears in the dialog box that is displayed if you choose the Save As... command while the glossary window is on your screen, or if you choose the Quit command.

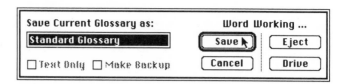

But setting up separate glossaries is straightforward. Just type in any other name in the text box in which Standard Glossary appears.

Standard Glossary is the only glossary you see when you choose the Show Glossary command in the Edit menu. To see a glossary saved under any other name, use the Show Glossary command to display the Standard Glossary window, then choose the Open command and select the name of the glossary that you want to see. It appears in the glossary window.

Searching for Text

One of the most useful time-savers of any word processor is the ability to search through an entire document and pick out each occurrence of a word, a code, or a punctuation feature that needs to be changed. The Search menu gives you three options: Find, Change, and Go To.

The Find command demonstrates the fundamental search process, so let's use it for learning how the Search commands work.

Using the Find Command

The Find dialog box gives you two refinements that help Word zero in on your target: Whole Word and Match Upper/Lowercase.

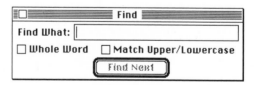

If you are searching for the word *each,* but you don't want to find words like *teacher, reaching,* or *peach,* you can click in the Whole Word check box. If you are looking for a particular combination of uppercase and lowercase letters, you can click in the Match box.

You start the process by pulling down the Search menu and choosing Find. When you see the insertion point blinking in the Find What text box, you type in the text you want to find, and click the Find Next button to start the search.

Each time the search process locates the word or text you entered, it stops at that location and highlights that text. If at any point in your search the highlighted text is not visible, it's because the Find dialog box is covering it. You have to drag the dialog box out of the way to see the highlighted text.

To continue the search after each stop, you click the Find Next button. Keep clicking the Find Next button each time until you see an alert box that announces, Search Complete.

This alert box indicates that, no matter where you started searching, the search has gone through the entire text and is back to the original insertion point.

Find is useful when you want to find each occurrence of a portion of text so that you can add information or record its location, depending on the context. For example, Find could be invaluable in creating an index for a book or long technical report.

Using the Change Command

When you want to change or replace a word everywhere it occurs in the text, the command to use is Change. The Change command can zip through an entire document and change every occurrence of a particular block of text or only those occurrences you select. The Change command adds several features to the basic search process.

≣□≣≣≣≣≣≣≣≣≣≣≣≣ Change ≣≣≣≣≣≣≣≣≣≣≣≣
Find What:
Change To:
☐ Whole Word   ☐ Match Upper/Lowercase
[Find Next] [Change, then Find] [Change] [Change All]

Just as with Find, you start by entering the text you want to find in the Find What text box. Then you type the replacement text into the Change To text box. The Whole Word and Match Upper/Lowercase options are the same as in the Find dialog box.

With a row of buttons at the bottom, the Change dialog box is much like a control panel. The Change All button activates a mode that scans the entire document, changing all occurrences. The Find Next button tells Word to stop at the next occurrence. When Word stops, you can click Find Next again without making a change or you can click Change. The Change Then Find button makes the change, then searches for the next occurrence.

You can limit the text-changing process to any portion of your document. Just select the block of text to be searched before choosing the Change command.

Using the Go To Command

The Go To command is particularly useful for longer documents: It takes you to the page you request. (Page numbers reflect pages as they will be printed.) For this reason, the Go To command can be a real time-saving convenience. It is just a matter of typing in the page number you want and clicking OK. It places your insertion point on the first line of the page you requested. If you are not sure of the page number, sometimes you can use the Find command to put you at the nearest subheading or at a unique word sequence near the location you want.

Saving Your Work
Frequently

One of the most frustrating ways to spend your word-processing time is redoing hours of work from scratch. This is likely to be the fate of anyone who has not yet learned the golden rule of computing: No document is safe until it is stored on disk. There are just too many things that can destroy hours of work in an instant: power outages, faulty disks, faulty user, obscure bugs in the software, even accidental exposure of a disk to a magnetic field.

It pays to make a habit of saving your work by simply choosing Save from the File menu (or pressing Command-S) regularly. Do it every ten minutes or every half hour, but do it regularly.

Even if you've saved your document, it is not really safe until it is stored on a separate backup disk (or two). Copy all changed files to a separate disk at the end of each word-processing session.

Time-Saving Tips for Printing Documents

Printing your documents can be a time-consuming process simply because printers can't print data as fast as computers can send it. It's frustrating to have the computer unavailable while printing is in progress. But there are ways to beat this game.

Printing from the Initial
Desktop

One way to save time with printing is to save the documents and print them all at once from the initial desktop. Finish editing all the files you want to print, then exit Word to the initial desktop. You can select all the files you want to print, even if their icons aren't adjacent, by holding down the Shift key while you click on each file icon. (*Note:* All selected files must be from the same application program.) Then choose Print from the File menu. The Mac loads Word and the first document, then displays a Print dialog box, allowing you to select various printing options. The options you choose will be used for all files to be printed, so choose wisely.

Check to make sure there is enough paper in the printer, and that the paper can feed freely so that nothing will get jammed. Then click OK and printing commences. You can walk away and let the printer run, but it is wise to keep an ear tuned and to check on the printer periodically while it is running.

Printing with a Print Buffer

For a few hundred dollars, you can purchase a print buffer, a device that accepts data as fast as the computer can send it. Data is stored in the buffer and passed on to the printer at the printer's own pace. When the computer is through sending data to the buffer, you regain control of the computer and the buffer continues to spoon-feed the printer. Some buffers are large enough to store several documents.

Printing Form Letters

If you send form letters to several different people, nothing will save you more time than the Print Merge... command from the File menu. Print Merge... can automatically insert names and addresses from a mailing list into a form letter, saving you from having to type and print each letter individually.

Print Merge... isn't like most commands that you can just choose at any time; you need to do some planning and take a few preliminary steps. Before you choose the Print Merge... command, you need to prepare two documents: a main document (such as a form letter) and a merge document (containing, for example, a mailing list).

For now, we'll only show you the basics needed to create a simple form letter. It won't take long for you to discover the time-saving potential of the Print Merge... command. If you want to learn more, be sure to read Chapter 9, where we'll take you step-by-step through a more sophisticated Print Merge... project.

Preparing the Main Document

You create the main document just as you would create any Word document, except that you put a placeholder called a field at each place where the information will change from one printout to the next. Each field is identified by a name of your choosing and is enclosed by international quotation marks (« and »). To type the « symbol, you hold down the Option key and press the backslash (\) key; to type the » symbol, you hold down the Option and Shift keys and press the backslash key.

The text inserted in place of a field will have whatever character format you give the field name. So, if you want the inserted text to be boldface and italic, for example, format the field name with boldface and italic when you type the main document.

You tell Word how to use the information in the fields by including instructions, which are also surrounded by international quotation marks. The DATA instruction, for example, identifies the merge document where Word can find the information you want inserted. Just type the word DATA (in any combination of capital and lowercase letters), a space, and the name of the merge document. The DATA instruction must always precede all other instructions and fields in the main document. It may be the only instruction you'll need in simple documents like the order-acknowledgment letter in Figure 4-6, which includes several fields and a DATA instruction.

Preparing the Merge Document A merge document supplies the information that allows Word to personalize each printing of the main document. It's fairly easy to assemble, since it's really nothing more than a series of lists. But you need to make sure that each list follows the same order.

To prepare a merge document, you first type a list of the field names you used in the main document, in the order you used them. This list of field names is called the header record. Then, for each letter, you type a list of the information you want Word to insert in place of the field names. These lists of field replacements are called data records.

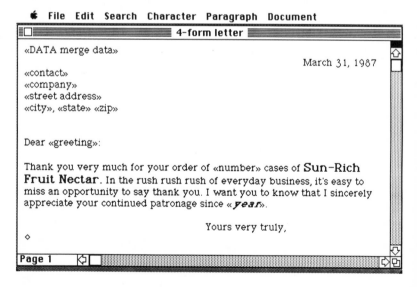

Figure 4-6. A sample letter containing fields and a DATA instruction

Use a comma or a single tab to separate one field from another in both the header record and each data record. If you want to start a new record, just press Return. If you want to start a new line, but not a new record, press Shift-Return. Figure 4-7 shows the merge document for the order-acknowledgment letter in Figure 4-6, with the Show ¶ command chosen so you can see where Return was pressed and where Shift-Return was pressed.

Printing a Form Letter

When you've finished preparing your main document and merge document, you're almost ready to print. First, make sure both documents are on the same disk. If you want to change the appearance of the printed page or if you just want to check the settings you selected previously, choose the Page Setup... command from the File menu. Then, open the main document and choose Print Merge... from the File menu. The Print Merge dialog box that appears is identical to the dialog box that appears when you choose Print... from the File menu. Choose your print options and click OK (or press Return). Word prints as many copies of the main document as there are data records in the merge document. Sample form letters, printed from the main document in Figure 4-6 and the merge document in Figure 4-7, are shown in Figure 4-8.

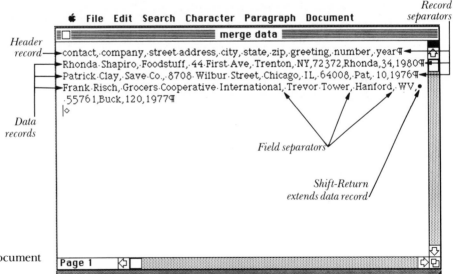

Figure 4-7. A merge document for a form letter

March 31, 1987

Rhonda Shapiro
Foodstuff
44 First Ave
Trenton, NY 72372

Dear Rhonda:

Thank you very much for your order of 34 cases of **Sun-Rich Fruit Nectar**. In the rush rush rush of everyday business, it's easy to miss an opportunity to say thank you. I want you to know that I sincerely appreciate your continued patronage since *1980*.

Yours very truly,

March 31, 1987

Frank Risch
Grocers Cooperative International
Trevor Tower
Hanford, WV 55761

Dear Buck:

Thank you very much for your order of 120 cases of **Sun-Rich Fruit Nectar**. In the rush rush rush of everyday business, it's easy to miss an opportunity to say thank you. I want you to know that I sincerely appreciate your continued patronage since *1977*.

Yours very truly,

March 31, 1987

Patrick Clay
Save Co.
8708 Wilbur Street
Chicago, IL 64008

Dear Pat:

Thank you very much for your order of 10 cases of **Sun-Rich Fruit Nectar**. In the rush rush rush of everyday business, it's easy to miss an opportunity to say thank you. I want you to know that I sincerely appreciate your continued patronage since *1976*.

Yours very truly,

Figure 4-8. Sample form letters

Time-Saving Tips for Managing Files

You can also save time by organizing and managing your disk files in an efficient way. You've already taken an important first step toward good disk file management in Chapter 2 by creating a data disk for storing only documents. To help you understand why, let's look at how the Macintosh stores information.

Computers store information in units called bytes, each of which represents one character. The place where the Mac stores information is called memory. A computer has two kinds of memory—read only memory and random access memory—each one serving different functions. Read only memory (or ROM) generally contains only information the Mac needs to perform certain basic operations, such as getting information from disks. The Mac has 64 kilobytes, or 64K, of ROM. (A kilobyte is 1,024 bytes.) Random access memory (or RAM) is where part of the Word program and your document are stored while you're working with them. You have 128K of RAM if you have a standard Mac, 512K if you have a Fat Mac.

Working with the information in RAM is fast, because the Mac has almost immediate access to everything that's stored there. But RAM isn't large enough to accommodate everything Word needs, plus your document. So, Word periodically has to go to a disk for more information. Another limitation of RAM is that it's not permanent: As soon as you turn off your Mac, the contents of RAM are gone. Of course, if you have saved your work on a disk, it doesn't matter. You just have the Mac transfer your document back into RAM after you turn on the Mac the next time.

Computers store information on disks in chunks called files. The size of a file is limited only by the capacity of the disk. Mac disks can store 400K of information. Files on your Word Master disk account for about 370K, leaving only about 30K for any documents you might want to store on it. Adding another claim to this relatively small remaining space are temporary files Word creates to store changes you make to your document. A page of text takes up about 3K, so, if you're lucky, you might find room on an unaltered Word Master disk for a seven-page document. Obviously, if you intend to do any serious word processing, you'll need more room. You provide yourself with more room by using a data disk.

But using data disks won't take care of all your space problems. Word still needs to use a certain amount of the 30K left on the master disk (even the working copy you're now using) for the temporary files we mentioned. And, if you're using a LaserWriter printer, you'll have to make some room on your Word disk for the 70 to 90K needed for the printer driver and the print fonts you'll have to transfer from the disk that comes with the LaserWriter. So, to accommodate all these extra files, it's a good idea to remove a few unneeded files from your Word Working Master disk.

Removing Unneeded Word Files

Some good candidates for removal from the Word Working Master are Help (37K), Memo (3K), printer drivers that you won't be using (1K each for daisy-wheel printer drivers, 17K for the original ImageWriter driver), and any print fonts you're sure you won't use (fonts generally range from 2K to 14K). Whatever you decide to remove, be sure you do it to a working copy of the master disk and not to your original Word Master disk. That way, should your needs change, you can always transfer a deleted file from the master to your working disk. And just to be on the safe side, you may want to make an extra, unaltered backup copy of the Word Master before you start deleting files.

Now which files should you remove and what are the consequences? The Help file is a tempting choice because it uses 37K of valuable disk space. This file contains the explanations Word displays when you choose the Help command from the Apple (&) menu or press Command-? and select a topic from the list in the Help dialog box. The Help feature is most valuable while you are still learning about Word. Once you have established a working rapport with the program, you can consider removing the Help file from the system disk. Simply drag the Word.Help icon to the Trash icon and release the mouse button. Then choose Empty Trash from the Special menu. Word functions fine without the Help file. If you later call for help, Word simply gives you the message, The Word.Help file is missing or altered.

You can remove printer drivers and Memo this same way, but removing fonts requires the use of the Font Mover program supplied on the system disk that came with your Mac. The procedure is discussed fully in Chapter 8.

Refinements on File Management

A disk can become considerably cluttered with a number of short files. If you don't take charge of the chaos, you may end up losing files or at least spending a lot of time looking for them. The Macintosh provides a means to group documents in its own version of the familiar file folder. Using folders can greatly speed up the process of storing and retrieving files.

Using File Folders

Every time you initialize a new disk, the system provides it with an icon labeled Empty Folder. When you select this icon and choose the Duplicate command from the File menu, or press Command-D, another

Figure 4-9. Folders stored within folders

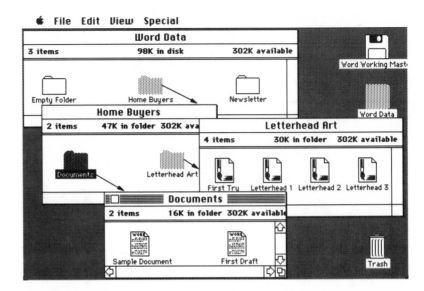

folder icon appears, labeled Copy of Empty Folder. You can create as many copies of Empty Folder as you need and relabel them as project folders, subject folders, any-category-you-wish folders. Then you can drag any file icon into the folder where you want it filed.

To see what is stored in a folder, double-click on the folder icon to display the folder window. If your organization system requires layers of subtopics, you can store folders within folders. For example, you could store a draft and a final version of the home-buyers' guide from Chapter 3 in one folder and different versions of the letterhead in another, as shown in Figure 4-9.

Organizing Disks by Project

As your proficiency with Word grows, and the range of applications you use it for increases, you'll find that having a single working copy of the master disk can be restrictive. One way to improve your efficiency is to create a separate Word Working Master disk for each major type of project or document. That way, you can load the working master disk that contains the printer drivers, type fonts, and special glossaries appropriate to that application.

To the extent that you can differentiate between projects or document types, you can set up your Word working master disks and data files accordingly. You can file your disks by project, keeping each version of the Word Working Master disk with the corresponding data disks. Then, when you pick up your disks to start a new session, you know that your basic tools are there for support.

Figure 4-10. An outline
template

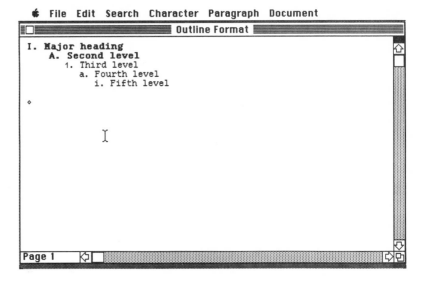

Building Your Own Templates   There is a way to refine this process even further and construct a file that's roughly equivalent to a style sheet, a feature of Word for the IBM PC. You can open a new, untitled file, type standard paragraphs you use all the time, and choose the formats you want from the Document, Paragraph, File, and Character menus. Then, save that file with the name Format 1 or Template A. You can create similar templates for all your standard document formats in the same manner. You can even type in standard headings, paragraphs, salutations, and other appropriate text. Figure 4-10 demonstrates how this technique could be used to set up a template for a report outline.

When you need to type one of the standard documents, just select the appropriate template, open it up on the screen, type in the details of this particular document, and save it under a different document name. In the Format 1/Template A example shown above, you can use Option-Command-click to transfer paragraph and character formats from any of the sample lines to your text.

Practice the techniques presented in this chapter using the sample document you created in Chapter 3 and explore any shortcuts that occur to you. When you feel comfortable with Word, turn to Chapter 5 to begin a closer look at the printing options available to you with Word and the Mac.

SECTION TWO

PRINTING WITH WORD

5 Choosing the right printer

Before you go out to buy a car, you have to make some decisions. For example, are you going to use it to haul firewood, to ferry your kids' swim team, or to take you to important business meetings? If you decide you're going to use it primarily to haul firewood, you'll probably buy a pickup truck, not a luxury car. But if it's going to serve as the team bus, you'll probably opt for a station wagon instead of a truck.

The process is the same when you are shopping for a printer. You need to ask yourself what your primary use will be and what you want the printer to do. Do you want your letters and reports to have the professional, executive typewriter look? Do your documents often include illustrations? Do you need a fast printer? A quiet printer? A printer that does a number of things well, no matter what the cost?

This chapter describes the different types of printer and helps you understand what they can do and how they do it. If you haven't yet bought a printer or you're thinking of buying another, the information in this chapter should help you decide which printer is for you.

Printers That Work with Word

In order to give the Mac access to a full range of printing features, particularly graphics printing, Apple wrote the Mac's printer-control software for the ImageWriter. This software, called the printer driver, is in the System folder on the Word Master disk. So, with the System folder, Word on the Mac is compatible with the ImageWriter.

Word adds to this compatibility by also including on the Word Master disk printer drivers for five major printers: Diablo 630, NEC 7710, AppleDaisy, Brother, and the typewriter. If the printer you want to use is on this list, it's compatible for use with Word on the Mac. If the printer you want to use isn't an ImageWriter and isn't on this list, you may still be able to use it if it is compatible with one of the printer drivers provided on the Word disk or with the ImageWriter printer driver. For example, Qume says its Letterpro 20 and Sprint 11 daisy-wheel printers are fully compatible with the AppleDaisy driver, one of the drivers on the Word disk. Almost any fully formed character printer can use the typewriter printer driver for standard text with no character formatting, such as boldfacing and underlining. You also may be able to use a printer driver provided by the printer manufacturer. In any case, be sure to test the printer or see it operated by the dealer the way you'll be using it before you buy, to make sure it does exactly what you want it to do with Word and any other software you intend to use.

A number of printer manufacturers make printers and other hardware that emulate the ImageWriter and use the ImageWriter printer driver. For example, the Blue Mac, a product of Riteman Computer Printers of Inglewood, California, and several C. Itoh printers emulate the ImageWriter. SoftStyle Inc. of Honolulu, Hawaii, has taken a different approach: it enables the popular Epson printer to emulate the ImageWriter with a printer circuit card, called HanZon.

Other printer manufacturers, such as Toshiba and NEC, provide their own printer drivers or modify the ImageWriter printer driver in order to make their products compatible with the Macintosh. In addition, several independent software developers sell software aimed at making various printers Mac-compatible. For example, SoftStyle offers a printer driver called Epstart for making Epson printers compatible (we demonstrate how to use Epstart in Chapter 7) and Creighton Development of Irvine, California, produces a stand-alone print utility called ProPrint that prints text files on a variety of fully formed character printers.

Microsoft's MacEnhancer, a peripheral device and software package, allows you to use Word on the Macintosh with a number of dot-matrix printers: Epson FX-80, Epson FX-100, Epson LQ-1500, Epson MX-80, Epson MX-100, Epson RX-80, Epson RX-100, IBM Graphics, C. Itoh ProWriter 8510, Okidata 92, Okidata 93, Toshiba P1340, and Toshiba P1351. The MacEnhancer also supports one ink-jet printer, the Hewlett-Packard ThinkJet.

Printer Types

If you haven't yet bought a printer, you may be unfamiliar with the three major printer types that you can use with Word on the Macintosh: dot-matrix, fully formed character, and laser. In the next few pages, we will give you enough information about how each works so you will have a basic understanding of the differences in the three technologies. We'll start with dot-matrix printers.

Dot-Matrix Printers

Dot-matrix printers are the most widely used type of printer today, probably because they are relatively inexpensive, reasonably fast, and impressively versatile. They print by impact—that is, a print head strikes an inked ribbon, which then presses against the paper to print an image. The print head contains one or more columns of tiny wires, called pins. These pins are fired at the ribbon in combinations that create patterns of dots as the print head moves across the page, as shown in Figure 5-1.

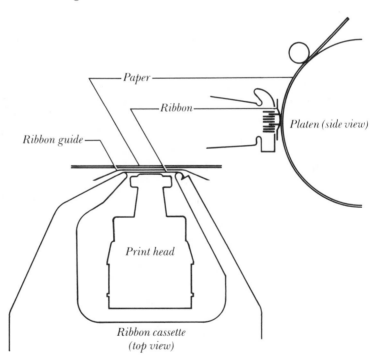

Figure 5-1. A dot-matrix print head

Dot-matrix printers print each text character according to a pre-defined dot pattern, or matrix. Printing matrices of dots to produce characters is what gives the dot-matrix printer its name. The name is somewhat misleading, since other types of printer, such as laser, ink-jet, and electrostatic, also form characters from matrices. However, the term "dot-matrix printer" is usually applied only to those printers that form matrices by firing pins at a ribbon.

Dot-Matrix Character Formation

In dot-matrix printing, the dot pattern for each character is a rectangular matrix stored in the printer's memory. The pattern for each character may vary from printer to printer. Figure 5-2 shows some sample matrices used by the ImageWriter.

The ImageWriter character matrix is nine dots tall and eight dots wide. But notice that the farthest right column of each matrix is blank. This blank column provides the space between adjacent characters. Vertical spacing between printed lines is controlled by the rate at which the paper feeds through the printer. The pre-set, or default, line-feed distance is ⅙ inch, but it can be varied by special programming in increments as small as ¹⁄₁₄₄ inch.

The matrices in Figure 5-2 represent only the dot patterns, not the spacing between dots. The vertical distance between dots is fixed by the distance between pins in the print head. This distance is typically ¹⁄₇₂ inch for nine-wire printers, such as the ImageWriter. Horizontal spacing between dot columns is not fixed; it is a function of the timing of pin firings and the speed of the print head as it moves across the page. On the ImageWriter, the distance between dot columns, called the pitch, can vary from ¹⁄₁₆₀ inch to ¹⁄₇₂ inch. Figure 5-3 shows elite proportional (the ImageWriter's tightest spacing) and elite extended (its loosest spacing).

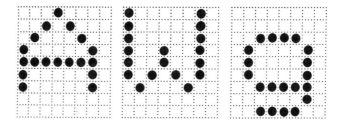

Figure 5-2. ImageWriter matrices for capital A, capital W, and lowercase g

Figure 5-3. The ImageWriter's tightest (top) and loosest (bottom) spacing

160 dots per inch (Elite Proportional)

72 dots per inch (Extended)

The default for horizontal spacing on the ImageWriter is ⅟₉₆ inch, which produces elite characters (12 characters per inch or 12 pitch). Word uses the elite characters in Draft-mode printing. Word's Standard mode uses a dot spacing of ⅟₈₀ inch.

Dot patterns are transferred to the printed page one column at a time as the print head moves horizontally across the paper. To print a capital W, as shown in Figure 5-4, the print head fires the top six pins, which prints the first column of the matrix, the downstroke of the W. Then the print head moves a small distance to the right (the distance depends on the pitch setting) and fires pin 7. This process of print-head movement and pin firing continues until each column of the letter is printed.

Screen Duplication with Dot-Matrix Printers

Word uses dot-matrix printers in two ways. In Draft mode, it uses the built-in characters and features (bold, underline, superscript, and subscript) of the printer. In Standard and High quality modes, the dots, or pixels, on the screen are duplicated on the paper by the pins of

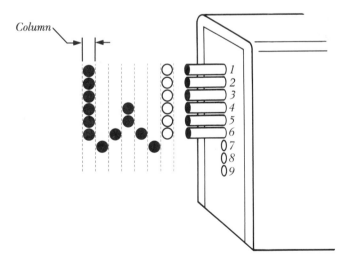

Figure 5-4. Pin-firing patterns for letter W

Figure 5-5. A 24-wire dot-matrix print head

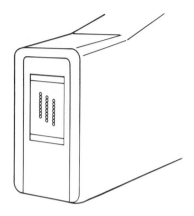

the print head using the graphics mode of the printer. In Standard mode, for example, Word assembles an image of each page in memory, with each unit, or bit, of information representing one pixel (this process is called bit-mapping). For every row of printing, Word activates the printer's graphics mode and transfers the appropriate dot patterns to the printer. Word print modes are explained in detail in Chapter 6.

The ImageWriter is considered a first-generation printer. A second generation of dot-matrix printers produces both smaller dots and greater density by using print heads with 24 thin wires (as small as $8/1000$ inch in diameter). The wires are arranged on the print head in two or three columns that are offset vertically as shown in Figure 5-5. This arrangement makes it possible to obtain a denser and smoother character with a single pass of the print head. The print quality represents a significant step toward the typewriter look produced by fully formed character printers.

Even though 24-wire printers have smaller, more densely packed pins and finer resolution than their 9-wire counterparts, Word treats them like 9-wire printers. Word uses the built-in ImageWriter printer driver, which Apple designed around a 9-wire printer, for 24-wire printers. Designing another driver to fully support 24-wire printers is an enormous task, not yet warranted by the limited market penetration of these printers. So, Word is likely to continue to treat all impact dot-matrix printers as 9-wire printers.

Ink-Jet Printers

As mentioned earlier in this chapter, ink-jet printers also form characters by printing dots in matrix patterns, just as impact dot-matrix printers do. But instead of using pins to print the dots, ink-jet printers use tiny droplets of ink. These droplets are sprayed directly onto the paper by the print head. The Hewlett-Packard ThinkJet, compatible with Word through the Microsoft MacEnhancer, uses an 11- by 12-character matrix.

Because the ink droplets tend to bleed into fuzzy dots on standard printer paper, most users of ink-jet printers prefer to use a specially coated paper that resists ink bleeding.

Fully Formed Character Printers

You should understand from the outset that fully formed character printers print text only; they cannot reproduce Macintosh screen fonts or graphics, although some can print some of Word's character formats, such as boldfacing and underlining. To approximate the printout from a fully formed character printer on the screen, Microsoft designed a completely new series of screen fonts (Dover).

Fully formed character printers are so called because the printing element utilizes the same kind of fully formed, raised characters that you see on a typewriter. These printers are also known as letter-quality printers because they produce print quality suitable for a business letter—the quality produced by an IBM Selectric typewriter.

The best-known fully formed character printers are the daisy-wheel printers. They use a flat, circular printing element, made of plastic or metal, with spokes radiating out from a hub in the center, much like petals on a daisy. At the end of each spoke is a single, raised, fully formed character. As illustrated in Figure 5-6, the daisy wheel is mounted on the print head in a vertical position.

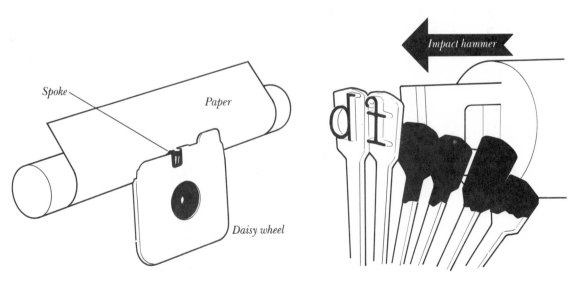

Figure 5-6. A daisy-wheel print head

Figure 5-7. A thimble print
element

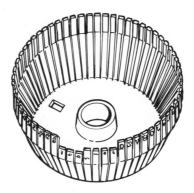

One motor moves the print head horizontally across a track and a second motor rotates the print wheel to the selected character. To print a character, an electromagnetically controlled hammer strikes a spoke against the ribbon to transfer the image to paper.

A variation on the daisy-wheel design, championed by NEC Information Systems, is the thimble print element shown in Figure 5-7. A thimble printer operates in much the same way as a daisy-wheel printer: The thimble is rotated to position the selected character in front of a hammer, which presses the raised character against the ribbon and paper.

One advantage of the thimble is that you can install and remove it easily without removing the ribbon and disengaging the print head. This can make a difference if you need to change print wheels often in order to print different character styles. However, some daisy-wheel printers now have the print wheel in a removable cartridge that takes approximately five seconds to replace.

Laser Printers

Recent breakthroughs in the technology and dramatic price reductions have made laser printers available to the desktop computer user. Laser printers combine office copier and laser technologies to produce letter-quality printing. Laser printers are faster and quieter than impact printers and they have the flexibility to handle the full range of Word's output.

As shown in Figure 5-8, the process starts with a laser source emitting a narrow beam of pulsating light, directed at a rotating, multi-faceted mirror. The mirror redirects the light pulses through two lenses and a reflecting mirror onto a rotating, cylindrical drum. The drum is coated with a photosensitive substance that holds a positive charge. The light pulses neutralize the positive charge of the photosensitive substance at every spot they strike on the drum, forming the image of whatever is being printed. As the drum turns, it comes

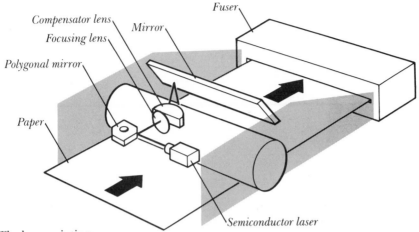

Figure 5-8. The laser printing process

into contact with a fine plastic powder, called toner, which has a positive charge. Since opposite electrical charges attract, the positively charged toner particles are repelled by the positively charged surface of the drum, but stick to each neutralized spot on that surface. As the drum rotates further, it comes into contact with paper that carries a negative electrical charge and the positively charged toner particles stick to the negatively charged paper. To complete the process, the paper is passed between two heated rollers that fuse the toner particles onto the paper at about 200 degrees Celsius. As the drum continues its revolution, the exposed section of the drum is then cleaned and recharged.

The print mechanism used in this process was developed by Canon for its personal copier. Both of the current entries in the low-cost laser market, Apple's LaserWriter and Hewlett-Packard's LaserJet, use this process. All the print-producing elements are contained in a disposable cartridge, including the photosensitive drum, electrostatic charging device, developer and toner assembly, and cleaner. Since these are the components with the most limited lifespans, replacing the cartridge when it runs out of toner takes care of nearly all maintenance.

The LaserWriter operates with ½ megabyte of ROM and 1½ megabytes of RAM. That is more than three times the memory of the 512K Macintosh computer and over 20 times the memory of the Hewlett-Packard LaserJet. This voluminous memory enables the LaserWriter to store a full page of high-resolution graphics (300 dots per inch, or dpi) in memory. The LaserJet can only store about a 5½-inch square at 300 dpi or a full page at 150 dpi.

The LaserWriter contains in its ROM a graphics language called PostScript. Developed by Adobe Systems, PostScript can control the placement of graphics and text on the page with such accuracy it has the potential to become a standard for graphics manipulation of high-resolution output devices. The combination of large memory capacity and the PostScript language speeds up the printing process, because the Macintosh can send condensed PostScript commands instead of lengthy bit maps (pixel-by-pixel representations) to the printer. The printer then creates an image of the page in printer memory.

HP's LaserJet stores dot patterns of its own fonts in fixed sizes, much like the Macintosh stores screen fonts. It generates patterns for other sizes from these fixed sizes. In contrast, the LaserWriter's ROM stores 13 fonts that are based on professional typesetting standards, as well as the PostScript programming language. It stores the outline of each character of each font in only one size and PostScript generates a dot pattern for virtually any size. In addition, Apple has a licensing agreement with Allied Linotype, one of the world's leading typesetting equipment firms and font copyright owners, giving Apple access to a type library of over 1300 typefaces.

The LaserWriter is ideally suited for a business-office situation, where its cost can be spread among several users. Using the AppleTalk network it can be shared by a number of Macs or other computers. It is considered by some to be the machine that will reshape business-office printing as the Mac is reshaping personal computers.

Printer Comparisons

Each of the three major printer types (dot-matrix, fully formed character, and laser) offers a range of features. In this section, we compare printer types on the basis of the main features you look for when buying a printer—quality, speed, noise level, versatility, and support.

Quality

The output quality of fully formed character printers is the standard against which other printers are measured. Comparable to the finest business typewriters, the print they produce is good enough to be referred to as letter-quality printing. Many people think it is the finest print quality available for word-processing applications this side of typeset print. For this reason, fully formed character printers are the

Figure 5-9. Sample printouts from the NEC 2010 (top) and Diablo 630 (bottom) fully formed character printers

`Letter Quality NEC 2010 Courier 12`

`Letter Quality Diablo 630 Pica 10`

likely choice where word processing is a high priority and quality is essential. What you sacrifice for this quality is speed, versatility, and graphics ability. Figure 5-9 shows the quality of printout from two popular fully formed character printers.

If you don't need the highest quality type, but you need speed, versatility, and graphics ability, you might want a dot-matrix printer. As already mentioned, Word offers three levels of quality with dot-matrix printers: Draft, Standard, and High. Draft mode is the lowest level of quality, using the built-in characters of the printer. Standard mode uses the graphics mode of the printer to reproduce the screen fonts on paper. High printing mode combines denser horizontal spacing with two-pass printing of each line to produce the best dot-matrix print possible with Word. We'll discuss these three modes in greater detail in Chapter 6. Figure 5-10 compares the three quality modes on two dot-matrix printers.

Dot placement has a big impact on the quality of output from dot-matrix printers. The ImageWriter was engineered to provide a very precise dot placement. Printers that do not meet the same standard of precision may leave gaps and streaks in your text and graphics.

Standard quality	*Draft quality*	*High quality*
Epson LQ-1500	Epson LQ-1500	Epson LQ-1500

Standard quality	*Draft quality*	*High quality*
ImageWriter	ImageWriter	**ImageWriter**

Figure 5-10. Samples of the Mac's three quality modes on two dot-matrix printers

Laser printers produce much better quality output than any of the dot-matrix printers, even the 24-wire machines. With a laser printer, the dots can be packed as densely as 300 per inch, compared with the ImageWriter's range of 72 to 160 dots per inch. The combination of smaller dots and precise placement enables laser printers to produce characters that are much closer to typeset quality. Even when reproducing Macintosh screen fonts, laser printers produce a crisper image than dot-matrix printers; their dot positioning is denser and the dots are finer. Figure 5-11 shows a LaserWriter printout of a Macintosh screen font and one of a font designed and installed on the Laser-Writer. Compare these to the dot-matrix characters in Figure 5-10.

As you can see in Figure 5-11, there are two distinct levels of resolution on the LaserWriter. For Macintosh screen fonts, each pixel is reproduced on the LaserWriter as a four-by-four matrix of dots. For the installed LaserWriter fonts, each dot is individually placed, producing crisp curves in the letter shapes.

Speed

Using impact printing, you give up speed in order to obtain quality. While most fully formed character printers plunk along at 12 to 55 characters per second (cps), dot-matrix printers are usually rated by their manufacturers at between 80 to 200 cps.

Using the manufacturer's rating is one way to judge a printer's speed. But a better way is to find performance test results in trade journals. Don't expect the two sources to agree, because they measure different things. The manufacturer's cps rating is a measure of the printer's output at the maximum speed, or burst speed, of the print head. Performance tests usually measure printed output, or throughput, which results in a lower number because it accounts for several factors. For example, in addition to the maximum speed at which characters are printed, throughput also reflects those times when the paper is advancing and characters aren't being printed. Also, the manufacturers' ratings represent only the fastest of Word's three print modes—Draft. To illustrate the differences between manufacturer and performance ratings and the effect of different print modes, we printed a 150-word sample (one screen full) on the ImageWriter in all three of Word's print modes. Although the ImageWriter is rated at a speed of 120 cps, the result of our test was 44 cps in Draft mode.

Figure 5-11. LaserWriter printout, comparing Macintosh New York font with LaserWriter installed Times font

```
New York Macintosh screen font
```

Times LaserWriter installed font

But even performance ratings don't reflect the time it takes the Macintosh to get ready to print, from the instant you click the OK button in the Print dialog box until the printer actually goes into action. During this time, the Macintosh processes all the dot patterns for the various type fonts, graphics, and formats you're printing, and sends them to the printer. The printer driver orchestrates this process and printer-driver efficiency varies from printer to printer and from program to program. For example, in the test run described above, the ImageWriter took 3 seconds to start printing in Draft mode, 12 seconds in Standard mode, and 15 seconds in High mode. In further testing, we found that a Diablo 630 daisy-wheel printer took 4 seconds, an Epson LQ-1500 in Standard mode took 19 seconds, and a LaserWriter printer took 20 seconds (although it is not absolutely clear when the LaserWriter starts printing and when it stops, since printing takes place inside the machine).

Laser printers are much faster than dot-matrix printers. Since laser printers print out an entire page at a time, they are rated in pages per minute rather than in characters per second. But by calculating the number of characters on an average page, comparisons can be made. For instance, we clocked one of the fastest dot-matrix printers at about two pages per minute, while the LaserWriter is rated at up to eight pages per minute, or about 300 cps. If you are printing out several copies of a document, the LaserWriter performs beautifully, once it starts printing. However, there is a considerable qualification to the LaserWriter's speed: Graphics slow down the process by which Word prepares for printing.

If you are printing one copy of a 20-page document, the through-put rate is considerably different from printing 20 copies of just one page, because the printer has to go through its setup procedure for each page. In another test, we took the three-page document created in Chapter 3, copied it in Word four times to create a 12-page document, and printed one copy on the LaserWriter. In this case, the three first pages took longer because of the graphic letterhead and logo; they took an average of 54 seconds. The other two pages averaged 22 seconds. The LaserWriter took less than 7 minutes to print 12 pages.

How fast is that? Well, the ImageWriter in Standard mode printed the same document in 12 minutes, the Diablo printed it in 15 minutes, and the LQ-1500, printing the document in Standard mode, took 23 minutes. Clearly, the contortions the Mac has to go through to print everything in graphics mode slow it down considerably.

Noise

Impact printers are inherently noisy. Most impact printers operate at between 65 and 80 decibels. In offices and other settings where distracting noise must be kept to a minimum, impact printers are often covered with soundproof hoods that can be purchased separately. Fully formed character and dot-matrix printers are equally noisy, though dot-matrix printers make a higher frequency buzzing sound that some people find less objectionable. Having heard many kinds and brands of printers, we've concluded that, regardless of decibel levels, the fully formed character printers make the most uncomfortable noise, and, among impact dot-matrix printers, the ImageWriter is the most comfortable to hear.

Laser and ink-jet printers, on the other hand, are very quiet, because they don't use impact. They make the whirring sounds typical of an office copier, with an occasional click.

Versatility

The ImageWriter is versatile, mostly because it reproduces, pixel by pixel, exactly what's displayed on the Mac's graphics-oriented screen. It can reproduce an impressive variety of type fonts, styles, and sizes, and can print down the length of a page instead of the width; it can print in columns, and it can combine text and graphics. It can be used for a wide range of commercial and professional printing projects, such as announcements, fliers, newsletters, menus, advertisements, price lists, maps, and greeting cards. Other dot-matrix printers can perform these same functions to the extent that they are compatible with the ImageWriter.

Fully formed character printers are not designed to take full advantage of the versatility of the Mac. They are basically relegated to printing text, with little or no provision for graphics printing. However, Word supports bold print, superscript, subscript, and underlining on fully formed character printers. The real variety in fully formed character printers, however, depends on the variety of print elements available. Some daisy-wheel and thimble printers have dozens of typefaces available, and others are limited. In any event, to change type styles, you must manually change print wheels, which gets to be a real chore if it happens several times in a document. The major limitation to fully formed character printers is their inability to print graphics or support other Word features, such as printing the length instead of the width of a page.

The LaserWriter, with its immense built-in computing power, has even more versatility than the ImageWriter. Some of its more exotic features, such as printing words at an angle, are not available via Word; you control these features by using the LaserWriter's built-in programming language, PostScript. With Word, the LaserWriter can print reductions down to 25 percent and enlargements up to 400 percent of screen size. You can print a document on short, wide pages, you can print on acetate to make a transparency for an overhead projector, you can have the Mac substitute LaserWriter fonts for fonts from other sources, and you can even have it smooth out jagged lines in your graphics.

Price

If a dot-matrix printer matches your printing needs, it will probably give you the most value per dollar. Dot-matrix printer prices range from under $400 to over $1000. But there is a dramatic difference in speed, quality, and versatility between the low and high end of the price range. It is to your benefit to realistically evaluate your requirements, especially as you learn more about what individual printers have to offer.

Significant reductions in prices of daisy-wheel printers have made them a hot item in recent years. At the upper end of the scale are some fine printers with price tags of over $2000. At the lower end, under $1000, there are some very acceptable, well-performing models. The more expensive models usually offer greater reliability, more speed, and more features.

Price is a major consideration with laser printers. The LaserWriter, at about $7000, is priced beyond the reach of most individual users. But business offices, printing services, and user groups may find the LaserWriter's superior quality well worth its considerable cost. The Hewlett-Packard LaserJet is less expensive, retailing for around $3500, which could make it a serious competitor for the upper portion of the printer market. However, to make it compatible with Word you will also need to purchase a Microsoft MacEnhancer.

Choosing Your Printer

Choosing a printer for use with Word on the Macintosh is simplified by the fact that the computer is optimized to print with the original Macintosh printer, the ImageWriter. The majority of software written for the Mac is designed to print on the ImageWriter or the LaserWriter. When selecting a printer for use with Word on the Macintosh, start by looking at what the ImageWriter has to offer. Then, consider other printers only if they exhibit a clear advantage over the ImageWriter for your use.

If you already have a dot-matrix printer, the advantage, pricewise, of using it with your Macintosh is quite clear. You simply need to know how to connect it and how it will perform with Word on the Mac. If you decide to purchase a different printer for some special feature, keep in mind that you are at the mercy of the printer-driver software. Test the printer out with Word and other programs you expect to use to make sure the features you want are fully implemented.

In time, you can expect good, compatible printer-driver software for a variety of dot-matrix printers, but that is not the case at this writing. It will always be pertinent for you to get a full disclosure of features and application programs not supported by the software for the printer you want to use. We will share some of the joys and agonies of interfacing printers other than the ImageWriter to the Mac and Word in Chapter 7.

If you need letter quality and low price, your best option is a fully formed character printer. Word supports a number of popular printers, and a majority of the fully formed character printers on the market are compatible with one of these standards. For this reason, your choice can be based on considerations such as price, speed, support, ease of use, documentation, and personal preference. The computer magazines are filled with comparative articles to keep you up to date on the latest in fully formed character printers.

If you want both high-quality print and versatility and you can afford it, go with a laser printer. Of the two choices at this writing, Apple's LaserWriter is a big step up in price but a bigger step up in printer technology.

In this chapter, we compared three major types of printer available for the Mac and Word. We looked at several factors to consider when buying a printer, including speed, compatibility, noise, quality, versatility, and price. Of course, the right printer for you depends on your needs and preferences.

In Chapter 6, we look at the printing process, which will be helpful background information for you when it comes time for you to connect your printer, the subject of Chapter 7.

6

The printing process

When you don't know what's going on inside the Mac and your printer, the long wait for the printer to start doing its job after you click the OK button in the Print dialog box probably seems like an unnecessary annoyance. Why doesn't it just start printing immediately, you might ask. Well, your printer has a lot to do to prepare for printing, as you'll learn in this chapter.

If you already know what happens during the printing process or you don't care to know, you can skip this chapter. But if you're the curious sort who just has to know how things work, stick around—this chapter's for you.

For the most part, there's not much you can do to change what happens inside the Mac during printing, unless you take up programming. But there is one thing that you can change. As you learned in Chapter 3, you have a choice in the Print dialog box of three Quality buttons: Draft, Standard, and High. Draft offers a substantially different method of printing than Standard and High, both in terms of what comes out of the printer and in terms of what happens inside the Mac. Clicking the Draft button results in draft printing. Draft printing prints only text; it does not reproduce graphics or character formatting, such as fonts, styles, and sizes. But when you click the Standard or High buttons, the Mac uses a different process, called spooled printing, that tells the printer to print a picture of what is on the screen, graphics and text alike.

We'll take a detailed look at each of these methods of printing a little later in this chapter. But first we need to cover a few basics of the printing process that apply to both draft and spooled printing.

Printing Basics

To understand the printing process, you need to understand some basics about how computers store and transfer information. You may already know some of these basics, but it will help you understand the entire process if you learn how the basics fit together.

Bits, Bytes, and ASCII

As you probably already know, computers store units of information as a series of high and low electronic impulses, which can be thought of as the numbers 1 and 0. Each of these basic units of information is called a bit. Eight bits strung together are called a byte, which is used to represent one keyboard character. When you click the OK button in the Print dialog box with Draft mode selected, the Macintosh sends strings of 1s and 0s, representing the characters that make up your document, to the printer.

The most widely used system for assigning specific strings of 1s and 0s to specific characters is the American Standard Code for Information Interchange (ASCII, pronounced *askee*), part of which is shown in Figure 6-1. With 256 combinations of eight 1s and 0s, the ASCII system not only provides a unique series of codes for a complete alphabet in upper- and lowercase, the numerals zero through nine, and most common keyboard symbols, it also has enough combinations left over so that there are codes to activate features common to most printers and other peripheral devices.

The Printer Driver and Printer Resource File

As mentioned in Chapter 5, the information the computer needs in order to communicate with a specific printer is stored in a file called the printer driver. The Macintosh stores the printer driver in a larger file, called the printer resource file. In addition to the printer driver, the printer resource file also contains the driver data record and the Print Manager. The driver data record contains information that the printer driver needs, such as commands that implement printer actions. The Print Manager acts as a traffic cop for the spooled printing process, as we'll discuss in more detail later in this chapter.

Data Transfer

The Macintosh sends data to the printer one bit at a time across a single wire of the printer cable, a data transfer method called serial data transfer. Most other computers today send data eight bits at a time across eight separate wires, a method called parallel data transfer. Parallel is generally faster and simpler than serial, but, in designing

Figure 6-1. Codes 32 through
126 of the American Standard
Code for Information
Interchange (ASCII)

ASCII Number	Character	ASCII Number	Character	ASCII Number	Character
032	(space)	064	@	096	`
033	!	065	A	097	a
034	"	066	B	098	b
035	#	067	C	099	c
036	$	068	D	100	d
037	%	069	E	101	e
038	&	070	F	102	f
039	'	071	G	103	g
040	(	072	H	104	h
041	)	073	I	105	i
042	*	074	J	106	j
043	+	075	K	107	k
044	,	076	L	108	l
045	–	077	M	109	m
046	.	078	N	110	n
047	/	079	O	111	o
048	0	080	P	112	p
049	1	081	Q	113	q
050	2	082	R	114	r
051	3	083	S	115	s
052	4	084	T	116	t
053	5	085	U	117	u
054	6	086	V	118	v
055	7	087	W	119	w
056	8	088	X	120	x
057	9	089	Y	121	y
058	:	090	Z	122	z
059	;	091	[	123	{
060	<	092	\	124		
061	=	093	]	125	}
062	>	094	^	126	~
063	?	095	—		

the Macintosh, Apple apparently favored serial for its ability to transmit data reliably over greater distances. Parallel is reliable only up to
about 20 feet; serial is reliable over hundreds of feet. Computers that
can transfer data reliably over greater distances are more suitable for
linking individual computers located in more than one office, called
interoffice networking, and linking more than one computer to a
printer, precisely the roles Apple envisions for the Mac.

Even when a computer and printer use the same type of interface, both must follow the same set of rules for sending and receiving data. This set of rules is called protocol.

Protocol

Protocol helps the Mac and the printer coordinate their activities by specifying the characteristics of data transfer, including how the computer signals the start and end of a byte, the speed at which the data is transmitted (or baud rate), and the method used to start and stop the flow of data (or handshaking). All of these characteristics are dictated by the printer driver.

The Mac uses a start bit in front and a stop bit at the end of each byte to tell the printer where bytes begin and end. The start and stop bits help coordinate the data transfer, which goes on at 9600 baud, or 9600 bits per second. These are the more straightforward elements of protocol; handshaking requires a bit more explanation.

The Macintosh can send data much faster than a printer can print and the area of the printer's memory where incoming data is stored, called the input buffer, is small. So, the Mac can send the printer only a small amount of data at one time and the printer must be able to signal when its input buffer is full and when it can begin receiving data again. This is the purpose of handshaking.

There are two types of handshaking—X-ON/X-OFF (software) and DTR (hardware)—and the Mac uses both. With software handshaking, the printer sends a 1 bit that tells the computer to stop sending data and a 0 bit that tells the computer to resume sending data. With hardware handshaking, one of the connector's pins is reserved for the handshaking signal. When there is an electrical current across this pin, the computer sends data and when there isn't a current, the computer doesn't send data.

Now that you know the basics of printing shared by both printing processes, we'll take you through draft printing.

Draft Printing

As we mentioned at the beginning of this chapter, draft printing will print only text. Since fully formed character printers also print only text, draft printing is your only choice if you're using a fully formed character printer. You can also use draft printing on a dot-matrix printer to get a fast, but rough, copy of your document.

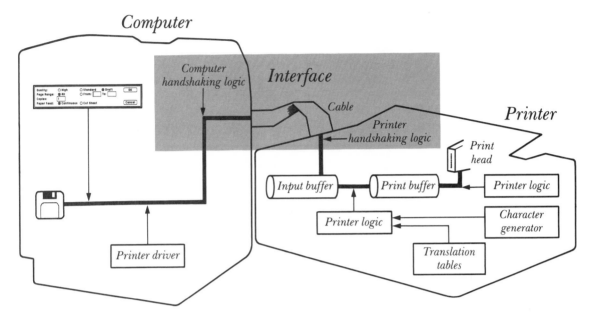

Figure 6-2. The Macintosh
draft printing process

In draft printing, the printer determines what the printed characters look like. If it's a fully formed character printer, the characters will look like the characters on the printing element. But if it's a dot-matrix printer, the characters will look like the dot patterns stored in the printer's memory. Because the Mac doesn't need to tell the printer what the characters look like, only which characters to print, draft printing is faster than spooled printing. The draft printing process is shown in Figure 6-2.

Data Conversion

In draft printing, after the Macintosh sends the strings of 1s and 0s to the printer, the printer must translate them into pin-firing patterns, if it's a dot-matrix printer, or, if it's a fully formed character printer, into hammer and printing element movement.

Printing

When you use draft printing on a fully formed character printer, the printed page can look like it was professionally typed on an electric typewriter. But when you use draft printing on the ImageWriter printer, the characters are printed in a relatively unattractive elite (12-characters-per-inch) monospaced font that's stored in the printer's memory. Spacing between words is uneven because the words are placed to align with where they would start if they were printed in Standard or High mode, and most Macintosh fonts are larger than the printer's built-in elite font.

Spooled Printing

Unlike draft printing, most of the calculations for spooled printing take place inside the Mac, rather than inside the printer. In draft printing, the Mac sends the printer strings of 1s and 0s that represent characters and the printer translates the strings into dots on the page. In spooled printing, as you'll learn in the following discussion, the Mac manipulates the data, creating pictures of the printed page, and sends the printer graphic information that can be quickly translated into dots on the page. We'll use the ImageWriter as an example, but the process, shown in Figure 6-3, is similar for any dot-matrix printer.

QuickDraw

When you create a Word document on the Macintosh, your document is stored not only as ASCII characters, but also as built-in Macintosh graphics commands called QuickDraw. QuickDraw tells the Mac how to draw basic graphics shapes, such as straight lines, arcs, and polygons, as well as text characters in a variety of fonts and styles. QuickDraw, in fact, is so much a part of the Macintosh that it's stored in the Mac's ROM, the most permanent part of the computer's memory.

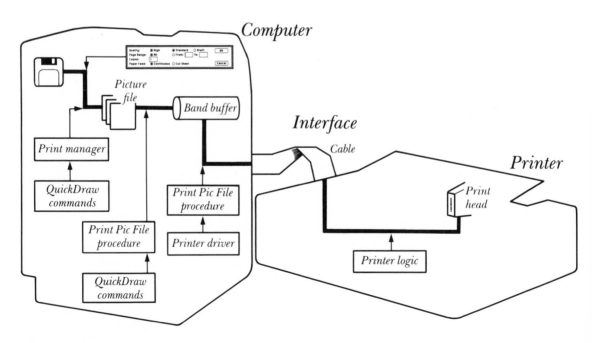

Figure 6-3. The Macintosh spooled printing process

Draft printing doesn't use graphics, so the Mac doesn't send Quick-Draw commands to the printer in draft printing. But QuickDraw commands do play a vital role in spooled printing, as you'll see in the next few pages.

The Picture File

When you click Standard or High and then OK in the Print dialog box, Word opens each page of your document and the Print Manager transcribes the page into QuickDraw commands. The Print Manager then creates a temporary file, called a picture file, for storing the Quick-Draw commands until they are sent to the printer.

The Print Pic File Procedure

After the picture file is created, Word uses another printer resource file program, known as the Print Pic File procedure, to execute the QuickDraw commands in the picture file to recreate the image of each page, with one bit representing one screen pixel. Since one bit can store the information needed to recreate one of two states represented by 1 or 0, each bit can represent not only whether a screen pixel is on or off, but also whether a pin on the printer's print head is fired or not fired. This one-to-one representation of the screen (bit-mapping) allows the Macintosh and a dot-matrix printer to recreate the screen image on paper. The image of a page created in the computer's memory is called a bit image.

Bands and the Band Buffer

There isn't room enough in the Mac's memory to store the bit image of an entire page. The information needed to create the bit image of a page can amount to as much as a quarter-megabyte (almost twice the total memory of the 128K Macintosh). So, Word divides each page into horizontal stripes, called bands, that are 32 dots tall. The printer driver transcribes each band into printer pin-firing commands and sends the transcribed band to the printer.

Standard Printing

Before printing starts, the Mac sends the printer a control code that tells the printer that what follows are graphics. The control code puts the printer in graphics mode—that is, the printer doesn't look in its memory for character matrices to print text; it simply uses the data being transmitted as pin-firing commands. Each byte tells the printer which of the top eight pins of the print head to fire (the bottom pin of the print head isn't used in graphics printing). The print head takes four passes across the page to print each band.

High-Resolution Printing

When you click High in the Print dialog box, text is printed with twice the usual number of dots per inch (graphics are not affected by high-resolution printing). The resulting text looks smoother than text that

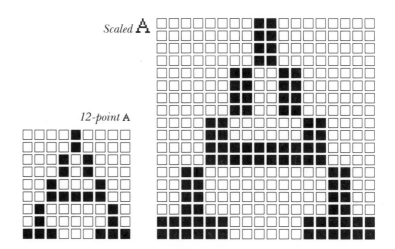

Figure 6-4. The Macintosh method for scaling fonts to a larger size

is printed by Standard and Draft. Word accomplishes this smoother-looking text by adding two steps to spooled printing, one at the page-imaging stage and one at the printing stage.

When the Print Pic File procedure executes the QuickDraw commands stored in the picture file, instead of providing the font size you called for, Word provides the same font, but at twice the point size, if that size is on your disk. For example, if you call for New York 12, Word uses New York 24, if it's on your Word disk. If the same font at twice the point size isn't on your Word disk, Word uses the nearest equivalent and adjusts, or scales, that equivalent font to twice the point size called for, as shown in Figure 6-4. Scaled sizes are more ragged than sizes already (installed) on your disk. So, it's important to have the same font at twice the size you call for on your disk if you plan to use high-resolution printing. You'll learn how to add fonts to your Word disk in Chapter 8.

If the printer printed the text with these double-sized characters, of course, your text would be twice the size you wanted (and probably wouldn't fit on the page). So, Word tells the printer to print each line in two passes of the print head, with a half-dot paper advance between each pass. It also tells the printer to advance across the page only half a dot at a time, instead of the usual full dot at a time. The result of both printer actions is text with four times the number of dots as text that is printed using Draft and Standard modes.

Now that you know a little more about printer basics, you might want to move on to Chapter 7, which focuses on the process of connecting and running specific printers with the Macintosh. It also deals with the printer drivers programmed into Word, as well as with many of the interfacing devices and programs on the market.

7

Connecting your printer

Connecting an ImageWriter printer to your Macintosh for use with Word is easy: You simply plug in the cable that's provided in the Image-Writer's accessory kit. But connecting any other brand of printer can be more difficult: You may need special cables, connectors, hardware adaptors, or printer-control software.

In this chapter, we'll explain step-by-step how to connect four popular printers to the Macintosh, using a different method for each: an NEC 2010 using one of Word's built-in printer drivers, a Toshiba P1340 using the Microsoft MacEnhancer, an Apple LaserWriter using its own unique connection process, and an Epson FX-80 using an independently produced printer driver.

The examples and descriptions we'll use in this chapter will resolve connection problems for the four major types of printer. There are so many printers on the market and so little standardization of connections that we could take the rest of the book to cover all of the possibilities adequately. But, instead, we'll start off this chapter with some general advice on connecting printers.

Connection Considerations

As explained in Chapter 6, printers and computers use either a serial or a parallel interface for transferring data to and from other devices. The Macintosh uses a serial interface, as does the ImageWriter, so you need either a printer with a serial interface or some method of making your printer compatible with a serial interface. That's the first connection consideration: serial and parallel interfaces.

But even if your printer and computer have the same type of interface, you still may have problems hooking them together if they have different types of connectors. For instance, if you look at the cable connecting a Mac and an ImageWriter, you'll notice there's a different type of connector on each end. These two types of connector represent two different industry standards established by the Electronics Industries Association (EIA). The connector on the Macintosh end of the cable uses the 9-pin RS-422 standard and the connector on the ImageWriter end uses the 25-pin RS-232C standard, as shown in Figure 7-1. You need either a printer with an RS-232C connector or an adapter that matches your printer connector. So the second connection consideration is the connector standard used by the printer and computer.

Connector standards describe several aspects of electronic communications, including the size and shape of the connector, and the function of the signal carried by each pin. One pin is assigned the function of receiving data, one the job of sending data, and one the duty of synchronizing the transfer of data. Unfortunately, not all manufacturers interpret the standards the same way. For instance, "sending data between a printer and a computer" can be interpreted two ways: sending from the computer to the printer and sending from the printer to the computer. As a consequence, even though two devices may use the same standard, the pin assignments may not be the same. What that means is if you have a male connector (the side with the pins) and a female connector (the side with the holes the pins fit into) that use different pin assignments, you need to reattach the wires in the cable to the pins of the connector to make the male and female compatible. You do that with a soldering gun.

If you're not proficient at soldering connectors, you'd be well advised to have your printer dealer supply the necessary cables and connectors when you buy your printer. If you already have your printer

Figure 7-1. An RS-232C connector (left) and an RS-422 connector (right)

and it has the wrong kind of connector, you can try to find a dealer who's willing to make the right connector for you or you can use a Smart Cable. A Smart Cable is a cable that has logic circuitry built into it. This circuitry can distinguish the most popular uses of the different pins and works with about 75 percent of the possible printer and computer combinations. The Smart Cable is produced by IQ Technologies, 11811 N.E. First Street, Bellevue, Washington 98005.

Once you've got your printer properly connected to your Mac, depending on the type of printer, you may need to change the settings of switches on the printer that control the parameters of communication with the computer. Check the printer manual or ask your dealer. These switches, called DIP switches (for dual inline pin), may also set the length of the sheet of paper (form length) and whether the printer or the computer advances the paper (line feed).

Again, the best approach is to let your printer dealer set the switches for you. But if that isn't possible, you can set the switches yourself by following the directions in the printer manual. In general, if you're connecting a printer to a Mac, set the line-feed switch to no feed, the baud rate to 9600, parity to even, stop bits to one, and the data transfer to eight-bit operation, because these are the parameters the Mac uses.

If you need to change DIP-switch settings, it is a good idea to turn off the printer before you make the changes. Most printers read the switch settings only when the power is *first* turned on.

Now that you understand a little more about the basics of connecting a printer, we'll look at how to hook up a specific printer: an NEC 2010 fully formed character printer, using a printer driver that's included on the Word disk.

Using a Word Printer Driver with the NEC 2010

As mentioned in Chapter 5, Word provides printer drivers for four of the most popular fully formed character printers, in addition to the ImageWriter printer driver; and it is possible to use these printer drivers with still other printers, with varying degrees of difficulty. For instance, you can use the NEC 7710 driver with an NEC 2010 printer by following the description we present in the next few pages.

Cables and Connectors

If you have an ImageWriter, you can use your ImageWriter cable and connectors to connect an NEC 2010 to your Macintosh. If you don't have an ImageWriter, you can get an accessory kit from NEC that includes cable, software, and documentation.

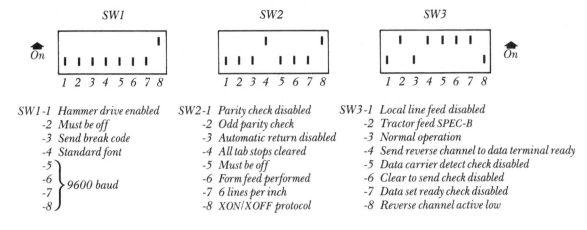

SW1-1 *Hammer drive enabled*
   -2 *Must be off*
   -3 *Send break code*
   -4 *Standard font*
   -5 ⎫
   -6 ⎬ *9600 baud*
   -7 ⎪
   -8 ⎭

SW2-1 *Parity check disabled*
   -2 *Odd parity check*
   -3 *Automatic return disabled*
   -4 *All tab stops cleared*
   -5 *Must be off*
   -6 *Form feed performed*
   -7 *6 lines per inch*
   -8 *XON/XOFF protocol*

SW3-1 *Local line feed disabled*
   -2 *Tractor feed SPEC-B*
   -3 *Normal operation*
   -4 *Send reverse channel to data terminal ready*
   -5 *Data carrier detect check disabled*
   -6 *Clear to send check disabled*
   -7 *Data set ready check disabled*
   -8 *Reverse channel active low*

Figure 7-2. The proper DIP-switch settings on an NEC 2010 for use with a Macintosh

Setting the Switches

DIP switches on the NEC 2010 are located on the interface module that plugs into the back of the printer. The default settings shown in the NEC Accessory Kit manual (and also shown in Figure 7-2, which was adapted from the illustration in the manual and used with the permission of NEC Information Systems) are the proper settings for the Macintosh, so there's no need to change them if you asked your dealer to set them for you.

Setting the Print-Element Dial

The print-element selection dial on the NEC 2010 is located on its front panel. The printer manual lists the proper settings for each pitch (characters per inch). To set up the printer for a 10-pitch thimble, for example, use the setting shown in Figure 7-3 (which was also adapted from an illustration in the NEC 2010 manual and used with the permission of NEC Information Systems).

Choosing the Printer Driver

You can take the final step in connecting an NEC 2010 printer anytime after you've opened Word and before you're ready to print.

Choose the Printer Setup... command from the File menu.

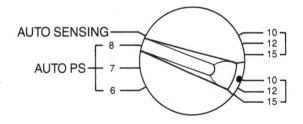

Figure 7-3. The proper setting on an NEC 2010 for a 10-pitch printing element

Figure 7-4. The default Printer
Setup dialog box

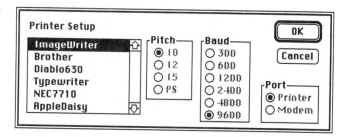

The dialog box shown in Figure 7-4 is displayed.

As we said earlier in this chapter, you can use the NEC 7710 printer driver for the NEC 2010, too.

> Click on NEC 7710 in the list box to choose the NEC 7710 printer driver.

The Pitch, Baud, and Port radio button groupings now change from dimmed to normal characters, indicating you can select from them.

> For a 10-pitch print element, click the 10 Pitch, the 9600 Baud, and the Printer Port radio buttons.

The dialog box will look as shown in Figure 7-5.

> Click OK.

Printing with the Newly Installed Printer

Now you can choose the Print... command from the File menu when you want to print. The dialog box that appears is the same as the dialog box that appears when you use the ImageWriter, except for one difference: The three Quality radio buttons aren't displayed, as you can see from the illustration in Figure 7-6 on the next page. Fully formed character printers such as the NEC 2010 print only in Draft mode, as mentioned in Chapter 6, so you don't have a choice of printing modes. If the options in the dialog box are to your liking, you are ready to print.

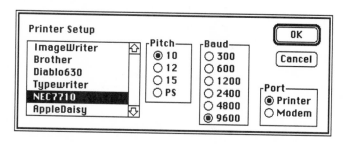

Figure 7-5. The Printer Setup
dialog box settings for an NEC
2010 with a 10-pitch thimble

Figure 7-6. The Print dialog
box displayed for fully formed
character printers

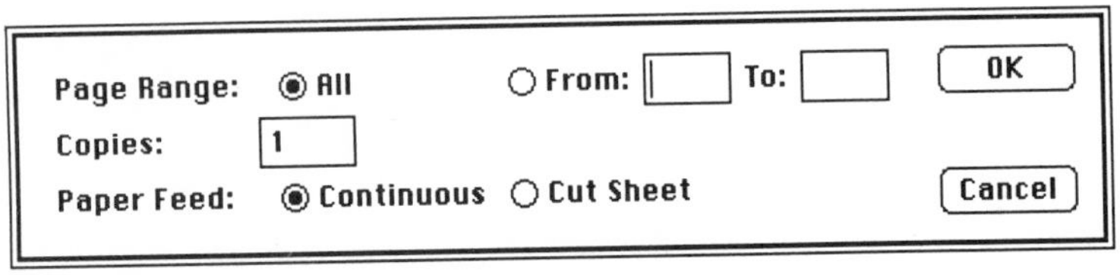

Page Range:	◉ All	○ From: [ ] To: [ ]	OK
Copies:	[1]		
Paper Feed:	◉ Continuous	○ Cut Sheet	Cancel

Choose the Print… command from the File menu.

Click the OK button to start printing.

Using the Microsoft MacEnhancer with the Toshiba P1340

Microsoft's MacEnhancer is a peripheral device, with accompanying software, that allows you to connect several kinds of printers to your Mac at the same time. The software that comes with the MacEnhancer contains printer drivers for a number of dot-matrix printers (9- and 24-wire) and the Hewlett-Packard ThinkJet ink-jet printer. The software also includes a terminal-emulation program that enables the Mac to communicate with other computers over phone lines.

The MacEnhancer itself is a box about three-fourths the size of the Macintosh keyboard, with four output ports across one side, as shown in Figure 7-7. One port is compatible with an IBM PC parallel interface, two are compatible with devices using an RS-232C interface, and one is compatible with printers using an RS-422 interface. With ports using three different types of interfaces, the MacEnhancer simplifies the job of finding a compatible cable and connector.

However, despite having three different connector types, the MacEnhancer doesn't completely resolve compatibility difficulties. For instance, the Toshiba P1340 we're using for our example isn't directly compatible with any of the four MacEnhancer ports. A specially made cable is needed to make the connection. As we advised earlier in this chapter, the best approach is to have a printer dealer make the cable for you. Actually, finding a dealer who'll sell you the right cable isn't as bleak as it sounds. Microsoft has provided IBM compatibility with the MacEnhancer, and chances are very good that your dealer will have the appropriate cable to hook up your printer to an IBM PC and therefore to the MacEnhancer.

Once you have the correct cable and connectors, you need to change the DIP switch settings. You can buy a Toshiba P1340 printer

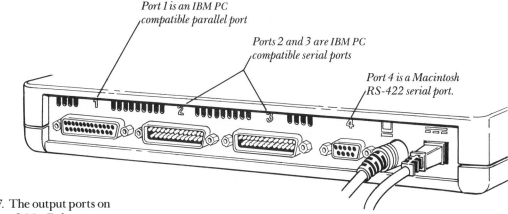

Port 1 is an IBM PC
compatible parallel port

Ports 2 and 3 are IBM PC
compatible serial ports

Port 4 is a Macintosh
RS-422 serial port.

Figure 7-7. The output ports on
the Microsoft MacEnhancer

with either a parallel or a serial interface. For a parallel interface
Toshiba P1340, set the switches, as shown in the printer manual, for
automatic character wraparound, automatic character wraparound
with a line-feed code, printing on receipt of a paper-movement command, no line feed with a carriage-return code, and automatic carriage return on receipt of a paper-movement command. If you are
connecting a Toshiba printer that has a serial interface to the Mac-
Enhancer, you may need to set additional switches that control the
communications parameters between the printer and the Macintosh.
The settings recommended by Microsoft are: even parity, one stop bit,
eight data bits, 9600 baud rate, and either X-ON/X-OFF or ready/busy
handshaking.

Now you can connect the MacEnhancer to the Mac, using either the
printer port or the modem port. If you want to use an ImageWriter
not connected to the MacEnhancer, connect it to the printer port and
the MacEnhancer to the modem port.

MacEnhancer Software

The MacEnhancer software is on two disks, one labeled System Disk
and the other labeled Program Disk. The Program Disk is for using
the Macintosh with a modem; the System Disk contains the printer-
connection program and printer drivers. You need to install the Mac-
Enhancer software on every system disk you intend to use with the
MacEnhancer.

In the case of the Word disk, you need to free up some space to provide enough room for the MacEnhancer software. Each printer driver you choose to install requires up to 18K of space and the installation software requires 14K, though you can recover 9K of that after the installation procedure. Removing the Word.Help file and the printer-driver folder (since you won't need any of Word's printer drivers with the MacEnhancer) should free up enough space.

Turn on the Mac, insert your Word Working Master disk, and remove Word.Help and the printer-driver folders by dragging them to Trash.

Eject the Word disk, insert the MacEnhancer disk and a blank disk, and make a copy of the MacEnhancer disk.

Using the MacEnhancer copy, open the MacEnhancer program by double-clicking on the program icon.

Your screen should look like the screen in Figure 7-8. As you can see, the initial screen is a representation of the Macintosh and the Mac-Enhancer.

In the upper left corner, beneath the icon of the Mac, click on the icon of the port to which you connected the MacEnhancer.

If you change ports or disconnect the MacEnhancer, the program will display an alert box that says it can't find the MacEnhancer. If that happens, reconnect the MacEnhancer and click the OK button.

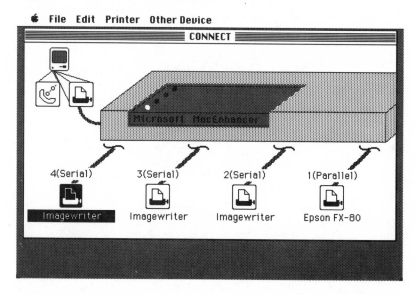

Figure 7-8. The MacEnhancer program initial screen

Click on the icon of the port (one of the four round-cornered boxes with an icon of a printer in it) to which you connected your printer.

Choose the name of the printer from the Printer menu.

If you had connected another kind of peripheral device, you could choose the name of the device from the Other Device menu. The name you choose appears beneath the port icon you selected. For example, if you had connected a Toshiba P1340 to port 1, you'd click on the port 1 icon, then choose Toshiba P1340 from the Printer menu, as shown in Figure 7-9.

If you are connecting the Toshiba to one of the serial ports instead of the parallel port, you need to take an extra step at this point: You need to set the communications parameters for your printer in the Configure dialog box.

To call for display of the Configure dialog box, double-click on the icon of the MacEnhancer port to which the printer is connected.

The Configure dialog box displays a series of radio buttons: Baud Rate, Bits per Character, Parity, Stop Bits, and Handshake. Remember to select the same settings in the Configure dialog box as you set on the printer.

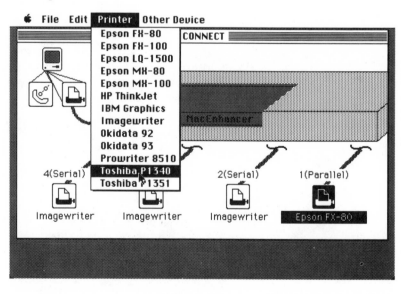

Figure 7-9. Choosing Toshiba P1340 from the Mac-Enhancer's Printer menu

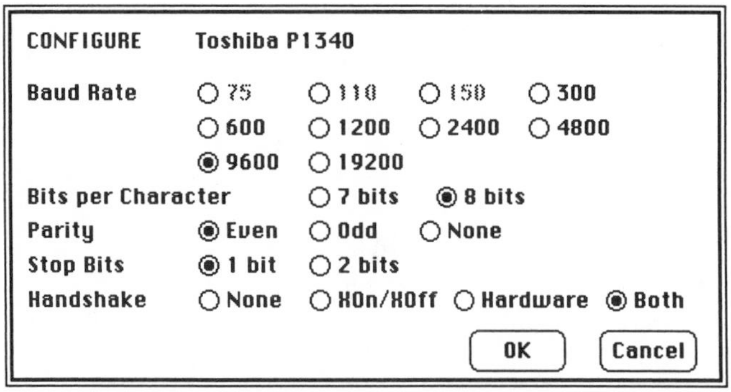

Figure 7-10. The Mac-
Enhancer's Configure dialog
box with the recommended
Toshiba P1340 selections

```
┌─────────────────────────────────────────────────────────┐
│  CONFIGURE      Toshiba P1340                             │
│                                                           │
│  Baud Rate      ○ 75    ○ 110    ○ 150    ○ 300           │
│                 ○ 600   ○ 1200   ○ 2400   ○ 4800          │
│                 ◉ 9600  ○ 19200                           │
│  Bits per Character     ○ 7 bits   ◉ 8 bits              │
│  Parity         ◉ Even  ○ Odd    ○ None                  │
│  Stop Bits      ◉ 1 bit ○ 2 bits                         │
│  Handshake      ○ None  ○ XOn/XOff ○ Hardware ◉ Both     │
│                                   ┌──────┐  ┌────────┐   │
│                                   │  OK  │  │ Cancel │   │
│                                   └──────┘  └────────┘   │
└─────────────────────────────────────────────────────────┘
```

If you selected the settings recommended earlier in this chapter for
serial printers, use the settings shown in Figure 7-10.

When you've made your selections, click the OK button.

But note: If you selected X-ON/X-OFF handshaking on the printer,
click the Both radio button beside Handshake in the Configure dialog
box; if you selected ready/busy handshaking on the printer, click the
Hardware button.

If you have additional printers connected to the MacEnhancer, you
need to go through the same procedure of clicking a MacEnhancer
port icon and choosing a printer name from the Printer menu (and,
perhaps, changing settings in the Configure dialog box) for each Mac-
Enhancer port used. But keep in mind that each printer driver you
add to a System disk takes up precious disk space. So, be judicious
about how many printers you connect to the MacEnhancer.

Now you're ready to save the settings you've selected onto each System disk you'll be using with the MacEnhancer. We'll describe how to
install the MacEnhancer on a Word disk, but the procedure is the
same for any other System disk.

With the MacEnhancer disk in one drive and your Word disk in the
other, choose Install from the File menu.

The dialog box shown in Figure 7-11 appears, displaying four buttons:
Install, Drive, Eject, and Cancel.

Click Drive to switch to the drive with Word, then click the Install
button.

Clicking Install copies a file titled Install MacEnhancer onto the
Word disk, along with the printer drivers for the printers you selected

Figure 7-11. The Mac-
Enhancer's Install dialog box

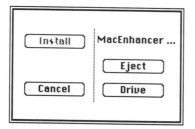

on the MacEnhancer initial screen. When it's done copying these files
the program asks if you want to install MacEnhancer on another disk.

> Click the No button.

You could follow the same procedure for any other System disk you
planned to use with the MacEnhancer by clicking the Yes button and
then clicking the Eject button instead of the Drive button and then inserting that disk. But there's one more step to take with the Word disk.

> Choose Quit from the File menu.
> Double-click the Word disk icon to open the disk directory window
> if it isn't open already.

You'll notice that Install MacEnhancer appears as a file icon in the disk
directory window of your Word disk.

> Double-click on the Install MacEnhancer icon.

This installs a new desk accessory called MacEnhancer in the Apple
menu. Once the MacEnhancer is installed as a desk accessory, you can
complete the last step.

> Delete the Install MacEnhancer file from the disk by dragging its icon
> to the Trash.

You can now choose MacEnhancer from the Apple menu. When
you do, the Macintosh displays a dialog box that shows the four Mac-
Enhancer ports, each labeled with the printer you connected to that
port. For our Toshiba P1340, we used port 1. If you had two or more
printers connected, you could simply switch from one to another.

If you want to connect another printer, you can redo the setup procedure. But if you plan to switch back and forth between the two
printer connection arrangements, a better solution is to prepare a second setup on a separate Word disk. That way, when you want to switch

from one MacEnhancer setup to the other, you can simply insert the other Word disk, instead of going back into MacEnhancer and changing the setup selections.

Removing the MacEnhancer desk accessory from the Apple menu is simple.

Insert the MacEnhancer disk, open the MacEnhancer program, and choose Remove from the File menu.

A dialog box similar to the Install dialog box is displayed, giving you four options: Remove, Drive, Eject, and Cancel.

Click Drive, then Remove.

Clicking Remove copies a program called Remove MacEnhancer that takes up about 3K of disk space.

Close the MacEnhancer program.

You'll see the icon for this new program in the disk directory window of the Word disk.

Double-click on the Remove MacEnhancer icon.

The MacEnhancer desk accessory is removed from the Word disk.

Connecting a LaserWriter

Connecting and setting up a LaserWriter for use with Word on the Mac is unlike connecting any other printer, in part because the LaserWriter printer is so different from other printers.

Connecting a LaserWriter to a Mac is simplified by purchasing two AppleTalk cables and connector sets: You just plug one of the AppleTalk connectors into the back of the LaserWriter and the other into either the printer port or the modem port on the Mac. AppleTalk is a system of cables and connectors that allows you to link as many as 32 Macintosh-compatible devices into one system. The AppleTalk cable and connector sets cost $50.

Every time you turn on the LaserWriter, it automatically prints a test sheet, similar to the one shown in Figure 7-12, that tells you the number of pages printed since the machine was built, the version of PostScript (its internal graphics programming language), and the current setting of the mode switch. If the test sheet looks too light or too dark, adjust the print-density dial on the back of the printer.

Figure 7-12. The test sheet the
LaserWriter prints each time
you turn it on

Installing the Software

The disk that comes with the LaserWriter contains its printer driver and its screen fonts. You need to install both on your Word disk or any other System disk you intend to use with the LaserWriter.

First, make a copy of the LaserWriter disk.

Installing the LaserWriter printer driver automatically removes any printer drivers other than the ImageWriter from your Word disk (if you clicked the ImageWriter button on the Install LaserWriter screen; otherwise, it removes ImageWriter, too). So, if there's any possibility you might need them, you need to save them on a separate disk.

Copy the printer drivers on the Word disk onto another disk.

Put the copy of the LaserWriter disk in one drive and the Word disk in the other.

Double-click on the Printer Installer icon in the LaserWriter disk directory window.

A dialog box, shown in Figure 7-13, appears, asking for the name of the disk you want the LaserWriter printer driver and fonts copied to, which printer driver you want copied (LaserWriter, ImageWriter, or both), and the font set you want copied (Minimal, Standard, or Complete). As you make your selections, the amount of disk space required to install your selections and the amount of disk space remaining are displayed in the dialog box.

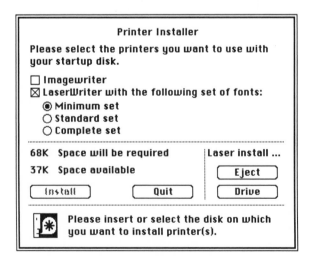

Figure 7-13. The LaserWriter's
Printer Installer dialog box

Choosing the Minimal font set installs Times, Helvetica, and Courier, each in 12-point size. Standard installs Times and Helvetica in 9, 10, 12, 14, and 18 points, and Courier and Symbol in 12 points. Complete installs Times, Helvetica, and Courier in 9, 10, 12, 14, 18, and 24 points, and Symbol in 9, 10, 18, and 24 points. The Complete set takes up to 150K of disk space and won't fit on the same disk as Word. If you want the Complete set, you'll have to store it on a disk other than your Word disk. But keep in mind that the LaserWriter's screen fonts appear only on the screen, not on the printout. The print fonts are permanently stored in the LaserWriter's memory. Screen versions of the LaserWriter fonts are intended only to give you a rough approximation of what the printed fonts will look like. The printed fonts, at a resolution of 300 dots per inch will, of course, be much smoother and of much better quality than the screen can reproduce. So, you don't need to install the Complete set to be able to print with them. And, if you decide later that you want more or fewer LaserWriter screen fonts, you can add or remove the fonts by using Font Mover, as discussed in detail in Chapter 8.

In addition to fonts and the printer driver, a file called Laser Prep and a desk accessory called Choose Printer are copied during the installation process. Choose Printer (5K) appears as a command in the Apple menu that lets you specify a printer and port prior to each printing. The Laser Prep file (21K), which is stored in the System folder, prepares the LaserWriter for printing only the first time you print. Since you won't need it again and since disk space may be severely limited with the LaserWriter installed, you can move Laser Prep to another disk to free up disk space.

Select the options you want in the Printer Installer dialog box.

Click the Install button.

Printing with the LaserWriter

When you're ready to print you need to tell the Mac you want to use the LaserWriter.

Choose the Choose Printer command in the Apple menu.

The dialog box shown in Figure 7-14 appears.

In the dialog box that appears, select the LaserWriter, select the port (printer or modem) to which the AppleTalk connector is attached, and click OK.

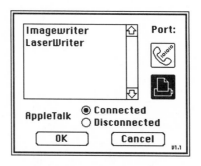

Figure 7-14. The LaserWriter's Choose Printer dialog box

Choose the Page Setup... command from the File menu to check the selected options.

The Page Setup dialog box is different when you have a LaserWriter connected than it is when you have other printers connected. For instance, the word *LaserWriter* appears in the upper left corner, telling you the LaserWriter is connected. The Page Setup dialog box, shown in Figure 7-15, also contains six groups of options: paper size, reduction or enlargement, orientation, font substitution, smoothing, and margins. The page size and margins groups are the same as in the Page Setup dialog boxes for other printers.

The Reduce or Enlarge text box allows you to reduce a screen image by as much as 25 percent of its screen size or enlarge it by as much as 400 percent. Just type in a number (representing a percentage) between 25 and 400. At the default setting of 100 percent, each pixel is reproduced on the LaserWriter as a square of 16 dots. Thus, at a 25-percent reduction, each pixel is a single dot on the printer.

Clicking the Portrait button beside Orientation prints your document so that the page is taller than it is wide; clicking Landscape prints it so that the page is wider than it is tall. Portrait is the same as Tall in the ImageWriter Page Setup dialog box and Landscape is the same as Wide.

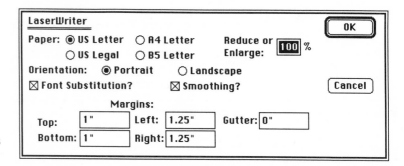

Figure 7-15. The LaserWriter's Page Setup dialog box

Figure 7-16. Printout with Smoothing? option (left) and without (right)

Clicking the Font Substitution? check box tells the LaserWriter to replace non-LaserWriter fonts on the screen with LaserWriter fonts on paper, using the printer's full resolution and graphics capability. For example, the LaserWriter replaces New York with Times, Geneva with Helvetica, and Monaco with Courier. If you don't click Font Substitution?, the LaserWriter reproduces non-LaserWriter fonts exactly as they appear on the screen.

The Smoothing? option calls on a marvelously complex piece of software that smooths the jagged edges of screen images caused by the corners of pixels where there should be a straight diagonal or curved line. As a result of smoothing, the printed image has relatively smooth diagonal and curved lines, as shown in Figure 7-16. Be aware, though, that smoothing affects only graphics, not text.

Select the Page Setup options you want.

Click the OK button, then choose Print... from the File menu.

The Print dialog box, shown in Figure 7-17, doesn't have the three Quality buttons the ImageWriter's Print dialog box has, but the other options are the same. As in the Page Setup dialog box, the word *LaserWriter* appears in the upper left corner.

Select the options you want and click the OK button.

While the printing process is going on, status messages are displayed on the screen and the status-indicator lights on the printer flash. A green flashing light indicates the printer is warming up, a

Figure 7-17. The LaserWriter's Print dialog box

LaserWriter

Copies: 1   Pages: ● All   ○ From: [   ] To: [   ]

Paper Source: ● Paper Cassette   ○ Manual Feed

OK

Cancel

steady green light tells you the LaserWriter is ready to print, flashing yellow means the printer is processing a page, steady yellow indicates the paper cassette is empty or not installed or the printer is set for manual paper feed, and a steady red light means the paper is jammed inside the printer. If you see a steady red light, consult your manual for methods of correcting the problem.

It can take up to several minutes for the LaserWriter to produce a single page. The advertised rate of eight pages per minute is the speed it produces a printout after the image of the page has been assembled in memory. The process of assembling an image in memory is a complex and time-consuming one. Images containing graphics and non-LaserWriter fonts take the longest to assemble. Assembling an image containing a LaserWriter font that's being used for the first time takes longer than images containing LaserWriter fonts that have been used before, because the printer must convert the outline form of the characters it has stored in memory into dot patterns.

Using an Independent Printer Driver with the Epson FX-80

As mentioned in Chapter 5, some independent software developers are producing printer drivers for a number of printers that wouldn't otherwise be compatible with Word on the Macintosh. Some, such as ProPrint from Creighton Development (mentioned in Chapter 5), let you use fully formed character printers from the initial desktop. You select the files you want to print, then choose a printing command from one of the menus. One drawback of ProPrint is that it can't print Word documents unless they were saved in Text Only format (by clicking the Text Only check box in the Save As dialog box).

Other programs modify the ImageWriter printer driver so that it will work for a different printer. For instance, Toshiba provides free of charge a printer driver that modifies the ImageWriter printer driver to allow you to connect its P1340, P1351, and P351 printers to the Mac. The Toshiba program is designed to get the most out of the 24-wire print head in Standard and High printing modes. To get a free copy of the program, contact the nearest Toshiba regional office: Irvine, California, (714) 250-0151; New Jersey, (201) 326-9777; or St. Louis, Missouri, (314) 991-0751. You can also get a Toshiba printer to produce near-letter-quality printouts by using ProPrint or by selecting the Apple Daisy driver in Word.

For this example, we're going to use a program called Epstart, sold by SoftStyle (also mentioned in Chapter 5), that allows you to connect an Epson FX-80 (or one of several other Epson printers) to a Mac by modifying the ImageWriter printer driver.

Since Epson printers come equipped with a parallel interface, you need either to purchase a serial interface card from an Epson dealer or to use a parallel-to-serial conversion device, such as the Mac-Enhancer. The serial interface card is a circuit board that is inserted inside the printer. The Epson documentation lists the switch settings. A conversion device is a better approach, because you don't need to fiddle with making the baud rate or handshake settings the same on the printer as on the Mac. We used a parallel-to-serial buffer made by Quadram for testing the Epson FX-80 example in this chapter. The Macintosh cable connects to the serial input port of the buffer and the parallel output cable of the buffer connects to the parallel input port of the printer.

You can leave the DIP switches, located behind the access hatch on the back of the printer, in the positions they were in when the printer came from the factory, but check to make sure switch 2-4 is off so that the printer doesn't advance the paper automatically. The Mac advances the paper. Now you're ready to install the printer driver on the Word disk.

> Insert the Epstart program disk in the internal drive, but don't insert the Word disk in the external drive.

The manual cautions that the installation process must take place entirely with the internal drive.

> Double-click on the Epstart icon in the disk directory window to open the program.

The Epstart window opens, displaying a representation of the two Macintosh ports.

> Click on the port to which you connected the printer, then choose the name of the printer you're using from the Printer menu.

For our example, we chose the Epson FX-80.

If you want to, you can change the baud rate from the default of 9600 by choosing a different speed from the Speed menu. But 9600 baud is a good choice, because it's the fastest data-transfer rate offered in the Speed menu, so it's best to leave it there. Now you're ready to install the setup you've chosen on the Word disk.

> Choose Eject Disk from the File menu and insert the Word disk in the internal drive in place of the Epstart disk.

The Epstart program modifies both the System file and the Image-Writer printer driver, changing the name of the printer driver to the name you selected. When the installation is completed, the Word disk is ready to use.

The Epstart printer driver can operate in all three Quality modes: Draft, Standard, and High. In Draft printing, Epstart picks a character size that's as close to the size of characters on the screen as possible.

If you want to change back to the ImageWriter printer driver, run the Epstart program again, but this time select the ImageWriter instead of the printer you used previously.

Now that you know how to connect your printer, we'll show you in Chapter 8 the quality of type you can access using Word on the Mac, both with and without a printer.

8   A word on type

It may seem a little strange to see a chapter on type in a book on word processing, but the Mac's ability to display different fonts, styles, and sizes of type on the screen has opened up the larger world of typesetting—at one time the exclusive domain of typographers—to Macintosh users.

In this chapter, we help you explore this new world. First, we show you where to find the growing variety of fonts you can use in your Word documents and demonstrate how to add them to your Word disk. Then, we look at some of the basic characteristics and categories of type. Next, we give some guidelines for using different fonts effectively. Finally, we discuss how you can use Word to get top quality results through typesetting.

Sources for Fonts

As you saw for yourself in Section One, Word gives you immediate access to six fonts when you choose Formats... from the Character menu. But you aren't limited to using only those six fonts. You can add fonts to your Word disk from several other sources: the System Disk that came with your Macintosh, other Macintosh application disks, independently produced font disks, the LaserWriter software, and do-it-yourself font software. We'll discuss these sources one at a time; but first we'll start by taking a closer look at the fonts that are on the Word disk when you buy it.

One final reminder before we get started: As mentioned in Chapter 6, only dot-matrix and laser printers can reproduce fonts as they appear on the screen. Though you can change fonts on a daisy-wheel or other fully formed character printer by changing the printing element, the fonts printed won't be the ones displayed on the Mac screen.

The fonts stored, or installed, in the System file of the Word Master disk when you first open Word are Chicago, New York, Geneva, Monaco, Dover, and Dover PS. The names of these fonts are displayed in the Font Names list box of the Character Formats dialog box. You can use the scroll arrows or scroll box to view the names of fonts at the bottom of the list.

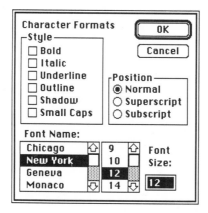

Some of these fonts have several installed sizes, which you can view in the Font Size list box. You can use the scroll arrows and scroll box in the Font Size list box, too. Clicking on the name of a font in the Font Name list box automatically displays the installed sizes of that font in the Font Size list box. The numbers displayed represent points, a standard of measurement in the printing world (one point equals about $1/72$ inch). Word's installed fonts and sizes are shown in Figure 8-1.

You can specify any other size from 4 to 127 points by typing a number in the Font Size text box that's displayed to the right of the Font Size list box. But as we explained in Chapter 6, if you specify a size that isn't installed, Word must scale an installed size, resulting in characters that are more ragged than the characters of an installed size.

Now we'll look at some sources for fonts that you can add to your Word disk.

Chicago 12

ABCDEFGHIJKLMNOPQRSTUVWXYZ
abcdefghijklmnopqrstuvwxyz
1234567890-=!@#$%^&*()_+[]\{}|;':",./<>?`~

New York 9

ABCDEFGHIJKLMNOPQRSTUVWXYZ
abcdefghijklmnopqrstuvwxyz
1234567890-=!@#$%^&*()_+[]\{}|;':",./<>?`~

New York 10

ABCDEFGHIJKLMNOPQRSTUVWXYZ
abcdefghijklmnopqrstuvwxyz
1234567890-=!@#$%^&*()_+[]\{}|;':",./<>?`~

New York 12

ABCDEFGHIJKLMNOPQRSTUVWXYZ
abcdefghijklmnopqrstuvwxyz
1234567890-=!@#$%^&*()_+[]\{}|;':",./<>?`~

New York 14

ABCDEFGHIJKLMNOPQRSTUVWXYZ
abcdefghijklmnopqrstuvwxyz
1234567890-=!@#$%^&*()_+[]\{}|;':",./<>?`~

New York 18

ABCDEFGHIJKLMNOPQRSTUVWXYZ
abcdefghijklmnopqrstuvwxyz
1234567890-=!@#$%^&*()_+[]\{}|;':",./<>?`~

continued

Figure 8-1. Word's system fonts,
in their installed sizes

New York 20

ABCDEFGHIJKLMNOPQRSTUVWXYZ
abcdefghijklmnopqrstuvwxyz
1234567890-=!@#$%^&*()_+[]\{}|;':",./<>?`~

New York 24

ABCDEFGHIJKLMNOPQRSTUVWXYZ
abcdefghijklmnopqrstuvwxyz12345
67890-=!@#$%^&*()_+[]\{}|;':",./<>?`~

Geneva 9

ABCDEFGHIJKLMNOPQRSTUVWXYZ
abcdefghijklmnopqrstuvwxyz
1234567890-=!@#$%^&*()_+[]\{}|;':",./<>?`~

Geneva 10

ABCDEFGHIJKLMNOPQRSTUVWXYZ
abcdefghijklmnopqrstuvwxyz
1234567890-=!@#$%^&*()_+[]\{}|;':",./<>?`~

Geneva 12

ABCDEFGHIJKLMNOPQRSTUVWXYZ
abcdefghijklmnopqrstuvwxyz
1234567890-=!@#$%^&*()_+[]\{}|;':",./<>?`~

Geneva 14

ABCDEFGHIJKLMNOPQRSTUVWXYZ
abcdefghijklmnopqrstuvwxyz
1234567890-=!@#$%^&*()_+[]\{}|;':",./<>?`~

Figure 8-1 (continued)

continued

Geneva 18

ABCDEFGHIJKLMNOPQRSTUVWXYZ
abcdefghijklmnopqrstuvwxyz
1234567890-=!@#$%^&*()_+[]\{}|;':",./<>?`~

Geneva 20

ABCDEFGHIJKLMNOPQRSTUVWXYZ
abcdefghijklmnopqrstuvwxyz 123456
7890-=!@#$%^&*()_+[]\{}|;':",./<>?`~

Geneva 24

ABCDEFGHIJKLMNOPQRSTUVWXYZ
abcdefghijklmnopqrstuvwxyz
1234567890-=!@#$%^&*()_+[]\
{}|;':",./<>?`~

Monaco 9

```
ABCDEFGHIJKLMNOPQRSTUVWXYZ
abcdefghijklmnopqrstuvwxyz
1234567890-=!@#$%^&*()_+[]\{}|;':",./<>?`~
```

Monaco 12

```
ABCDEFGHIJKLMNOPQRSTUVWXYZ
abcdefghijklmnopqrstuvwxyz
1234567890-=!@#$%^&*()_+[]\{}|;':",./<>?`~
```

continued

Figure 8-1 (continued)

Dover 8

```
ABCDEFGHIJKLMNOPQRSTUVWXYZ
abcdefghijklmnopqrstuvwxyz
1234567890-=!@#$%^&*()_+[]\{}|;':",./<>?`~
```

Dover 10

```
ABCDEFGHIJKLMNOPQRSTUVWXYZ
abcdefghijklmnopqrstuvwxyz
1234567890-=!@#$%^&*()_+[]\{}|;':",./<>?`~
```

Dover 12

```
ABCDEFGHIJKLMNOPQRSTUVWXYZ
abcdefghijklmnopqrstuvwxyz
1234567890-=!@#$%^&*()_+[]\{}|;':",./<>?`~
```

Dover PS 12

```
ABCDEFGHIJKLMNOPQRSTUVWXYZ
abcdefghijklmnopqrstuvwxyz
1234567890-=!@#$%^&*()_+[]\{}|;':",./<>?`~
```

Figure 8-1 (continued)

System Disk Fonts

The System Disk that came with your Macintosh (we'll refer to this as the Macintosh System Disk, to avoid confusion with any other disk with a System file) also contains several fonts, some of which are not on the Word disk. These additional fonts are Athens, Cairo, London, Los Angeles, San Francisco, Toronto, Seattle, and Venice, shown in Figure 8-2. The names and number of fonts on your System Disk may vary, depending on which version you have.

Fonts on Other Application Disks

Some applications for the Macintosh also include unique fonts. For example, Word has two unique fonts (Dover and Dover PS). At one time, Microsoft Multiplan was the only program that contained Seattle, but Seattle is now included on the System Disk.

Athens 18

ABCDEFGHIJKLMNOPQRSTUVWXYZ
abcdefghijklmnopqrstuvwxyz
1234567890-=!@#$%^G*()_+[]\{}|;':",./<>?`~

Cairo 18

London 18

ABCDEFGHIJKLMNOPQRSTUVWXYZ
abcdefghijklmnopqrstuvwxyz
1234567890-=!@#$%&*()_+[]\{}|;':",./?

Los Angeles 12

ABCDEFGHIJKLMNOPQRSTUVWXYZ
abcdefghijklmnopqrstuvwxyz
1234567890-=!@#$%^&*()_+[]\{}|;':",./<>?~

continued

Figure 8-2. Macintosh System
Disk fonts in their installed
sizes

Los Angeles 24

ABCDEFGHIJKLMNOPQRSTUVWXYZ
abcdefghijklmnopqrstuvwxyz
1234567890-=!@#$%^&*()
_+[]\{}|;':",./<>?~

San Francisco 18

ABCDEFGHIJKLMNOPQRSTUVWXYZ
abcdefghijklmnopqrstuvwxyz
1234567890-=!@#$%&*()_+[]\{}|;':",./<>?

Seattle 10

ABCDEFGHIJKLMNOPQRSTUVWXYZ
abcdefghijklmnopqrstuvwxyz
1234567890-=!@#$%^&*()_+[]\{}|;':",./<>?`~

Seattle 20

ABCDEFGHIJKLMNOPQRSTUVWXYZ
abcdefghijklmnopqrstuvwxyz
1234567890-=!@#$%^&*()_+[]\
{}|;':",./<>?`~

continued

Figure 8-2 (continued)

Toronto 9

ABCDEFGHIJKLMnOPQRSTUVWXYZ
abcdefghijklmnopqrstuvwxyz
1234567890-=!@#$%^&*()_+[]\{}|;':",./<>?`~

Toronto 12

ABCDEFGHIJKLMnOPQRSTUVWXYZ
abcdefghijklmnopqrstuvwxyz
1234567890-=!@#$%^&*()_+[]\{}|;':",./<>?`~

Toronto 14

ABCDEFGHIJKLMnOPQRSTUVWXYZ
abcdefghijklmnopqrstuvwxyz
1234567890-=!@#$%^&*()_+[]\{}|;':",./<>?`~

Toronto 18

ABCDEFGHIJKLMnOPQRSTUVWXYZ
abcdefghijklmnopqrstuvwxyz
1234567890-=!@#$%^&*()_+[]\{}|;':",./<>?`~

Toronto 24

ABCDEFGHIJKLMnOPQRSTUV
WXYZabcdefghijklmnopqrstu
vwxyz1234567890-=!@#$%^&*
()_+[]\{}|;':",./<>?`~

Figure 8-2 (continued)

continued

Venice 14

A B C D E F G H I J K L M N O P Q R S T U V W X Y Z

a b c d e f g h i j k l m n o p q r s t u v w x y z

1 2 3 4 5 6 7 8 9 0 - = ! # $ % ^ & * ( ) _ + [ ] \ { } | ; ' : " , . / < > ? ` ~

Figure 8-2 (continued)

Independently Produced Fonts

Several independent software developers are now offering an impressive variety of fonts for the Mac. Most are for display or are highly stylized—what might be called novelty typefaces. But there are also some very readable text fonts for letters and manuscripts. And there are some specialty fonts, such as foreign alphabets, scientific notation, and cartoon symbols, as you can see from the sampling in Figure 8-3—Congo, Columbia, and Border from UltraFonts by 21st Century Software, and Images from Fluent Fonts by Casady Computing.

Most of the fonts are offered on disks that cost between $20 and $50 each and include several fonts. We urge you to be cautious about loading up on a stock of fonts you may never use. Disk space is precious, and the best typographers insist the best results come from judicious use of a few good typefaces. Some of the independently produced font disks for the Macintosh at this writing are: *UltraFonts* and *Technical & Business* from 21st Century Software, 2306 Cotner Ave., Los Angeles, California 90064, (213) 829-4436; *Mac the Knife, Vol. 2* from Miles Computing, Inc., 21018 Osborne St. #5, Canoga Park, California 91304, (818) 341-1411; and *Fluent Fonts* (two-disk set) from Casady Company, P.O. Box 223779, Carmel, California 93922, (408) 646-4660. These are the independent developers whose products we use as examples throughout much of the rest of this chapter, but there are many others producing equally fine quality fonts. Check the advertisements in computer magazines for the names of others. More font marketers appear almost every month.

Congo 18 (also available in 12 and 24)

ABCDEFGHIJKLMNOPQRSTUVWXYZ
abcdefghijklmnopqrstuvwxyz
1234567890-=!@#$%&*()_+'’\“”'|;':",./,.? ~

Columbia 18 (also available in 12 and 24)

ABCDEFGHIJKLMNOPQRSTUVWXYZ
abcdefghijklmnopqrstuvwxyz
1234567890-=!@#$%&*()_+'’\“”|;':",./,.?`~

Border 9

Images 12

Figure 8-3. A sampling of
independently produced fonts

LaserWriter Fonts

Apple's LaserWriter printer has its own four fonts: Helvetica, Times, Courier, and Symbol, as shown in Figure 8-4. Each of the first three fonts comes in four standard styles: Roman, Italic, Bold Roman, and Bold Italic. Symbol includes Greek, mathematical, legal, and decorative characters.

Helvetica 9

ABCDEFGHIJKLMNOPQRSTUVWXYZ
abcdefghijklmnopqrstuvwxyz
1234567890-=!@#$%^&*()_+[]\{}|;':",./<>?'~

Helvetica 10

ABCDEFGHIJKLMNOPQRSTUVWXYZ
abcdefghijklmnopqrstuvwxyz
1234567890-=!@#$%^&*()_+[]\{}|;':",./<>?'~

Helvetica 12

ABCDEFGHIJKLMNOPQRSTUVWXYZ
abcdefghijklmnopqrstuvwxyz
1234567890-=!@#$%^&*()_+[]\{}|;':",./<>?'~

Helvetica 14

ABCDEFGHIJKLMNOPQRSTUVWXYZ
abcdefghijklmnopqrstuvwxyz
1234567890-=!@#$%^&*()_+[]\{}|;':",./<>?'~

Helvetica 18

ABCDEFGHIJKLMNOPQRSTUVWXYZ
abcdefghijklmnopqrstuvwxyz
1234567890-=!@#$%^&*()_+[]\{}|;':",./<>?'~

---

continued

Figure 8-4. LaserWriter fonts

Helvetica 24

ABCDEFGHIJKLMNOPQRSTUVWXYZ
abcdefghijklmnopqrstuvwxyz123
4567890-=!@#$%^&*()_+[]\{}|;':",./<>?'~

Times 9

ABCDEFGHIJKLMNOPQRSTUVWXYZ
abcdefghijklmnopqrstuvwxyz
1234567890-=!@#$%^&*()_+[]\{}|;':",./<>?'~

Times 10

ABCDEFGHIJKLMNOPQRSTUVWXYZ
abcdefghijklmnopqrstuvwxyz
1234567890-=!@#$%^&*() +[]\{}|;':",./<>?'~

Times 12

ABCDEFGHIJKLMNOPQRSTUVWXYZ
abcdefghijklmnopqrstuvwxyz
1234567890-=!@#$%^&*()_+[]\{}|;':",./<>?'~

Times 14

ABCDEFGHIJKLMNOPQRSTUVWXYZ
abcdefghijklmnopqrstuvwxyz
1234567890-=!@#$%^&*()_+[]\{}|;':",./<>?'~

Times 18

ABCDEFGHIJKLMNOPQRSTUVWXYZ
abcdefghijklmnopqrstuvwxyz
1234567890-=!@#$%^&*()_+[]\{}|;':",./<>?'~

continued

Figure 8-4 (continued)

Times 24

ABCDEFGHIJKLMNOPQRSTUVWXYZ
abcdefghijklmnopqrstuvwxyz 123
4567890-=!@#$%^&*()_+[]\{}|;':",./<>?'~

Courier 9

```
ABCDEFGHIJKLMNOPQRSTUVWXYZ
abcdefghijklmnopqrstuvwxyz
1234567890-=!@#$%^&*()_+[]\{}|;':",./<>?'~
```

Courier 10

```
ABCDEFGHIJKLMNOPQRSTUVWXYZ
abcdefghijklmnopqrstuvwxyz
1234567890-=!@#$%^&*() +[]\{}|;':",./<>?'~
```

Courier 12

```
ABCDEFGHIJKLMNOPQRSTUVWXYZ
abcdefghijklmnopqrstuvwxyz
1234567890-=!@#$%^&*() +[]\{}|;':",./<>?'~
```

Courier 14

```
ABCDEFGHIJKLMNOPQRSTUVWXYZ
abcdefghijklmnopqrstuvwxyz
1234567890-=!@#$%^&*() +[]\{}|;':",./<>?'~
```

Courier 18

```
ABCDEFGHIJKLMNOPQRSTUVWXYZ
abcdefghijklmnopqrstuvwxyz 123
4567890-=!@#$%^&*() +[]\{}|;':",./<>?'~
```

continued

Figure 8-4 (continued)

Courier 24

```
ABCDEFGHIJKLMNOPQRSTUVWXYZ
abcdefghijklmnopqrstuvwxyz
1234567890-=!@#$%^&*()_+[]\{}|;
':",./<>?`~
```

Symbol 9

ΑΒΧΔΕΦΓΗΙϑΚΛΜΝΟΠΘΡΣΤΥςΩΞΨΖ
αβχδεφγηιφκλμνοπθρστυϖωξψζ
1234567890−=!≅#∃%⊥&*()_+[]∴{}|;ϑ:∀,./<>? ‾~

Symbol 12

ΑΒΧΔΕΦΓΗΙϑΚΛΜΝΟΠΘΡΣΤΥςΩΞΨΖ
αβχδεφγηιφκλμνοπθρστυϖωξψζ
1234567890−=!≅#∃%⊥&*()_+[]∴{}|;ϑ:∀,./<>? ‾~

Symbol 18

ΑΒΧΔΕΦΓΗΙϑΚΛΜΝΟΠΘΡΣΤΥςΩΞΨΖ
αβχδεφγηιφκλμνοπθρστυϖωξψζ
1234567890−=!≅#∃%⊥&*()_+[]∴{}|;ϑ:∀,./<>? ‾~

Symbol 24

ΑΒΧΔΕΦΓΗΙϑΚΛΜΝΟΠΘΡΣΤΥςΩΞΨΖ
αβχδεφγηιφκλμνοπθρστυϖωξψζ123456
7890−=!≅#∃%⊥&*()_+[]∴{}|;ϑ:∀,./<>? ‾~

Figure 8-4 (continued)

Public Domain Fonts

Dozens of Mac fonts are in the public domain—that is, no one holds the rights to sell them. Some are what's known as honorware: You are asked to donate a certain amount to the developer, though you are under no legal obligation to do so. Others are what's called freeware: You are under no obligation, legal or otherwise, for the use of them.

You can obtain public domain fonts through user groups, electronic bulletin boards, and commercial information services. Strictly speaking, the fonts aren't free from any of these sources. You must provide a disk to put them on and, in the case of bulletin boards and information services, there are also connect fees and long-distance telephone charges.

Do-It-Yourself Fonts

If, despite the variety of fonts available, you still don't find a font you like, you can design your own. Apple has provided its software developers with a program, called FontEditor, that enables them to design and edit fonts. With FontEditor, you can start with an existing font, scale it to the size you want, and then modify it in a mode similar to the FatBits mode of MacPaint. Or you can start from scratch. When you're satisfied, you can store your font in a font library on a separate disk, on the Word Working Master disk, on the MacPaint disk, or on any other system disk.

Apple may or may not release its FontEditor for public distribution, but, if it doesn't, you will probably be able to find sources for similar programs. Ann Arbor Softworks, Inc., 308½ South State Street, Ann Arbor, Michigan 48104, issues a font-producing program called Font Blaster, in connection with its Animation Toolkit program. Another source is Altsys Corp., P.O. Box 865410, Plano, Texas 75086, which offers a font editor called FONTastic.

Using Font Mover

With such a variety of fonts available, you may eventually want to use one or two in your Word documents. Even if you're not tempted by the smorgasbord of fonts, sooner or later you'll probably need to free up some space on your Word disk, and one of the best ways of doing that is by removing some of the fonts you never use from your Word disk's System file. In either case, you'll need Font Mover, a utility program on the Macintosh System Disk. Font Mover allows you to add and remove fonts from the System file of any application. You can't open System files or manipulate their contents in the usual ways. Font Mover gives you access to the fonts in these files, allowing you to remove them or to transfer them to other System files by means of an intermediary file called Fonts. We'll see how in a minute.

You don't need to use Font Mover to add LaserWriter fonts to your Word disk. They are added to the Word System file automatically by an installation utility provided with the LaserWriter. But you can use Font Mover to add and remove LaserWriter fonts one at a time.

Creating a Fonts Disk

Standard practice for using Font Mover is simply to copy Font Mover and its accompanying Fonts file from the Macintosh System Disk to an application disk, such as Word, then to transfer fonts from the Fonts file to the application's System file, or vice versa, directly on the application disk. But, because there is so little available space on the Word disk, we recommend instead that you copy Font Mover and the Fonts file to a third disk, a disk without a System file of its own. Using a third disk not only avoids the need to create a large amount of extra space on the Word disk, but gives you a start on creating a font library.

To give you an idea of the space limitations on the Word disk, even if you removed the Help file, Memo, and the printer drivers file, just the Word program and the System file would take up all but about 70K of space. Font Mover (13K) and the Fonts file (56K) together require 69K, and that doesn't take into account the space needed for working with Font Mover. Even using a third disk for Font Mover and the Fonts file, you'll need at least 50K on your Word Working Master disk for storing new fonts. If you want to follow the step-by-step instructions we're about to give, check your working master disk to see that you have at least 50K of space. Available disk space is displayed in the upper right corner of the disk directory window. If you need more space, see Chapter 4 for suggestions on freeing up disk space.

When you're satisfied you have enough room to work with, replace the Word disk with the Macintosh System Disk and initialize a blank disk as follows.

Insert the Macintosh System Disk in one drive and a blank disk in the other drive.

Click the Initialize button in the first dialog box displayed, then type *Fonts* in the Please Name This Disk text box of the second dialog box displayed.

Now you're ready to put the Font Mover on the new Fonts disk.

Drag the Font Mover and Fonts file icons from the Macintosh System Disk directory window to the Fonts disk icon and wait while the Mac copies the two Files.

Next, restart the system with the Word disk as the system disk.

> Eject both disks and turn off the computer.
>
> Insert the Word Working Master disk in the internal drive and the Fonts disk in the external drive.
>
> Turn on the computer.
>
> Open the Fonts disk directory window and double-click on the Font Mover icon.

Opening Font Mover automatically loads two font files as well: the fonts from the System file on your Word Working Master and the file named Fonts that you just copied. The Font Mover window, shown in Figure 8-5, displays two list boxes, with the System-file fonts listed in the box on the left and the Fonts-file fonts listed in the one on the right. Between these two list boxes are four buttons: Help, Copy, Remove, and Quit.

You can always check in with Help to get help, but, if you stay with this chapter, you will get help as you need it. To activate the Copy and Remove buttons, you must first select a font in one of the files by clicking on its name. So find a font in the Fonts file that you want to copy into your Word System file.

> Click on the font you want to copy.

There, the Remove button brightens up, and the Copy button comes to life, with a series of arrows pointing to the left. Now, it's time for a caution about disk space. Before you copy a font, you should make sure there's enough space on the disk to which you're copying. Every time you copy a font, you use up 2K to 13K of available disk space.

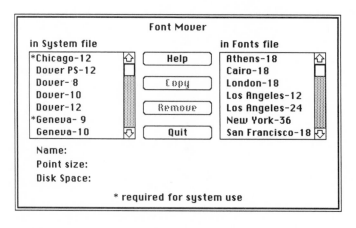

Figure 8-5. The Font Mover window

When you select a font, its disk space (in bytes) is displayed at the bottom of the screen, along with its name, point size, and a sample of it, so you can quickly tell how many bytes you are about to add to the disk.

Whether or not you are sure of how much disk space you have, go ahead and copy the font.

Click on the Copy button.

If you have enough disk space, you see your chosen font appear in the System-file box. If you don't have enough disk space, an alert box is displayed. If, for example, you tried to copy 36-point New York and didn't have enough disk space, you'd see an alert box, stating: Insufficient disk space to copy New York-36.

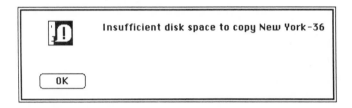

If you get this message, you'll have to click the OK button, then go back and remove some fonts or extraneous files from your Word disk. To free up some disk space, we'll put the Remove button to work now just to show you how to use it.

Caution: Remove does just what it says. Once a font is removed, you can't get it back unless you've made a copy of it. It's best to remove a font from the System file that is also in the Fonts file, so that you know it can easily be replaced.

Select a font in the System file and click the Remove button.

Four of the fonts in the System file are required for system use: Chicago-12, Geneva-9, Geneva-12, and Monaco-9. (In the System-file section of the Font Mover window, these fonts are identified with asterisks.) You cannot remove these fonts from the System file, because the Mac uses them for such things as menu labels, file names, dialog- and alert-box messages, and icon titles. So there is no point in keeping them on the Fonts disk as part of a font library file: They are a part of every System file and will always be available to you, no matter what system disk you use to start your Macintosh.

For this exercise, remove a font or two from your System file so that you have disk space to try out your Font Mover. Note that the larger point sizes take up more disk space. For example, 9-point New York requires 2032 bytes of disk space, while 36-point New York requires 13,780 bytes. If you weren't able to copy a font the first time because of inadequate disk space, try again after having removed some fonts using the Remove button.

If you want to copy more than one font into your System file and there is sufficient disk space, you can copy them all at the same time. Just hold down the Shift key as you click each font name in the Fonts-file section of the Font Mover window. Each font you click will stay highlighted until you click Copy or Remove.

Shift-click on font names to select more than one.

When you are finished copying or removing fonts, close the Font Mover window.

Click the Quit button.

Creating a Font Library

We strongly recommend that you prepare a set of disks containing Font Mover and fonts arranged in useful files. These disks will make up your font library. With a little bit of planning, you can minimize the space taken up by fonts on your working master disk, and you can minimize the time you spend fussing with Font Mover when you want to use a font that isn't on your working master. Setting up your own font library on your new Fonts disk gives you these and other advantages, as you will discover in the next few pages.

Before starting, you need to consider how you want to organize your library. You might want to group similiar fonts together. You could start with separate files for each of the fonts that take up the most room, such as New York, Geneva, and Toronto, which are available in eight different point sizes. Next, you could reserve one of the files for fonts that look good for text or are available in only a few sizes, such as Athens, Dover, and Dover PS, plus Monaco, which comes only in point sizes 9 and 12. In another file, you might group the exotic fonts, such as San Francisco, Los Angeles, Venice, London, and Cairo. Arranged this way, your Fonts disk directory window might look like the one in Figure 8-6.

Figure 8-6. A basic font library

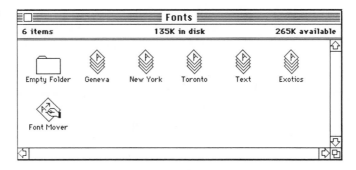

Or you could group your font files by the types of documents that you write regularly. For example, a technical report might require mathematical symbols from the LaserWriter utility font, but children's stories would not. So, you could put the utility font and a text font for technical reports in one file and simply a text font for children's stories in another file. Of course, Font Mover works just fine for other applications programs, not just Word. So, in setting up your font library categories, you might also set up special files for MacPaint or MacDraw documents.

As we explained in Chapter 6, when you print in high-quality mode, your Macintosh looks for a font twice the size of the selected font and then scales it to half size for printing. If you are going to use high-quality printing, keep pairs of sizes together in the same file. For example, if you're going to print 10-point New York in high-resolution mode, you'll need to be sure that 20-point New York is stored in the same library file so that they can be transferred together into your System file.

When you have a plan for organizing your font files, you are ready to build your font library, starting with the fonts in Word's System file. As we said before, when you open Font Mover, it automatically loads the Fonts file. If you change the name of the Fonts file so that there is no file called Fonts available, Font Mover will open a new, blank Fonts file. You can call the old file anything but Fonts. We will use the name Fonts Source.

> Click the I-beam pointer immediately to the right of the icon name *Fonts,* type a space and then *Source.*

Now you have no file named Fonts. So open Font Mover again to create a new Fonts file.

> Double-click on Font Mover.

You are ready to start your first permanent font-library file. For example, you could copy all the New York fonts into the new file and give it the charming and clever title New York.

> Select the fonts you want to store in the blank file and copy them from the System file to the Fonts file.
>
> Click on Quit.
>
> Drag the I-beam pointer across the icon name *Fonts,* and type *New York* to rename the file.

You can repeat this process for each font style in the System file.

Now you can expand your library to include the fonts from the Macintosh System Disk that you stored in the Fonts Source file. To do that, you first need to move them into Word's System file. So far, you've only moved fonts from the Fonts file to the Word System file and from the System file to a new, blank Fonts file. But it's just as easy to move fonts from an existing file, such as the one you renamed Fonts Source, to the System file. Just open the file.

> Double-click on the Fonts Source file icon.

The Font Mover window opens again with Fonts Source file in the right window. Now you have all the tools you need to complete your library. You can copy fonts from the Fonts Source file to the System file. Then you can open successive new, blank Fonts files and copy the fonts from the System file to create a series of appropriate library files.

> Shift-click on the names of fonts in the Fonts Source list box, then click on Copy.
>
> Click on Quit.
>
> Double-click on the Font Mover icon.
>
> Copy the new fonts from the System file into library files.

Once all fonts are located in library files, you can trash the Fonts Source file, and you can remove all but the four required fonts from the Word System file. From this point on, you can double-click on any of the library files to start the Font Mover and then copy that set of fonts into the System file when you want to use them. In some application programs, such as MacPaint, the font menu is limited to about 20 fonts. In Word, you can load fonts into the System file until you are out of disk space.

If you want to use an independently produced font, you could simply insert your font library disk in one drive and the independent font disk in the other drive, then drag the file containing the font you want to use to your font library disk. But a better approach is to put Font Mover on the independent font disk and create new font files arranged the way you plan to use them.

> Drag Font Mover from the System Disk directory window to the independent font disk directory window.
>
> Double-click on the font file containing fonts you want to use.

Font Mover opens, with the specified font file in the list box on the right side of the Font Mover window, and the System Disk System file on the left side.

> Click on the font or Shift-click on the fonts you want to use.
>
> Click the Copy button.

The specified fonts are copied into the System file.

> Click the Quit button.
>
> Double-click on the Font Mover icon.

Font Mover opens with a blank Fonts file in the list box on the right side of the window.

> Click on the font or Shift-click on the fonts you want to copy from the System file into the new Fonts file.
>
> Click the Copy button.
>
> Click the Quit button.
>
> Rename the new Fonts file.
>
> Eject the System Disk and insert your font library disk.
>
> Drag the new Fonts file icon to the font-library disk window.

If you use Font Mover to install independently produced fonts on your Word disk, there is a possibility you might later choose one font and see a totally different font displayed. This possibility exists because of a lack of standardization in the marketplace. The Macintosh distinguishes between fonts not by name, but by an identification number within the software for each font. Each identification number is intended to be unique, with no other font having that same number. But, unfortunately, this is not always the case with independently produced fonts. Since there is no clearinghouse for assigning Macintosh font numbers, two developers could unknowingly assign the same identification number to two different fonts. If you installed one of these fonts, then the other, the second font installed would be the font the Mac would identify with the shared number. The Mac would display both font names in the Fonts list box, but would display only the second font no matter which one you chose.

One final suggestion to make your font handling easier: If you are working with several different projects that use different font selections, you can make a Word Working Master disk for each project. Just give each disk a different identifying title and a different set of fonts in its System file.

And, whatever else you do, make backup copies of your library disk or disks. One erroneous click on Remove could be disastrous without a backup copy.

Type Characteristics and Categories

You might want to take some time now to learn a little more about the characteristics and terminology of type. With the brief background presented in the next few pages, you'll be better able to use the fonts available for the Macintosh to create attractive, professional-looking printed projects, such as those described in Section Three of this book. We don't intend what follows to be a course on typography; there are small libraries of books on type design and typography. But, since the Mac has opened the door to this larger world, you should know what's on the other side. Then, if you're interested in learning more, you can always read further.

First, we'll look at the major characteristics of type. Then, we'll present a simple classification system that can help you make some sense out of the bewildering variety of fonts available.

Type Characteristics

Typography is far from being an exact science. Even the term "font" may mean different things to different typographers. On the Macintosh, a font is a general character design (for example, New York) in a range of sizes (for example, 9-, 10-, 12-, 14-, 18-, 20-, and 24-point) and a range of styles (Plain, Bold, Italic, Underline, Outline, Shadow, Small Caps, Superscript, and Subscript). But some typographers use the term "font" to mean a single design and style (for example, New York Bold or New York Italic), while others refer to a single design in a range of styles as a typeface, a case, or a family of type. For clarity, we'll stick with the Macintosh definition of a font.

To aid your understanding of some other terms we'll use, take a look at the labels on the diagram in Figure 8-7. You might think of this as an anatomy lesson—the anatomy of type.

Each character usually consists of a series of vertical, horizontal, diagonal, or curved lines, or strokes. In some fonts, long strokes may end with a short cross stroke, or serif. Fonts that contain these cross strokes are called serif fonts; fonts without serifs are called sans serif. The bottoms of most letters form a horizontal line, the baseline. The parts of letters, such as the *y* and *p,* that extend below the baseline are called descenders. The tops of most lowercase letters also appear to form a horizontal line, the mean line. Portions of letters, such as *t* and *l,* that extend above the mean line are called ascenders. The distance between the baseline and mean line, the x-height, may vary from one font to another. The size of a font, measured in points, is approximately the distance from the bottom of the descenders to the tops of the ascenders and uppercase letters. (As you may recall from earlier in this chapter, a point is about ½2 inch.)

Individual characters in most Macintosh fonts vary in width, with a *w* taking up more horizontal space than an *i.* This variation in character width is called proportional spacing (the PS in Dover PS, one of the fonts on your Word Master disk, stands for proportionally spaced). A few fonts, such as Dover (without the PS), give the same amount of horizontal space to every character, much like the characters on a typewriter. These fonts are called monospaced.

Type Categories

Now that you're familiar with some of the terminology of type, you can take a more coherent look at the many fonts available for the Macintosh, in some basic categories. There are several systems for classifying fonts, ranging from two to over a hundred classifications. But we think a simple system of six categories, based on the fonts currently available for the Macintosh, is the most helpful. The six categories are: serif, sans serif, script, novelty, foreign language, and symbols.

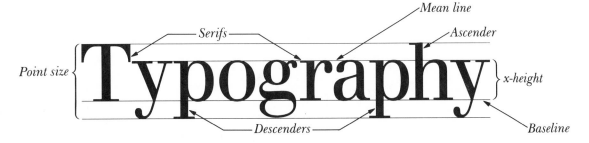

Figure 8-7. The anatomy of type

Figure 8-8. Independently produced serif fonts with strokes of varying widths

Bodoni 14 (also available in 9, 10, 12, 18, 20, 24, and 36)

ABCDEFGHIJKLMNOPQRSTUVWXYZ
abcdefghijklmnopqrstuvwxyz12345
67890-=!@#$%^&*()_+[]\{}|;':",./<>?`~

Manhattan 12 (also available in 24)

ABCDEFGHIJKLMNOPQRSTUVWXYZ

abcdefghijklmnopqrstuvwxyz

1234567890-=!@#$%[&*()_+[]\⟨⟩⟨⟩|;':",./<>?`~

Serif Fonts

Serifs are a feature that plays a major role in determining type categories. Among the serif fonts currently available are: New York, Dover, and Dover PS from your Word Master disk, and Toronto and Athens from the Macintosh System Disk.

In traditional, non-dot-matrix type design, many serif fonts have tapered serifs and thick and thin strokes. Designing typefaces for the Macintosh that can reflect these refinements is seriously constrained by the limited number of screen pixels and printer dots available. Word's New York font, which is patterned after Times Roman, is a traditional serif font. Similar independently produced serif fonts—Bodoni from Fluent Fonts and Manhattan from Mac the Knife—are shown in Figure 8-8.

Other serif fonts designed for the Macintosh have strokes of uniform thickness, rather than both thick and thin strokes. Some have uniformly thick strokes, with stubby serifs, such as Athens from the System Disk and Oblique from Fluent Fonts, shown in Figure 8-9.

Oblique 18

ABCDEFGHIJKLMNOPQRSTUV
WXYZabcdefghijklmnopqrstuv
wxyz1234567890-=!@#$%^&*
()_+[]\{}|;':",./<>?`~

Figure 8-9. Independently produced serif font with uniformly thick strokes

Toronto and the two Dover fonts have uniformly thin strokes one pixel wide, which works well for matrix-pattern font designs where strokes are horizontal and vertical. Similar independently produced fonts—Ease from Fluent Fonts, Seine from UltraFonts, and Washington DC from Mac the Knife—are shown in Figure 8-10.

Ease 18 (also available in 9, 10, 12, 20, and 24)

A B C D E F G H I J K L M N O P Q R S T U V W X Y Z

a b c d e f g h i j k l m n o p q r s t u v w x y z 1 2 3

4 5 6 7 8 9 0 - = ! @ # $ % ^ & * ( ) _ + [ ] \ { } | ; ' : " , . / < > ? ` ~

Seine 24 (also available in 12 and 18)

A B C D E F G H I J K L M N O P Q R S T U V W X

Y Z a b c d e f g h i j k l m n o p q r s t u v w x y z

1 2 3 4 5 6 7 8 9 0 - = ! @ # $ % & * ( ) _ + ' ' \ " " " | ; ' : " , . / , . ? ~

Washington DC 18 (also available in 9, 12, and 24)

A B C D E F G H I J K L M N O P Q R S T U V W X Y Z

a b c d e f g h i j k l m n o p q r s t u v w x y z

1 2 3 4 5 6 7 8 9 0 - = ! @ # $ % ^ & * ( ) _ + [ ]

\ { } | ; ' : " , . / < > ? ` ~

Figure 8-10. Independently produced serif fonts with uniformly thin strokes

Figure 8-11. The LaserWriter's serif font with strokes of varying widths

Times 10

ABCDEFGHIJKLMNOPQRSTUVWXYZ
abcdefghijklmnopqrstuvwxyz
1234567890-=!@#$%^&*() +[]\{}|;':",./<>?'~

The LaserWriter resolution of 300 dots per inch enables it to reproduce the tapered serifs and thick and thin strokes of the widely used Times Roman font, even in smaller point sizes, with remarkable precision, as you can see from the sample of the LaserWriter's Times shown in Figure 8-11.

Some serif font designs for the Mac are patterned after typewriter fonts. The LaserWriter Courier font, shown in Figure 8-12, simulates a familiar IBM typewriter font.

Sans Serif Fonts

Sans serif fonts generally have uniformly thin strokes. Geneva and Monaco from the Word Master disk, Seattle from Multiplan, and the independently produced fonts in Figure 8-13 on the following page—Nordic and Slim from Fluent Fonts, and Montreal and Stuttgart from Mac the Knife—are examples of sans serif fonts with uniformly thin strokes.

Courier 18

ABCDEFGHIJKLMNOPQRSTUVWXYZ
abcdefghijklmnopqrstuvwxyz
1234567890-=!@#$%^&*() +[]
\{}|;':",./<>?'~

Figure 8-12. The LaserWriter's serif font with uniform strokes

Nordic 18 (also available in 9 and 12)

ABCDEFGHIJKLMNOPQRSTUVWXYZ

abcdefghijklmnopqrstuvwxyz

1234567890-=!@#$%^&*()_+[]\{}|;':",./<>?`~

Slim 36 (also available in 18)

ABCDEFGHIJKLMNOPQRSTUVWXYZ

abcdefghijklmnopqrstuvwxyz123

4567890-=!@#$%^&*()_+[]\{}|;':",./<>?`~

Montreal 18 (also available in 9, 12, and 24)

ABCDEFGHIJKLMNOPQRSTUVWXYZ

abcdefghijklmnopqrstuvwxyz

1234567890-=!@#$%^&*()_+[]\

()|;':",./<>?`~

Stuttgart 18 (also available in 9, 12, and 24)

ABCDEFGHIJKLMNOPQRSTUVWX

YZabcdefghijklmnopqrstuvwxyz123

4567890-=!@#$%^&*()_+[]\{}|;':",./<>?'~

Figure 8-13. Independently produced sans serif fonts with uniformly thin strokes

Figure 8-14. Independently produced sans serif font with uniformly thick strokes

Greenbay 18

ABCDEFGHIJKLMNOPQRSTUVW
XYZ abcdefghijklmnopqrstuv
wxyz1234567890-=!@#$%^&*()
_+[]\{}|;':",./<>?`~

Some sans serif fonts have uniformly thick strokes, such as Greenbay from Mac the Knife, shown in Figure 8-14.

A few sans serif fonts, such as Chicago from the Word Master disk, and the independently produced fonts shown in Figure 8-15 — Hudson from UltraFonts and Sydney from Mac the Knife — are patterned after traditional serif fonts, using thick and thin strokes effectively. However, notice that even though they are based on serif fonts, Hudson and Sydney do not have serifs.

Sydney 12 (also available in 24)

ABCDEFGHIJKLMNOPQRSTUVWXYZ
abcdefghijklmnopqrstuvwxyz123
4567890-=!@#$%^&*()_+[]\{}|;':",./<>?`

Hudson 18 (also available in 12)

ABCDEFGHIJKLMNOPQRSTU
VWXYZabcdefghijklmnop
qrstuvwxyz1234567890-=!@
#$%&*()_+""\"" |;':",./,.? ~

Figure 8-15. Independently produced sans serif fonts with strokes of varying widths

Script Fonts

Script fonts are styled after handwriting and frequently have connecting letters. None of the fonts on the Word Master disk is script and only a few script fonts are currently available from independent developers. Script fonts are designed in two distinctly different styles. One style has abrupt strokes and strong contrast in stroke width, as though drawn with a brush or a quill pen, such as Tokyo from Mac the Knife, shown in Figure 8-16. The other type has a more graceful appearance, with uniformly thin strokes, such as Florence from Mac the Knife, also shown in Figure 8-16.

Novelty Fonts

Font designers are having a field day coming up with fonts that are intended to express a particular mood, to be used for a particular purpose, or just to get attention. Such fonts defy traditional definitions and can only be described as novelty fonts. Out of 82 fonts available from six commercial sources, 43 can be categorized as novelty. Los Angeles, San Francisco, and London from the System Disk are examples of novelty fonts. Other examples, which are shown in Figure 8-17, on the next page, are Chubby, Eire, Stripe, Canterbury, and Mazel Tov from Fluent Fonts, Amazon from UltraFonts, and Carmel from Mac the Knife.

Tokyo 14

A B C D E F G H I J K L M N O P Q R S T U V W X Y Z

a b c d e f g h i j k l m n o p q r s t u v w x y z 1 2 3

4 5 6 7 8 9 0 - = ! # $ % ^ & * ( ) _ + [ ] \ { } | ; ' : " , . / < > ? ` ~

Florence 12 (also available in 24)

A B C D E F G H I J K L M N O P Q R S T U V W X Y Z

a b c d e f g h i j k l m n o p q r s t u v w x y z 1 2 3

4 5 6 7 8 9 0 - = ! @ # $ % ^ & * ( ) _ + / / \ ( ) / ; ' : " , . / < > ? ` ˙

Figure 8-16. Independently produced script fonts

Chubby 24

ABCDEFGHIJKLMNOPQRST
UVWXYZABCDEFGHIJKLMNOPQR
STUVWXYZ1234567890-=!@#
$%^&*()_+[]\{}|;':",./<>?`~

Eire 12 (also available in 24)

ABCDEFGHIJKLMNOPQRSTUVWXYZ

ABCDEFGHIJKLMNOPQRSTUVWXYZ

1234567890-=!●#$%^&*()_+[]\{}▓;':",./●◉?`

Stripe 24

ABCDEFGHIJKLMNOPQRSTUV
WXYZABCDEFGHIJKLMNOPQ
RSTUVWXYZ1234567890-=!
@#$%^&*()_+[]\{}|;':",./<>?`

continued

Figure 8-17. Independently
produced novelty fonts

Canterbury 24 (NOTE: Type in lowercase letters only; uppercase, number, and symbol keys produce an empty box.)

Mazel Tov 14 (NOTE: Type in lowercase letters, numbers, and symbols only; uppercase keys produce an empty box.)

A B C D E F G H I J K L M N O P Q R S T U V W X Y Z

1 2 3 4 5 6 7 8 9 0 - = ! @ # $ % & * ( ) _ +   ; ' : " . , / < > ?

Amazon 18 (also available in 12 and 24. NOTE: Type in lowercase letters, numbers, and symbols only; uppercase keys produce an empty box.)

ABCDEFGHIJKLMNOPQRSTUVWXYZ
1234567890-=!@#$%Ĝ*()_+'"\""”|;':",./,.?

Carmel 24

ABCDEFGHIJKLMNOPQRSTUV

WXYZ abcdefghijklmnopqrstuvw

xyz 1234567890-=!@#$%&*()_+[]\{}|;':
",./<>?`~

Figure 8-17 (continued)

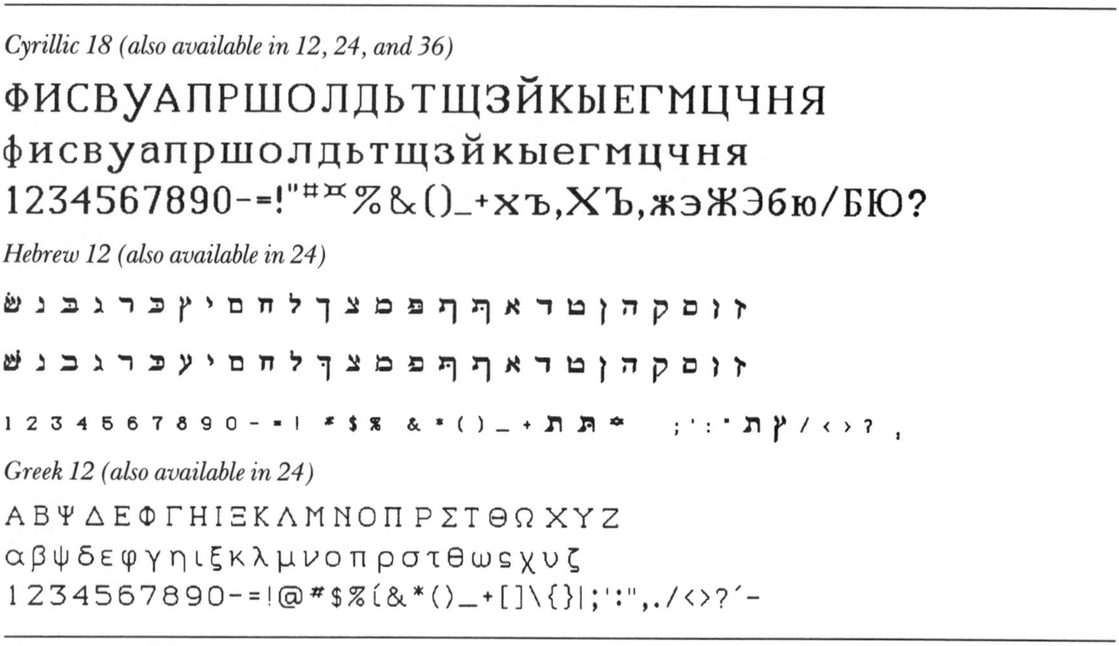

Cyrillic 18 (also available in 12, 24, and 36)

ФИСВУАПРШОЛДЬТЩЗЙКЫЕГМЦЧНЯ
фисвуапршолдьтщзйкыегмцчня
1234567890-=!"#¤%&()_+хъ,Хъ,жэЖЭбю/БЮ?

Hebrew 12 (also available in 24)

זוסקהנטדאתפמצדלחסיעכרגבנש

זוסקהנטדאתפמצדלחסיעכרגבנש

1 2 3 4 5 6 7 8 9 0 - - ׀ ₪ $ ₪ & ∗ ( ) _ + ת ת   ת ת   ;ʹ:ʹ ת ק / ‹ › ? ,

Greek 12 (also available in 24)

Α Β Ψ Δ Ε Φ Γ Η Ι Ξ Κ Λ Μ Ν Ο Π Ρ Σ Τ Θ Ω Χ Υ Ζ
α β ψ δ ε φ γ η ι ξ κ λ μ ν ο π ρ σ τ θ ω ς χ υ ζ
1234567890-=!@#$%{&*()_+[]\{}|;':",./<>?´−

Figure 8-18. Independently produced foreign-language fonts

Foreign-Language Fonts

There's no need to go back to pen and paper if you want to write in Hebrew or Greek, or to use a Cyrillic alphabet. Several independent developers specialize in or offer some foreign-language fonts. Examples shown in Figure 8-18 include Hebrew, Cyrillic, and Greek from Fluent Fonts.

There are limitations to using some of these fonts, however. For instance, though Hebrew is written from right to left, the cursor moves from left to right. Also, some foreign-language characters don't correspond directly to the English characters of the keyboard, making it necessary for you to translate foreign characters to English-character keys as you type.

Symbol Fonts

Some fonts aren't alphabetical and numerical characters, but symbols, ranging from the lighthearted to the serious. Examples of symbol fonts include Cairo from the Macintosh System Disk and the fonts in Figure 8-19 offered by independent developers—Math, Electronic, Science, and Borderline from Fluent Fonts.

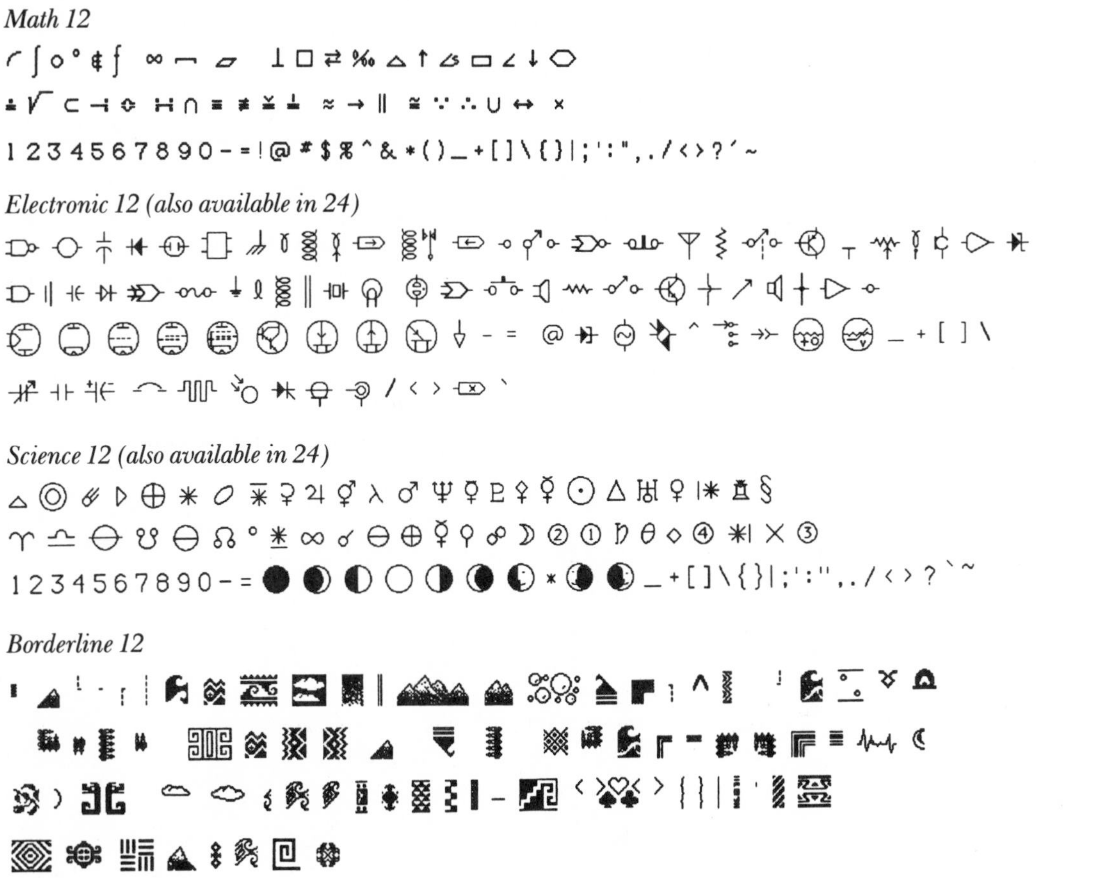
Math 12
1 2 3 4 5 6 7 8 9 0 - = ! @ # $ % ^ & * ( ) _ + [ ] \ { } | ; ' : " , . / < > ? ' ~
Electronic 12 (also available in 24)
Science 12 (also available in 24)
1 2 3 4 5 6 7 8 9 0 - =
Borderline 12

Figure 8-19. Independently produced symbol fonts

Using Type

Knowing some of the terminology and characteristics of type doesn't guarantee you'll be able to use type in attractive ways, any more than knowing art terminology would assure that you'd be able to paint a masterpiece the first time you picked up a palette and brush. Typography, like art, is a matter of experience, creativity, and personal taste. But there are some general principles that can help guide you toward a more pleasing use of type.

Before you make any decisions about what kind of type you're going to choose, you should ask yourself how the type will be used. What is the purpose of the document? Do you want it to convey a particular mood? Who will be the audience? Is space a factor? Will the type be used for text or display (display is a catchall term used to describe anything that isn't text: for example, headings and advertisements)?

Type is used differently for text than for display. Readability is the overriding consideration when choosing type for text. Your reader should be able to read text quickly and be able to distinguish one character from another easily. Fonts familiar to the reader also aid readability. In general, you want text type to be as invisible as possible; the reader shouldn't focus more on the type than on the thoughts expressed.

Display type has a different function: to attract attention. In other words, type that works well for display probably wouldn't be a good choice for a legal document.

With these considerations in mind, you can begin making choices on the font, size, and style that best suits your needs. We'll look at choosing a font first.

Choosing a Font

As we mentioned earlier, it's best to find a few good fonts and stick with them, particularly for text.

Of the categories we presented earlier in this chapter, only a few are suitable for use, particularly in text, in more than an isolated instance. Your subject matter could require use of a foreign-language or symbol font, for instance, but those fonts have very limited use. That leaves only two categories for most text and display uses: serif and sans serif.

Serif Versus Sans Serif

Most typographers agree that serif fonts are the best choice for text. Serifs add to the uniqueness of each letter, which helps the reader distinguish between letters and aids readability. Compare the serif and sans serif samples in Figure 8-20, which contains only the upper half of a word. You may find the serif sample easier to read because the serifs help you identify what each letter is even though you can't see the

Figure 8-20. Serif letters (top) are easier to identify than sans serif letters (bottom).

Figure 8-21. Serif letters (top) keep your eyes moving horizontally better than sans serif letters (bottom).

This is a demonstration of readability. The top text is New York, a serif font. The bottom text is Geneva, a sans serif font.

This is a demonstration of readability. The top text is New York, a serif font. The bottom text is Geneva, a sans serif font.

entire letter. But in some cases, dot-matrix serif fonts may be harder to read because it is difficult to reproduce smooth tapers on serifs.

Serifs also tend to pull the reader's eyes along the line, aiding what is called horizontal flow, or horizontal movement of the reader's eyes. You'll probably find the serif sample paragraph in Figure 8-21 easier to read than the sans serif sample, because the serifs tend to keep your eyes moving horizontally.

But some typographers maintain that sans serif fonts can also be used for text, if the text line is fairly short. The purpose or mood of your document or your personal preference may convince you a sans serif font is best for your text, and that could be the right choice.

Choosing a Style

You can apply the style options in the Character menu to any font in any combination of boldface, italic, underlining, outlining, shadow, small capitals, superscript, and subscript. These style options multiply the number of typefaces at your command. Sometimes they have a functional use, such as italics for the title of a literary work, and other times they can be used to create a mood or add emphasis to a particular point.

You can use boldface to add emphasis in either display lettering or text. But you should use restraint in boldfacing text. Boldface characters have a tendency to lose definition and fill in between strokes, especially in smaller point sizes. A new ribbon or a low-quality printer can make this problem even worse. Compare the sample boldface and regular text in Figure 8-22 for readability.

Figure 8-22. Boldface type (bottom) is more difficult to read than regular type.

This is a demonstration of readability. The top text is in New York plain. The bottom text is in New York bold.

This is a demonstration of readability. The top text is in New York plain. The bottom text is in New York bold.

Figure 8-23. Italics used for display type

ITALICS: DOUBLE WINNER

Italics can be used for *emphasis* in a heading or as a portion of text.

Italics also emphasize words, but aren't as distracting as boldface. Italic type is the standard method for marking titles, quotations, and instructions. You can also choose italics for display type, as shown in Figure 8-23.

Many of the old typewriter uses for underlining can be done by other style options, but underlining is still useful for some circumstances, such as blanks in forms, and emphasis.

Small capital letters can be used to soften the appearance of words that must be written in all capital letters. For example, you might use the Small Caps command for a series of acronyms for government agencies, such as the FBI, IRS, HEW, and TVA.

Outlining and shadow characters might seem to have unlimited potential for clever uses, but they are, in reality, used more by beginners than by professionals. As with novelty fonts and the other style options, outlining and shadow characters are effective only when used sparingly, as you can see from the example of shadow and outlining in Figure 8-24.

Choosing a Size

Word apparently finds 12-point type the most legible for text, because that's the default size for all of the fonts that come on the Word disk. But, as mentioned earlier in this chapter, you can change the size of any font by clicking on another size in the Font Size list box of the Format Character dialog box or by typing any other size from 4 to 127 in the text box.

The best size for a particular piece of type depends on a number of factors, including how it's being used, who will be reading it, and how it will be printed. Larger sizes can add emphasis to display type and smaller sizes can save space or denote a different kind of text, such as a footnote. But smaller type sizes are more difficult to reproduce on lower-quality printers, and some readers have difficulty reading the smaller type sizes.

The key to using such features as outline and shadow styles is restraint. A particular novelty type or font style can lose its effectiveness if it is overdone.

Figure 8-24. Shadow and outlining can be overdone.

Figure 8-25. The London and
Venice fonts clash.

𝕷𝖔𝖓𝖉𝖔𝖓

Venice

Combining Fonts

Though it's best to limit your fonts to a well-chosen few, you don't need to stick with just one font. But care must be taken to combine fonts that work well together. With the many fonts now available for using with Word on the Mac, picking compatible font combinations is a challenge. The following are some guidelines that should help.

Avoid mixing fonts with pronounced curves, exaggerated serifs, and other unusual features. For example, as shown in Figure 8-25, London and Venice clash because the most identifiable features of each are different.

Don't mix fonts with contrasting character shapes, such as a narrow, or condensed, font with a wide, or extended, font. Figure 8-26 shows that Stuttgart doesn't look good with Slim. Don't combine two sans serif fonts, such as Geneva and Micro, also shown in Figure 8-26.

Typeset Quality

The selection of fonts isn't your only consideration when determining whether your document is suitable for your purpose. The quality of the printing is the most significant factor.

Microcomputer printers provide you with a choice of quality that should satisfy most word-processing needs. But some of your word-processing efforts may call for the ultimate in printed quality—typesetting. As good as printer output has become, it still can't compare with a professionally typeset document. And it's not difficult to understand why: While the ImageWriter prints 80 dots per inch and the

Stuttgart   Geneva

Figure 8-26. The Stuttgart and
Slim fonts clash, as do the
Geneva and Micro fonts.

Slim   Micro

Figure 8-27. Sample text
printed on the ImageWriter,
NEC 2010 Spinwriter, and
LaserWriter printers, and by
the Mergenthaler Linotron
202 typesetting machine

ImageWriter Quality

Letter Quality

LaserWriter Quality

Typeset Quality

LaserWriter prints 300 dots per inch, the top professional typesetting equipment can print 1500 or more dots per inch. Figure 8-27 compares typeset print with three types of printer output.

Not only are typeset characters smoother and crisper, but the spaces between lines, words, and even specific pairs of letters can be controlled with precision, as you can see from the samples in Figure 8-28. Notice that the spacing between words in the typeset sample is more even than in the LaserWriter sample. That's because the typesetter has greater control over the spaces between words, which must be varied from line to line to make the lines the same length in justified text. Also notice that there appears to be more space between the *W* and *o* of *Word* than between most other pairs of letters of the Laser-Writer sample, but the space between the same two letters of the typeset sample appears to be the same as all others. Actually, all the spaces between letters in the LaserWriter sample are the same size, but the space between letters such as the *W* and *o* looks larger because of the large visual gap between the rightmost diagonal stroke of the *W* and the leftmost point on the *o*. Typesetters can move pairs of letters such as *W* and *o* closer together by a process called kerning, so that they *appear* to have the same amount of space between them as other pairs of letters.

Figure 8-28. Spacing is more
even with typeset print
(bottom) than with Word-
generated LaserWriter
print (top).

Word controls spacing between characters, words, and lines of text automatically. Typesetters allow precise character positioning to remove obtrusive white space between characters, words, and lines of text.

Word controls spacing between characters, words, and lines of text automatically. Typesetters allow precise character positioning to remove obtrusive white space between characters, words, and lines of text.

The Word Processor/
Typesetter Link

To get professional typesetting, you could pay $30 or more to have a single page of text typeset through the traditional process. But when you consider that a phototypesetting system may cost from $30,000 to $150,000 and that it requires trained professionals to program the proper formatting codes for each document, that shouldn't be surprising. In the traditional process, a double-spaced manuscript is submitted to the typesetting house, notated with symbols designating such things as font, size and style, spacing, alignment, and indents. The typographer retypes the manuscript, replacing the manuscript's symbols with formatting and style codes that can be understood by the particular typesetting machine the typesetting house is using.

But using your Macintosh, you can substantially reduce these costs by doing some of the typographer's work yourself. There are two ways you can do this.

First, you can submit your manuscript over phone lines, on disk, or in other machine-readable form, and eliminate the need for the typographer to retype the entire document. This process, sometimes called conversion typesetting, at least eliminates the need to retype the document. You create a manuscript on your word processor and store it on a magnetic disk. You can submit the disk, in which case the typesetting house processes it through a media reader/converter, creating a new disk or tape that is used to drive a typesetting machine. Or, you can transmit the information on the disk by means of a modem and a telephone—a process that's called telecommunication. The modem converts the digital signals on your disk into sound frequencies for transmission by telephone lines. A modem on the other end of the phone line then converts these sound frequencies back into digital signals. Transmitting your finished text over phone lines is faster than sending a disk, saves time, reduces mistakes because it eliminates redundant steps, and helps to avoid the problem of mismatched hardware. Most typesetting houses are set up to accept text over phone lines and some can accept text day or night, either to their in-house computer or to a time-sharing service.

The second method, which can save even more time and money, is to add to the document the codes that directly control the typesetter. But this method requires considerably more effort on your part, and requires that you learn to use complex coding that a typographer would otherwise insert for you. Figure 8-29 shows the coding necessary to produce just a few typeset paragraphs.

Figure 8-29. Text with typesetting instructions (top) and
the resulting typeset printout
(bottom)

Text with typesetting codes

[LL27][RLI][DRH50,0,27][rt]
[RLD26][TB1,0,15,J][TB2,17,10,L]
[MCO][CT1][FT685][PS10][LS11]WORD SPACING [FT683]is the amount of white
space between words. It is one of the most critical factors affecting high quality
typography and readability.[QL][rt]
[MCR[CT2][SB12,8,32]Standard word spacing[QL][rt]
[SB10,7,18]Medium word spacing[QL][rt]
[SB8,6,15]Tight word spacing[QL][rt]
[MCX][RLD26][DRH50,0,27][rt]
[ALD3][rt]
[MCO][CT1][FT685]LETTER SPACING [FT683]is the amount of white space
between letters that can be added or subtracted to justify a line of type.[QL][rt]
[MCR[CT2][LT3,1]Standard letter spacing[QL][rt]
[LT2,1]Medium letter spacing[QL][rt]
[LT1,1]Tight letter spacing[QL][rt]
[MCX][RLD26][DRH50,0,27][rt]

Typeset printout

WORD SPACING is the amount of white space between words. It is one of the most critical factors affecting high quality typography and readability.	Standard word spacing Medium word spacing Tight word spacing
LETTER SPACING is the amount of white space between letters that can be added or subtracted to justify a line of type.	Standard letter spacing Medium letter spacing Tight letter spacing

A reasonable compromise used by many typesetting houses and their clients is to set up a coding system whereby the author types simple codes into the manuscript. The typographer sets up a translation table in the typesetter's computer that converts these codes into instructions the typesetting machine understands. Once the translation table is worked up, the process can be handled with little human intervention. Figure 8-30 shows a manuscript with simplified codes, the translation table, and the resulting typeset text from a process used by type-a-graphic typesetters, 201-8011 Leslie Road, Richmond, British Columbia V6X 1E4, Canada, (604) 270-4433.

Figure 8-30. A document with simple codes, a partial translation table, and the final typeset document

Original with simple codes

@1The typefaces shown here are available now and may be accessed using the Macintosh and @bSet & Send software@m. Soon, dozens of additional typefaces will be available.<
@1Below, is a simulation of a Compugraphic MCS typesetting screen with the complex codes needed to produce just two paragraphs of the material shown above; compare the skill level needed to set the same @bquality type@m using Microsoft Word, Set & Send software and the mouse on your Macintosh . . . plus you'll save over 50% of the cost of conventional typesetting.<

Translation table

@1 = <LL27<FT683<PS10<LS11>EM space
@b = <FT685>
@m = <FT683>
<   = QL, Return

Typeset printout

The typefaces shown here are available now and may be accessed using the Macintosh and **Set & Send software**. Soon, dozens of additional typefaces will be available.
Below, is a simulation of a Compugraphic MCS typesetting screen with the complex codes needed to produce just two paragraphs of the material shown above; compare the skill level needed to set the same **quality type** using Microsoft Word, Set & Send software and the mouse on your Macintosh . . . plus you'll save over 50% of the cost of conventional typesetting.

Submitting a manuscript in machine-readable form and coding your document can result in savings of up to 50 percent over the costs of traditional typesetting. These are techniques available to users of all microcomputers, not just to users of the Macintosh. They don't take advantage of the formatting capabilities of Word or the type-style selection and graphics abilities of the Mac. But several typesetting companies have developed software that takes advantage of the Mac's ability to display type fonts on the screen by finding a typeset font replacement for Mac screen fonts, though not all are able to ensure that lines break at the same place on the screen and in the printout.

By being able to translate screen fonts into real fonts, you can control the typesetting machine without complicated coding: You simply select font and style combinations from menus. In theory, you could translate a Mac typeface, such as Monaco Italics Outline, to any of the thousands of real typefaces available. More likely, your typographer will have developed a set of comparable equivalents that have been found to work well.

Font translation represents a major step forward in putting the Mac user in charge of typesetting, but it doesn't take care of all the formatting information needed by the typesetter. However, there are programs being developed that let you select format options from a menu rather than type in codes. One of the first programs to do this, called Set and Send (Set and Send Software, 201-8011 Leslie Road, Richmond, British Columbia V6X 1E4, Canada, (604) 270-4433), displays a menu, from which you select your options. It then makes a new copy of your Word file, with the full typeset codes inserted into the document in place of the Mac options. This text is then transmitted to the typesetting house and typeset directly, with little or no operator intervention. This method clearly illustrates the trend: With each software innovation, you receive more control for less effort.

You and Your Typographer

If you decide to use your Word program to produce a typeset document, your first step is to find the right typesetting house. The right typographer is one who is working with other microcomputer word processors. Count yourself blessed if you find one who is interfacing with a Macintosh: Most typesetting houses that can interface with a microcomputer do so only with the IBM PC models. If you want to do a thorough job of searching for the right typographer, the names and addresses of over 600 typesetting shops with interfacing capability are listed by city in *The Interface Data Book for Word Processing/Typesetting* by Ronald Labuz (R. R. Bowker and Company, 1984).

Typesetting houses offer a wide range of services and they operate with different equipment systems, some very specialized and some very comprehensive. Before coming to final agreement with a typographer, it is advisable to see samples of typeset output.

When your printed text comes back from the typesetter, you'll likely need to take an additional step before your document is complete. Your text is typeset on long sheets, called galleys, which must be cut and pasted in the page layout you've designed. This pasted-up version is then taken to a printer, who uses it as the master copy in the photo-offset printing process. Printing houses, like typesetting houses, offer a variety of services.

In this chapter, we have given you a sampling of the staggering array of type fonts now available to you to use with your Word program and shown you how to use Font Mover for organizing and handling those fonts. We discussed some of the anatomy, terminology, classifications, and distinguishing characteristics of type. We talked about selecting type for specific applications, about typeset-quality printing, and about using Word as the first step in the typesetting process.

With your Word program on your Macintosh computer, you have a unique and remarkable system for creating professional documents and publications. In Chapters 9 through 13, you will see examples of Word applications using letter-quality, dot-matrix, and laser printers. You will have a chance to follow along as we use some of the unique features of Word to create a form letter, a report, a newsletter, a business form, and a brochure, sometimes with an unexpected twist.

SECTION THREE

PROFESSIONAL PRINTING PROJECTS

9

A form letter

For our first project, let's take another look at Word's Print Merge feature. The Print Merge... command can save you considerable time when you need to write letters to a number of people and the information varies little from letter to letter, as you saw in Chapter 4. But Print Merge... also can vary the information a great deal from letter to letter, allowing you to tailor each letter to the recipient without having to type each letter individually. As you'll see in this chapter, the ability to make a form letter appear to be a personalized letter is a handy tool in business correspondence.

To illustrate this more-sophisticated use of Print Merge..., this chapter offers an example of how a form cover letter could be tailored to each of its recipients. For the sake of the example, imagine that you are Wallace J. Pence, owner of The Management Efficiency Group, a small management consulting firm. You need to prepare a cover letter that will accompany a brochure announcing a new series of seminars on employee productivity. In the past, you simply photocopied a standard form letter, such as the one in Figure 9-1, and put a copy in each envelope with a brochure. But response to past mailings hasn't been what you'd hoped. So you've decided to personalize the letters by highlighting particular aspects of the seminars you think would interest particular recipients of the mailing. In addition, you want to include some background information about your firm in the letters to potential new clients, as in Figure 9-2, and you want to express appreciation by means of a special discount in the letters to existing clients, as in Figure 9-3. Instead of typing each letter individually, you've decided to print out the letters using the Print Merge... command. To give the letters a personally typed appearance, you plan to print them on a fully formed character printer.

The Management Efficiency Group
1202 Center Street
Riverdale, Pennsylvania 67301

March 25, 1984

Dear Business Person:

The Management Efficiency Group, TMEG, is proud to announce "Management and Motivation," a new seminar series focusing on improving productivity through increased employee communication and involvement. Nationally recognized human relations authority, Robert B. Hager, will be the featured speaker. See the enclosed brochure for details.

TMEG has provided consulting services in the areas of productivity, organizational development, and management information systems to leading companies for 14 years. Our seminars consistently receive high marks from businesses we have assisted. Our unique group workshop process is enriched by informative presentations from top business authorities.

If you are interested in attending this seminar, please fill out the registration form and return it with the advance registration fee. This will be one of the best investments you will ever make.

Sincerely,

Wallace J. Pence

Figure 9-1. A form letter that looks like a form letter

```
                      The Management Efficiency Group
                            1202 Center Street
                         Riverdale, Pennsylvania 67301


March 11, 1986


J. D. Cook
Cook Industries
10 Ash Street
Munson, TN 40484

Dear Mr. Cook:

    The Management Efficiency Group (TMEG) is proud to announce "The
Productivity Mother Lode," a new seminar series focusing on higher
productivity through planning and communication. An expert panel will be
led by the renowned team of communications specialists, Joan A. Nesbitt
and J. Arthur Paddington. See the enclosed brochure for details.

    The Management Efficiency Group has provided consulting services in
the areas of productivity, organizational development, and management to
firms like yours for the past 15 years. Our satisfied clients include
Smith-Horner, Wesse Bros, Ross & Sons, and Banta Industries.

    Our seminars receive consistently high marks from business leaders
across the land. Our unique group workshop process is enriched by
informative presentations from leading business authorities.

    To reserve your seat, please fill out the enclosed registration form
and return it along with the advance registration fee. We believe this
will be one of the best investments you'll ever make.

            Sincerely,


            Wallace J. Pence
```

Figure 9-2. A form letter, customized for a potential client

```
                    The Management Efficiency Group
                           1202 Center Street
                      Riverdale, Pennsylvania 67301


  March 11, 1986


  Jane Applegate
  Dumar Mfg.
  1446 Front Street
  Sandy, FL 85675

  Dear Jane:

     The Management Efficiency Group (TMEG) is proud to announce "The
  Productivity Mother Lode," a new seminar series focusing on higher
  productivity through planning and communication. An expert panel will be
  led by the renowned team of communications specialists, Joan A. Nesbitt
  and J. Arthur Paddington. See the enclosed brochure for details.

     Because you are one of our most valued clients, we are delighted to
  extend a special offer to your firm. For every two employees of your
  company who register for this seminar, an additional employee may
  register for free. This is our way of saying "Thank you" for your
  continuing patronage.

      You will find particular value in the topic "Production,
  Performance, and Profits" by Paul Hoffman, former director of operations
  for ITB Corp. Mr. Hoffman is a specialist in evaluating and improving
  productivity.

     To reserve your seat, please fill out the enclosed registration form
  and return it along with the advance registration fee. We believe this
  will be one of the best investments you'll ever make.

                         Sincerely,



                         Wallace J. Pence
```

Figure 9-3. A form letter, customized for an existing client

Planning Your Documents

As we pointed out in Chapter 4, before you actually choose Print Merge..., you need to create a main document (such as the main text of a letter) and a merge document (a list of the information you want inserted into the main document). For more elaborate merge printing projects, such as the seminar cover letter, you can also create text files containing information you want inserted into the main document. For instance, to insert a paragraph of background information about your consulting firm into the letters going to potential clients, you need to create the paragraph and save it as a separate file. Then, when you create the main document, you include an instruction, similar to the DATA instruction used in Chapter 4, that inserts the saved paragraph in only those letters addressed to potential clients. To allow Word to distinguish between which recipients are to receive the background information and which are not, you need to include the status of each recipient (current or potential) in the merge document. By the same token, since you would like to direct each recipient's attention to the seminar speaker in his or her field of interest, you also need to include each recipient's field of interest in the merge document.

The major limitation on files used in the merge operation is that they must all be on the same disk. You could create these files in any order, but we'll show you how to create the merge document, then the text files, then the main document.

Creating the Merge Document

The merge document for your seminar cover letter is, essentially, a mailing list. In fact, you could use a mailing list compiled in a database program, such as Microsoft File. (Database programs are frequently used to compile mailing lists.) You'd simply type the information in the database program in the same order you plan to use it in the merge operation (the order you'd use in the data records if you were using Word) and save the file as a text file. Then you could use this text file as your merge document in Word. However, it would have to be saved on the same disk as the main document and other files used in the merge operation.

To review briefly what you learned in Chapter 4 about creating a merge document: The first line of the merge document, called the header record, establishes the order and the name of each item of information, or field, that appears in the succeeding lines, called the data record. You type a comma or press Tab to start a new field, and you press Return to start a new record. If the information in a field contains a comma, you need to enclose the entire field in quote marks, so Word knows that comma is part of the information and not a field separator.

You're now ready to create the merge document for the seminar cover letter. Figure 9-4 shows how part of The Management Efficiency Group's mailing list might look on the Macintosh screen, with the Show ¶ command chosen so you can see where to press Return (the ¶ marks) and where to type spaces (the dots). Notice there are spaces at the ends of some of the lines and that the following lines begin new fields. Word breaks lines, or word wraps, on spaces, but ignores spaces at the beginnings and ends of fields. So, the spaces shown in Figure 9-4 specify that lines break between fields, which makes the display more readable.

> Open a Word file and type the merge document shown in Figure 9-4.
>
> Save the merge document as Maillist.

The merge document for The Management Efficiency Group's cover letter contains only the information required in the main document. But you don't need to limit the fields to only those you're using in a particular merge operation. You can have as many fields as you like and use only those you need. As a result, you can use the same

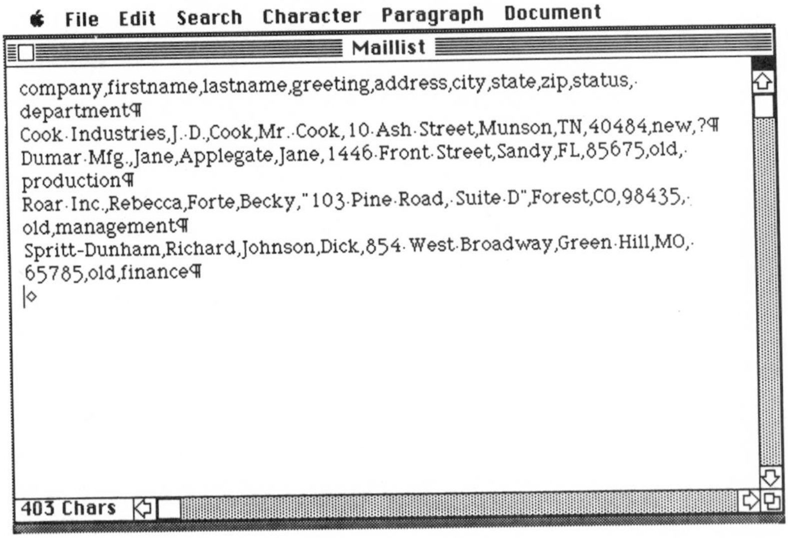

Figure 9-4. A merge document for The Management Efficiency Group's cover letter

merge document for a number of merge operations. In addition, the fields don't need to be in the same order that they're used in the main document, though, as mentioned earlier in this chapter, the fields in the data records must be in the same order as the header record.

Now that your merge document is complete, you can create the paragraphs that will vary from letter to letter, depending on the recipient's area of interest and status with your firm.

Creating Text Files

As you can see from the merge document, you can create two different paragraphs for the status field, one for potential customers (identified as new) and the other for existing customers (identified as old). The department field has four different types of entry: finance, production, management, and an unknown area or interest. So, you need to create six different paragraphs to cover all the options of these two fields. Don't press Return at the end of each paragraph or you'll get an extra blank line in the printout. When you've finished, save each paragraph as a separate file.

Type the following, without pressing Return, and save it as a file named Newcust.

The Management Efficiency Group has provided consulting services in the areas of productivity, organizational development, and management to firms like yours for the past 15 years. Our satisfied clients include Smith-Horner, Wesse Bros., Ross & Sons, and Banta Industries.

Type the following, without pressing Return, and save it as a file named Oldcust.

Because you are one of our most valued clients, we are delighted to extend a special offer to your firm. For every two employees of your company who register for this seminar, an additional employee may register for free. This is our way of saying "Thank you" for your continuing patronage.

Type the following, without pressing Return, and save it as a file named Maninfo.

You will be particularly interested in the presentation by Thomas J. Pauls, author of the best-selling book "The Supermanager." Mr. Pauls has a degree in psychology, an MBA from Harvard Business School, and serves as a consultant to several Fortune 500 companies.

Type the following, without pressing Return, and save it as a file named Prodinfo.

You will find particular value in the topic "Production, Performance, and Profits" by Paul Hoffman, former director of operations for ITB Corp. Mr. Hoffman is a specialist in evaluating and improving productivity.

Type the following, without pressing Return, and save it as a file named Fininfo.

You will be particularly interested in "The Financial Aspect of Motivation" by Robert H. Landman, former head of the SEC and currently Professor of Financial Systems at Harvard Business School. He has written several books on financial organizations.

Type the following, without pressing Return, and save it as a file named Geninfo.

Our seminars receive consistently high marks from business leaders across the land. Our unique group workshop process is enriched by informative presentations from leading business authorities.

By replacing one additional paragraph—the first paragraph—with a variable, you will be able to use the main document for cover letters for future seminars. So, create one more text file.

Type the following, without pressing Return, and save it as a file named Intro.

The Management Efficiency Group (TMEG) is proud to announce "The Productivity Mother Lode," a new seminar series focusing on higher productivity through planning and communication. An expert panel will be led by the renowned team of communications specialists, Joan A. Nesbitt and J. Arthur Paddington. See the enclosed brochure for details.

Creating the Main Document

Your main document is the form letter with placeholders, or instructions, indicating where the information in the merge and text files will be printed. If you could see it all on the screen at one time, the main document would look like the sample in Figure 9-5. Don't worry about what everything means at this point: We'll explain how to create the document a step at a time. The full document is included here just so you can see what the final product will look like.

Inserting the DATA Instruction

As you may recall from Chapter 4, the main document always starts with the DATA instruction, to tell Word the name of the merge document where the data to be inserted can be found. Merge instructions

«DATA Maillist»

The Management Efficiency Group
1202 Center Street
Riverdale, Pennsylvania 67301

«SET date=? What is the date?»
«date»

«firstname» «lastname»
«company»
«address»
«city», «state» «zip»

Dear «greeting»:

   «INCLUDE Intro»

   «IF status = "new"»«INCLUDE Newcust»«ELSE»«INCLUDE
Oldcust»«ENDIF»

   «IF department = "finance"»«INCLUDE Fininfo» «ELSE»«IF
department = "management"»«INCLUDE Maninfo» «ELSE»«IF
department = "production"»«INCLUDE Prodinfo» «ELSE»«INCLUDE
Geninfo» «ENDIF»«ENDIF»«ENDIF»

   To reserve your seat, please fill out the enclosed registration form
and return it along with the advance registration fee. We believe this
will be one of the best investments you'll ever make.

            Sincerely,

            Wallace J. Pence

Figure 9-5. The main
document for the seminar
cover letter

are enclosed by special merge characters (international quotation marks). To type an open merge character («), press Option and backslash. To type a close merge character (»), press Shift, Option, and backslash.

> Open a new Word file and type:
>
> *«DATA Maillist»* [Return]

The next step is to add the company letterhead of The Management Efficiency Group.

> Type the following:
>
> *The Management Efficiency Group* [Return]
> *1202 Center Street* [Return]
> *Riverdale, Pennsylvania 67301* [Return]
>
> Highlight the letterhead and choose Centered from the Paragraph menu.

The SET and ASK Instructions

The next item in the letter is the date. You could just type in the date, but if you do, you might forget to change it the next time you use this main document to print a cover letter. Instead, you can use Word's SET instruction to display a reminder, or prompt, for the current date.

The SET instruction sets the contents of a field at the same value for the duration of the merge-printing operation. You can use the SET instruction in two ways: You can have Word prompt you with an on-screen message for the information you want to appear throughout the merge printing, or you can set the information ahead of time. For example, if you wanted to set the date ahead of time, you'd type *«SET date=September 3, 1985»* and September 3, 1985 would be inserted wherever you typed *«date»* in the main document. But instead, you want Word to prompt you for the current date whenever you print the cover letter.

> Type the following:
>
> *«SET date=? What is the date?* [Return]
> *«date»* [Return]

You can use any wording you want between the two question marks. The message will appear on the screen just the way you type it.

Another instruction that prompts you for information is the ASK instruction. You set up the ASK instruction prompt in the same way you set up the SET prompt, but the ASK prompt pops up as each copy of your document is printed, allowing you to vary the information from one copy to the next.

Now you can type in the field names for the name, company, and address, then the salutation.

Press Return twice, then type:

«firstname» «lastname»[Return]
«company»[Return]
«address»[Return]
«city», «state» «zip»[Return][Return]
Dear «greeting»:[Return]

Testing Your Merge Operation

It's a good idea to perform a test printing of the merge operation now, before you're finished, to make sure that the operation works properly up to this point. If you wait until the end to print, errors are harder to locate because there are more steps to retrace.

Choose the Print Merge… command from the File menu.

Type the current date when Word prompts you for it.

You should get one printed copy for each data record in the merge document, similar to the one shown in Figure 9-6, and the correct date should appear in the proper place on the pages. If the printing doesn't go according to plan, check to make sure the merge characters and spacing are exactly as we've shown them along the way. Also check to make sure the field names are typed exactly the same in the main document and in the merge document. Check the spaces, commas, and quote marks in the merge document, too.

```
                    The Management Efficiency Group
                           1202 Center Street
                      Riverdale, Pennsylvania 67301


     March 11, 1986


     J. D. Cook
     Cook Industries
     10 Ash Street
     Munson, TN 40484

     Dear Mr. Cook:
```

Figure 9-6. A sample of a test printing of the seminar cover letter

The INCLUDE Instruction

Now you've come to the body of the letter. This is your first opportunity to use some of the text files you created earlier. The way you insert text from a text file is by using the INCLUDE instruction.

The text you saved in the Intro file isn't formatted for the letter's style, so you need to add the formatting now.

> Choose Show Ruler from the Edit menu or Formats... from the Paragraph menu and set the first line indent to 0.25.
>
> Press Return and type the following:
>
> *«INCLUDE Intro»*[Return]

You might want to make another test printing now to make sure you've successfully completed this important step.

Conditional Instructions

As mentioned earlier in this chapter, Word can insert information in some merge-printed copies and not insert that information in other copies, based on terms, or conditions, you set ahead of time. You set these conditions using instructions appropriately called conditional instructions. Conditional instructions follow the rules of a branch of mathematics called logic. They always begin with IF and end with ENDIF. In essence, a conditional instruction tells Word, "If the specified condition exists, take the specified action." The unwritten alternative in this simplified conditional instruction tells Word that if the specified condition doesn't exist, do nothing. But you can specify an alternative action as well by using ELSE between the IF and ENDIF instructions. That's what you want to do in the seminar cover letter: You want Word to print the Newcust file if the recipient is a potential client and the Oldcust file if the recipient is a current client. And Word can find out whether the recipient of a specific letter is old or new by the status field in the merge document.

> Type the following:
>
> *«IF status = "new"«INCLUDE Newcust» «ELSE» «INCLUDE Oldcust» «ENDIF»*[Return]

Notice that the word *new* is enclosed by quote marks. The quote marks are required around all text conditions (but not around field names and file names).

Conditional instructions can also be used within other conditional instructions. In fact, that's what you need to use so that Word prints a different paragraph for each different department field in the data records. You want those in management to get the Maninfo paragraph, those in finance to get the Fininfo paragraph, those in production to get the Prodinfo paragraph, and those in other departments to get the Geninfo paragraph.

Type the following:

«IF department = "Finance"»«INCLUDE Fininfo» «ELSE»«IF department = "management"»«INCLUDE Maninfo» «ELSE»«IF department = "production"»«INCLUDE Prodinfo» «ELSE»«INCLUDE Geninfo» «ENDIF»«ENDIF» «ENDIF»[Return]

When conditional instructions are contained within other conditional instructions, each ELSE alternative action refers to the closest preceding IF condition.

Be careful about where you put spaces and where you press Return in conditional instructions. For example, if you put any extra spaces between the IF and INCLUDE portions of the conditional instruction just given, the first line indent of the inserted paragraph would be larger than that of other paragraphs. And if you pressed Return anywhere but where indicated, you'd get an extra blank line on each copy of the letter printed. Now is a good time to test your merging once more to make sure you haven't included any extra spaces or returns. Then finish the letter by typing the last paragraph and closing.

Type the following:

To reserve your seat, please fill out the enclosed registration form and return it along with the advance registration fee. We believe this will be one of the best investments you'll ever make.[Return]
Sincerely,[Return] [Return]
Wallace J. Pence[Return]

Save the main document as a file named Main on the same disk with the merge document and text files.

Now you can do your final merge printing. The result should look like the samples in Figure 9-7.

Choose Print Merge... from the File menu.

In this chapter, you've seen how, with a little planning, you can use the Print Merge... command to let Word do the repetitive work in what might otherwise be a large typing project. Now you can turn to Chapter 10, where we describe a report project that employs a number of Word features.

```
                    The Management Efficiency Group
                          1202 Center Street
                       Riverdale, Pennsylvania 67301


        March 11, 1986


        Rebecca Forte
        Roar Inc.
        103 Pine Road, Suite D
        Forest, CO 98435

        Dear Becky:

           The Management Efficiency Group (TMEG) is proud to announce "The
        Productivity Mother Lode," a new seminar series focusing on higher
        productivity through planning and communication. An expert panel will be
        led by the renowned team of communications specialists, Joan A. Nesbitt
        and J. Arthur Paddington. See the enclosed brochure for details.

           Because you are one of our most valued clients, we are delighted to
        extend a special offer to your firm. For every two employees of your
        company who register for this seminar, an additional employee may
        register for free. This is our way of saying "Thank you" for your
        continuing patronage.

           You will be particularly interested in the presentation by Thomas J.
        Pauls, author of the best selling book "The Supermanager." Mr. Pauls has
        a degree in psychology, an MBA from Harvard Business School, and serves
        as a consultant to several Fortune 500 companies.

           To reserve your seat, please fill out the enclosed registration form
        and return it along with the advance registration fee. We believe this
        will be one of the best investments you'll ever make.

                      Sincerely,



                      Wallace J. Pence
```

Figure 9-7. Sample merge-
printed cover letters

continued

```
                    The Management Efficiency Group
                          1202 Center Street
                      Riverdale, Pennsylvania 67301


March 11, 1986


Richard Johnson
Spritt-Dunham
854 West Broadway
Green Hill, MO 65785

Dear Dick:

   The Management Efficiency Group (TMEG) is proud to announce "The
Productivity Mother Lode," a new seminar series focusing on higher
productivity through planning and communication. An expert panel will be
led by the renowned team of communications specialists, Joan A. Nesbitt
and J. Arthur Paddington. See the enclosed brochure for details.

   Because you are one of our most valued clients, we are delighted to
extend a special offer to your firm. For every two employees of your
company who register for this seminar, an additional employee may
register for free. This is our way of saying "Thank you" for your
continuing patronage.

   You will be particularly interested in "The Financial Aspect of
Motivation," by Robert H. Landman, former head of the SEC and currently
Professor of Financial Systems at Harvard Business School. He has
written several books on financial organizations.

   To reserve your seat, please fill out the enclosed registration form
and return it along with the advance registration fee. We believe this
will be one of the best investments you'll ever make.

                    Sincerely,



                    Wallace J. Pence
```

Figure 9-7 (continued)

10

A report

In this chapter, we present some of Word's features that are very handy for writing reports: indenting entire paragraphs (called nesting paragraphs), creating footnotes and running heads, and setting up tables of information.

The project we will use to demonstrate these techniques is a style guide for writers, which can be thought of as a type of report. Let's assume that you're the editor-in-chief of a small publishing house and you're preparing this style guide for your authors. You plan to print it out on an ImageWriter, as shown in Figure 10-1, to give your typographer an idea of what you want the finished product to look like. After you've incorporated your typographer's comments, you'll insert the proper codes and deliver the guide on disk for typesetting. Then you can distribute the typeset guide to authors and your staff.

In addition to indenting paragraphs, creating footnotes and running heads, and setting up tables, this project will also show you how to insert blank lines throughout the document, how to change fonts, how to determine where one page will end and another will begin without actually printing the document, and, finally, how to create a letterhead that extends the width of the page, which introduces Word's multiple-column formatting feature, a feature used quite prominently in the final three projects in this book. As we mentioned in Chapter 4, writing and word processing are keyboard-intensive operations. So, we'll use the keyboard instead of the mouse whenever possible.

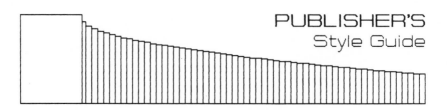

PUBLISHER'S
Style Guide

A key to quality in publishing is consistency of style. The term style, in the publishing context, refers to two different things: the personal writing style of the author and the set of conventions that the publishing house has chosen to adopt as its own house style. Author style includes such things as the use or nonuse of contractions ("you've," "we'll," and so on), and the patterns authors usually follow when putting words and phrases together. House style includes such things as punctuation, spelling, and capitalization conventions, and how figures and captions are handled. Most publishing houses base their house style on a manual catering to their particular kind of publishing, rather than creating their own style from scratch.[1]

The following section is intended to establish some guidelines and to answer some, but not all, questions about our house style. These style guidelines are not intended to serve as the last word on the matter; they aren't rigid laws that cannot be broken. If house style doesn't make sense for a particular book, we can make exceptions, and where house style seriously conflicts with author style, we usually respect author preferences.

Before we deal with the nitty-gritty of house style, here are some general suggestions to bear in mind while you are writing your book:

Keep words and sentences short, simple, and easy to understand.

Avoid excessive use of the passive voice.

Watch out for ambiguity. Precision is important in any type of writing, but especially so in technical writing.

---

[1]Our house style is based on The Chicago Manual of Style, University of Chicago Press, 1982.

continued

Figure 10-1. A publisher's style guide printed on an ImageWriter

Publisher's Style Guide   2

You will find that many of the marks your editor makes on your manuscript are made in the interests of helping you improve the clarity, accuracy, and consistency of your manuscript. Other marks probably relate to the house style conventions discussed below.

Capitalization

We follow these rules on capitalization:

Capitalize all nouns and adjectives formed from proper names (such as names of companies) and trademarks.

For example: Gaussian, Simpson, Cartesian, Coca Cola, Pepsi, Microsoft.

A sentence--but not a paragraph--may begin with a lowercase letter if necessary. But you may want to reword the sentence.

For example: "a was the first letter to appear on the CRT." Or "An 'a' was the first letter to appear on the CRT."

A single word or phrase introduced by a colon should always begin with a lowercase letter, unless the first word is a proper name or would otherwise begin with a capital letter.

For example: "You have two choices: a black-and-white or a color monitor."

If a colon introduces a complete sentence, the first word after the colon is capitalized.

For example: "We have come to the following conclusion: The first manuscript is the best."

Capitalize specific references to other parts of your book or of other works. General references should be lowercase.

For example: "This is shown in Figure 5-4." But: "It is shown in the figure below."

Spelling

Always use the preferred spelling--the first entry--in your dictionary and use American rather than British spellings.[2]

---

[2]We use Webster's Ninth New Collegiate Dictionary, Merriam-Webster Inc., 1983.

continued

Figure 10-1 (continued)

Publisher's Style Guide   3

Hyphenation

When in doubt, consult the dictionary. However, here are some general rules:

Avoid hyphenation unless closing up would produce a double letter.

For example: "non-negotiable."

Hyphenate if closing up would change the meaning of a word.

For example: "un-ionized."

Hyphenate if a prefix or suffix is added to a proper noun.

For example: "non-Simpson."

Hyphenate if a prefix or suffix is added to two or more words, and hyphenate them all.

For example: "non-time-dependent."

If a modifier is made up of two or more words, it is generally hyphenated, unless it is the complement of the verb "to be."

For example: "She used a double-sided disk." But: "The disk was double sided."

If the first word of a compound modifier is an adverb ending in "ly," do not hyphenate.

For example: "frequently used codes."

Use hyphens in lists of compound modifiers with common elements.

For example: "5-, 7-, and 9-inch gaps."

When spelling out fractions, hyphenate them.

For example: "one-half."

Abbreviations

The following are some general rules on abbreviations:

Don't use abbreviations and symbols in text; always use the full word.

For example: " Figure 6-1," not "Fig. 6-1." And: "37 percent," not "37%."

continued

Figure 10-1 (continued)

Publisher's Style Guide   4

Keep acronyms to a minimum and use them only when it is reasonable to suppose that the reader will have no trouble recognizing them later in the text. Always spell out an acronym, no matter how common, the first time it is used.

For example: " This kind of file is called an ASCII text file. (ASCII stands for American Standard Code for Information Interchange.)"

An acronym takes the article (a or an) that agrees with the way it is commonly spoken.

For example: "a RAM." But: "an LED."

When units of measure are preceded by numerals, use abbreviations.

For example: "8 in." and "14 MHz."

Note: Most abbreviations are not followed by periods unless leaving off the period causes confusion, as in the use of "in." for inches.

Numbers

Here are a few rules to follow for the use of numbers in technical manuscripts:

Dates are written as follows:

April 15............................not..................April 15th
twentieth century.........not..................20th century
sixties and seventies....not..................60's and 70's
1930s................................not..................1930's

Spell out the numbers zero through ten and use numerals for numbers 11 or greater.

For example: "16-bit" and "two bytes."

However, use numerals when there is a list of numbers some of which are greater than ten (for example: 2, 45, and 9870), when numbers are used as chapter, table, or graphic numbers (for example: Chapter 2, Table 4-10, Figure 7-23), and when numbers are used with units of measure (for example: 2 MHz, 8-bit, 5 1/4-inch).

When one number follows another, use a numeral for one and spell out the other.

For example: "seven 8-inch disks."

Figure 10-1 (continued)

Typing the Text

Take a little time now to type some of the text for the style guide. You don't need to type the entire guide, just enough to give you an adequate amount of text to work with—say, a page or two. Don't worry about making it look like the finished product; we'll show you how to add formatting and headings later in the chapter. First, as always, insert your Word Working Master disk and a data disk and open a new Word document. Then just start typing.

Insert your Word Working Master disk and a data disk, double-click the Word disk icon to open the disk directory window (if it isn't open already), and double-click on the Word program icon to open a new document.

Type the following:

A key to quality in publishing is consistency of style. The term style, in the publishing context, refers to two different things: the personal writing style of the author and the set of conventions that the publishing house has chosen to adopt as its own house style. Author style includes such things as the use or nonuse of contractions ("you've," "we'll," and so on), and the patterns authors usually follow when putting words and phrases together. House style includes such things as punctuation, spelling, and capitalization conventions, and how figures and captions are handled. Most publishing houses base their house style on a manual catering to their particular kind of publishing, rather than creating their own style from scratch.[Return]

The following section is intended to establish some guidelines and to answer some, but not all, questions about our house style. These style guidelines are not intended to serve as the last word on the matter; they aren't rigid laws that cannot be broken. If house style doesn't make sense for a particular book, we can make exceptions, and where house style seriously conflicts with author style, we usually respect author preferences.[Return]

Before we deal with the nitty-gritty of house style, here are some general suggestions to bear in mind while you are writing your book:[Return]

Keep words and sentences short, simple, and easy to understand. [Return]

Avoid excessive use of the passive voice.[Return]

Watch out for ambiguity. Precision is important in any type of writing, but especially so in technical writing.[Return]

You will find that many of the marks your editor makes on your manuscript are made in the interests of helping you improve the clarity, accuracy, and consistency of your manuscript. Other marks probably relate to the house style conventions discussed below. [Return]

Capitalization[Return]

We follow these rules on capitalization:[Return]

Capitalize all nouns and adjectives formed from proper names (such as names of companies) and trademarks. For example: Gaussian, Simpson, Cartesian, Coca Cola, Pepsi, Microsoft.[Return]

A sentence—but not a paragraph—may begin with a lowercase letter if necessary. But you may want to reword the sentence. For example: "a was the first letter to appear on the CRT." Or: "An 'a' was the first letter to appear on the CRT."[Return]

A single word or phrase introduced by a colon should always begin with a lowercase letter, unless the first word is a proper name or would otherwise begin with a capital letter. For example: "You have two choices: a black-and-white or a color monitor."[Return]

If a colon introduces a complete sentence, the first word after the colon is capitalized. For example: "We have come to the following conclusion: The first manuscript is the best."[Return]

Capitalize specific references to other parts of your book or of other works. General references should be lowercase. For example: "This is shown in Figure 5-4." But: "It is shown in the figure below."[Return]

Spelling[Return]

Always use the preferred spelling—the first entry—in your dictionary and use American rather than British spellings.[Return]

Hyphenation[Return]

When in doubt, consult the dictionary. However, here are some general rules:[Return]

Avoid hyphenation unless closing up would produce a double letter. For example: "non-negotiable."[Return]

Hyphenate if closing up would change the meaning of a word. For example: "un-ionized."[Return]

Hyphenate if a prefix or suffix is added to a proper noun. For example: "non-Simpson."[Return]

Hyphenate if a prefix or suffix is added to two or more words, and hyphenate them all. For example: "non-time-dependent."[Return]

If a modifier is made up of two or more words, it is generally hyphenated, unless it is the complement of the verb "to be." For example: "She used a double-sided disk." But: "The disk was double sided."[Return]

If the first word of a compound modifier is an adverb ending in "ly," do not hyphenate. For example: "frequently used codes."[Return]

Use hyphens in lists of compound modifiers with common elements. For example: "5-, 7-, and 9-inch gaps."[Return]

When spelling out fractions, hyphenate them. For example: "one-half." [Return]

Abbreviations [Return]

The following are some general rules on abbreviations: [Return]

Don't use abbreviations and symbols in text; always use the full word. For example: "Figure 6-1," not "Fig. 6-1." And: "37 percent," not "37%." [Return]

Keep acronyms to a minimum and use them only when it is reasonable to suppose that the reader will have no trouble recognizing them later in the text. Always spell out an acronym, no matter how common, the first time it is used. For example: "This kind of file is called an ASCII text file. (ASCII stands for American Standard Code for Information Interchange.)" [Return]

An acronym takes the article (a or an) that agrees with the way it is commonly spoken. For example: "a RAM," but "an LED." [Return]

When units of measure are preceded by numerals, use abbreviations. For example: "8 in." and "14 MHz." [Return]

Note: Most abbreviations are not followed by periods unless leaving off the period causes confusion, as in the use of "in." for inches. [Return]

Numbers [Return]

Here are a few rules to follow for the use of numbers in technical manuscripts: [Return]

Dates are written as follows: [Return]

April 15 not April 15th [Return]

twentieth century not 20th century [Return]

sixties and seventies not 60's and 70's [Return]

1930s not 1930's [Return]

Spell out the numbers zero through ten and use numerals for numbers 11 or greater. For example: "16-bit" and "two bytes." [Return]

However, use numerals when there is a list of numbers some of which are greater than ten (for example: 2, 45, and 9870), when numbers are used as chapter, table, or graphic numbers (for example: Chapter 2, Table 4-10, Figure 7-23), and when numbers are used with units of measure (for example: 2 MHz, 8-bit, 5¼-inch). [Return]

When one number follows another, use a numeral for one and spell out the other. For example: "seven 8-inch disks." [Return]

When you're finished typing, save the text on disk as *Style Guide* or some other appropriate name.

Press Command-S to choose Save from the File menu.

In the Save Document As dialog box, type *Style Guide* in the Save Current Document As text box, click the Drive button, then click the Save button.

Adding Blank Lines

Right now, the text looks uniform—so uniform, in fact, it's difficult to see where one paragraph ends and another begins. Being able to see where paragraphs begin and end will be important when it is time to do the formatting we'll demonstrate later in the chapter. So, add a blank line between each paragraph now to visually break up the text.

Adding one blank line between each paragraph could take quite a while if you went through the document pressing Return at the end of each paragraph. But you can do the same thing in two quick steps by selecting the entire document and using Command-Shift-O (the letter, not zero).

Move the pointer into the selection bar, press the Command key and click the mouse button to select the entire document.

Press Command-Shift-O to insert a blank line in front of every paragraph.

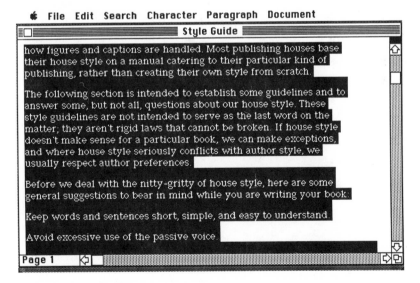

You could accomplish this same feat by choosing the Formats... command from the Paragraph menu and typing *1* in the Space Before text box. But Command-Shift-O is much quicker.

Indenting Entire Paragraphs

Indenting an entire paragraph a fixed amount from the left margin is a standard method of visually setting off that paragraph from the rest of the text and sometimes of indicating that the paragraph is subordinate to the preceding one. An indented paragraph, also known as a nested paragraph, may also have its own indented, subordinate paragraph, such as in an outline format. The style guide has two levels of paragraph indentation.

You could indent a paragraph by selecting it, then choosing the Formats... command from the Paragraph menu and typing a new left indent amount in the Left Indent text box. But Word offers a shortcut: the Command-Shift-N key combination. Pressing Command-Shift-N indents the selected paragraph half an inch to the right of the preceding paragraph. The new indent remains in effect until you press Command-Shift-M, which moves the left margin half an inch to the left, if the page setup will allow it.

Searching for Paragraphs to Indent

To find the paragraphs for the first level of indent, you could simply scroll through the text until you find the first paragraph you want to indent, then scroll to the next one, and so on. But, the paragraphs you want to indent are all preceded by a colon and a paragraph mark, so it's easier to use the Find... command from the Search menu to find each occurrence of a colon followed by a paragraph mark. You can't type a paragraph mark in the Find What text box of the Find dialog box, because pressing Return (the way you enter a paragraph mark in text) is the keyboard method of telling Word to carry out the command. Instead, you use two special characters in place of pressing Return: a caret and a *p*. You get a caret (^) by pressing Shift-6.

Press Command-F to choose Find... from the Search menu, type : ^*p* in the Find What text box.

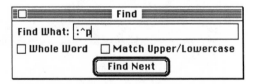

Click the Find Next button.

Click the close box for the Find dialog box and select the desired paragraphs following the colon.

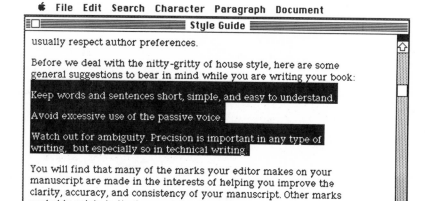

Press Command-Shift-N to indent these paragraphs.

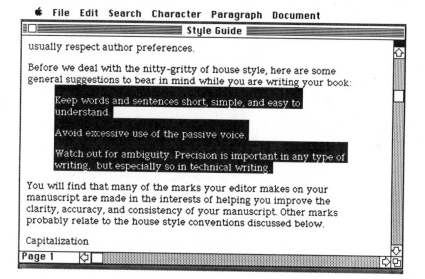

You're ready to move on to the next set of indented paragraphs, but there's no need to retype the symbols you're searching for: They are still in the Find dialog box when you choose Find... again.

Press Command-F to choose Find... and press Enter to find the next occurrence of :¶.

Close the Find dialog box, select the subordinate paragraphs following the colon, and press Command-Shift-N.

Repeat this procedure for the rest of the document.

Next, you want to set up the examples in the text as separate paragraphs. Again, you could scroll through the text, making changes as you encounter them. But a faster way is to use the Change... command from the Search menu.

Press Command-H to choose Change... from the Search menu, type *For example* in the Find What text box, press Tab to move to the Change To text box, type *^pFor example*, click the Match Upper/Lowercase check box, and click the Change All button.

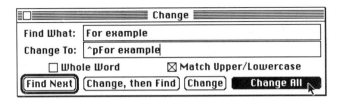

All of the examples are set up in separate paragraphs without your having to do anything more. Now, to indent these example paragraphs an extra half-inch and to reduce the point size to make them appear subordinate to the paragraphs above them, just use Find... the same way you did earlier when you indented the first group of paragraphs. Again, there's no need for you to retype the search text; it's already in the Find What text box. And Match Upper/Lowercase is already selected.

Press Command-F to choose Find... and press Enter to find the next occurrence.

Close the Find dialog box, select the entire paragraph, and press Command-Shift-N to indent the paragraph another half inch.

Press Command-D to choose Formats... from the Character menu, click 10 in the Font Size list box, and click OK.

Repeat this procedure for the rest of the document.

Changing Fonts from the Keyboard

The headings in your style guide will stand out more if they are a larger size and a different font. Assuming you haven't substantially changed your System file by adding and removing a lot of fonts, your text so far is probably in the default New York font. So let's change the headings to Geneva, using the keyboard command for changing fonts: Command-Shift-E, then a number. The number you type represents the position of the font in the Font Name list box (in the Character Formats dialog box you see when you choose Formats... from the Character menu), starting at 0. If you haven't added or removed any fonts from the System file, the numbers and fonts correspond as follows: 0 Chicago, 1 New York, 2 Geneva, 3 Monaco, 4 Dover, and 5 Dover PS. If you've added or removed fonts, you may want to check the Character Formats dialog box (press Command-D) before proceeding. You can use the numbers 6 through 9, as well, if you have that many fonts in your System file. But if you have more than ten fonts in your System file, you can request only one of the first ten with the Command-Shift-E-number key combination.

Scroll to the first heading (*Capitalization*) and select it.

Press Command-Shift-E, then press 2.

After you press Command-Shift-E, you have about nine seconds to press a number key before you hear a beep, which means that you have to press Command-Shift-E again.

Next, change the font size from 12 to 14. The key combination Command-Shift-> increases the font size without your having to choose Formats... from the Character menu and click or type a different size. Likewise, Command-Shift-< decreases the font size. But Command-Shift-> and Command-Shift-< only allow you to move, in sequence, among the following sizes: 7, 9, 12, 14, 18, 24, 36, 48, 60, and 72. If you want a font size that isn't in this list, you need to access it with the Character Formats dialog box.

Press Command-Shift-> once to increase the font size to 14 points.

Finally, make the heading boldface by using the key combination Command-Shift-B.

Press Command-Shift-B to choose Boldface.

Now copy the character formatting of the first heading to all of the other headings.

Scroll to the next heading and select it.

Scroll back up to the first heading.

Press Option-Command and click to copy the character formatting of the first heading to the second.

Repeat the same procedure for the other headings.

Setting Up a Table

The examples of how dates should be written (under the *Numbers* heading) will be easier to read if set up as a three-column table. Setting up a table in Word is similar to setting up a table on a typewriter, in that you use tabs to separate the columns. But Word makes measuring easier. First, let's indent the table so that it is subordinate to the paragraph it follows.

> Scroll to the line reading *Dates are written as follows:* and select the four lines that follow it.
>
> Press Command-Shift-N.

Each of the four lines you've selected ends with a paragraph mark. Since you added a blank line ahead of every paragraph in the document, each of these lines also has a blank line ahead of it. But you don't want blank lines in your table, so delete the paragraph marks and add a new-line mark instead, by pressing Shift-Return.

> Press Command-Y to choose Show ¶.
>
> Click the insertion point at the start of the second line, press Backspace to delete the paragraph mark, and press Shift-Return to add a new line mark.
>
> Repeat this procedure for the other two lines.

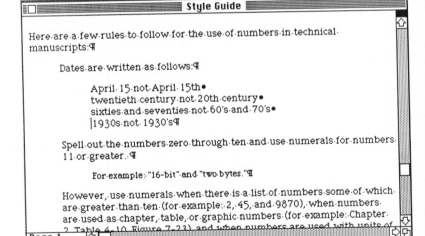

Now you can tell Word where to position the columns of the table by using the Tabs... command from the Paragraph menu. For separating tab columns, Word offers four different options: blank space, dots, dashes, and a solid underline. These tab column separators are called leaders. We think dots make suitable leaders for the date table, but you can use a different kind if you want.

Select the whole table.

Press Command-T to choose Tabs... from the Paragraph menu.

In the Tabs dialog box, click the dotted-line button in the Leader box, click a tab at 2¾ inches on the ruler, click another tab at 3¾ inches, and click OK.

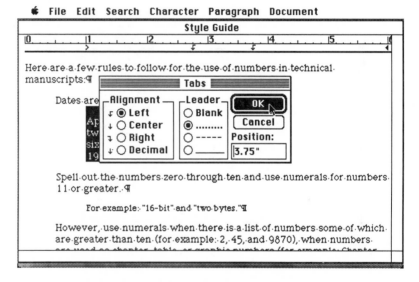

Now all you need to do is tell Word where in the table you want the tabs. This is simple to do while you still have the table selected. You want tabs to replace the spaces on either side of the word *not* in all four lines. You can do this with the Change... command, using a special character code to insert the tabs just as you used special characters to search for paragraph marks. The code is *^t*.

Press Command-H to choose Change... from the Search menu.

Type the following in the Find What text box:

[Space]*not*[Space]

Press Tab, type *^tnot^t* in the Change To text box, and click Change Selection.

Click the Change close box.

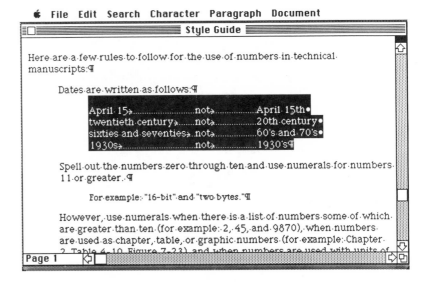

Creating a Footnote

Footnotes are a valuable tool that allows you to pass along additional information or cite your source for a particular statement. Word lets you include footnotes, either on the page where the reference appears or at the end of the document. We will demonstrate how to add two footnotes to the style guide so that each appears on the page where it is referenced. The first footnote reference is at the end of the first paragraph, so return to the top of the document and then locate the end of the first paragraph.

> Scroll to the top of the document by dragging the scroll box to the top of the scroll bar.
>
> Click the insertion point at the end of the first paragraph, between the period and the paragraph mark.

Now, choose the Footnote... command from the Document menu.

> Press Command-E to choose Footnote... from the Document menu.

In the dialog box that's displayed, you are offered a choice between the Auto Numbering check box and the Footnote Reference Mark text box. The default is Auto Numbering, which inserts a number, in numeric order starting at 1, at each footnote reference location. You want automatic numbering for the style guide, but if you wanted a different kind of footnote reference mark—you can use up to 10 characters— you could type that mark in the Footnote Reference Mark text box. As soon as you start typing in the text box, the check disappears from the Auto Numbering check box. Both kinds of reference marks appear in your text in superscript.

> Press Enter (instead of clicking OK) to accept the Auto Numbering option.

Word splits the screen in two, with the document window remaining open at the top of the screen and a footnote window appearing at the bottom. The footnote window is similar to a document window. You can type any amount of text in it, you can close it by dragging the window split bar to the bottom of the scroll bar, and you can open it by pressing Shift and dragging the window split bar from the top of the scroll bar. To create the text for the first footnote, just type it in the footnote window.

> Type the following:
>
> *Our house style is based on The Chicago Manual of Style, University of Chicago Press, 1982.*[Return]

 File   Edit   Search   Character   Paragraph   Document

```
▤▯▤▤▤▤▤▤▤▤▤▤▤▤▤▤▤ Style Guide ▤▤▤▤▤▤▤▤▤▤▤▤▤▤▤▤

= A·key·to·quality·in··publishing·is·consistency·of·style.·The·term·style,·in·the·
publishing·context,·refers·to·two·different·things:·the·personal·writing·style·
of·the·author·and·the·set·of·conventions·that·the·publishing·house·has·
chosen·to·adopt·as·its·own·house·style.·Author·style·includes·such·things·as·
the·use·or·nonuse·of·contractions·("you've,"·"we'll,"·and·so·on),·and·the·
patterns·authors·usually·follow·when·putting·words·and·phrases·together.·
House·style·includes·such·things·as·punctuation,·spelling,·and·capitalization·
conventions,·and·how·figures·and·captions·are·handled.·Most·publishing·
houses·base·their·house·style·on·a·manual·catering·to·their·particular·kind·of·
publishing,·rather·than·creating·their·own·style·from·scratch.[1]¶

[1]Our·house·style·is·based·on·The·Chicago·Manual·of·Style,·University·of·
Chicago·Press,·1982.¶
|◇

footnote
```

The second footnote is referenced at the end of the only paragraph under the *Spelling* heading. The footnote window is still open, so you don't need to reopen it. Just mark the location for the next footnote reference and choose Footnote... again.

Scroll to the end of the paragraph on spelling and click the insertion point between the period and the paragraph mark.

Press Command-E to choose Footnote... and press Enter to carry out the command with the default setting.

Type the following:

We use Webster's Ninth New Collegiate Dictionary, Merriam-Webster Inc., 1983.[Return]

Now that you're finished typing your footnote text, you can close the footnote window.

Drag the window split bar to the bottom of the scroll bar.

Finally, you need to tell Word where to print the footnotes with the Division Layout... command from the Document menu.

Choose Division Layout... from the Document menu, click the On Same Page radio button in the Footnotes Appear box, and press Enter (instead of clicking OK).

Looking at Page-Break Locations

Right now, you have no way of telling where one page will end and another will begin when you print your document. So, you have no way of knowing if, for instance, the date table you created will end up split between two different pages, an arrangement that would make it difficult to read the table. To allow you to spot such problems, Word offers a command that lets you see how the pages will break before you print: Repaginate from the Document menu. Let's use Repaginate now to see how it works.

Press Command-J to choose Repaginate from the Document menu.

Watch the page numbers change in the box at the lower left of the screen as Word divides the document into pages. When Word has finished paginating the style guide, you can scroll through the document and see where page breaks will occur. Page breaks are marked by an equal sign in the left margin beside the first line of each new page. Go to the top of the document, then scroll down until you see the first page-break mark.

> Drag the scroll box to the top of the scroll bar, then click on the bottom scroll arrow to locate the first page-break mark (=).

You want to make sure the heading *Capitalization* appears on the same page as the paragraph that follows it, since it would be hard to read the guide if a heading appeared at the bottom of one page and the text it pertains to appeared on the next page. You can prevent division of the headings and paragraphs, no matter how many changes you later make above or below them, by using either of two check boxes in the Paragraph Formats dialog box: Keep With Next ¶ and Keep Lines Together. Now let's use the Keep With Next ¶ button to keep the *Capitalization* heading and the two paragraphs following it together.

> Select the *Capitalization* heading and the paragraph that follows it.
>
> Press Command-M to choose Formats… from the Paragraph menu, click the Keep With Next ¶ check box, and click OK.

```
╔══════════ Paragraph Formats ══════════╗
║ Left Indent:  [     ]  Line Spacing: [     ]   ┌── OK ──┐ ║
║ First Line:   [     ]  Space Before: [     ]   │        │ ║
║ Right Indent: [     ]  Space After:  [     ]   └ Cancel ┘ ║
║ ┌────────────────────┬────────────────────────┐          ║
║ │ ○ Left    ○ Right  │ ⊠ Keep with next ¶     │          ║
║ │ ○ Centered ○ Justified │ ▩ Keep lines together │        ║
║ └────────────────────┴────────────────────────┘          ║
╚═══════════════════════════════════════════╝
```

Now let's do the same for the other four headings, keeping them together with the paragraphs that follow them.

> Select the next heading, press Command-M, click the Keep With Next ¶ button, and click OK.
>
> Repeat this procedure with the other three headings.

By the same token, the example paragraphs should appear on the same page as the paragraphs that precede them. So, use the same procedure for the examples.

> Select the paragraph above the first example, press Command-M, click Keep With Next ¶, and click OK.
>
> Repeat this procedure for the rest of the examples.

If you wanted to, you could use Find..., and type *For example* in the Find What text box to move quickly from one example paragraph to the next.

You also want to avoid having the date table divided between two pages. This would not be a good arrangement for ease of reading. You want to make sure the table is printed on one page. The best way to do that is with the other button we mentioned in this section: Keep Lines Together.

> Select all four lines in the table.
>
> Press Command-M, click the Keep Lines Together button, and click OK.

Now ensure that the table and the paragraph preceding it appear on the same page.

> Select the paragraph above the table, press Command-M, click Keep With Next ¶, and click OK.

Another way to keep certain paragraphs or elements together is to specify where page breaks will occur. You do that by pressing Shift-Enter at the point where you want a page break. But if you specify a page-break location with Shift-Enter, then add or delete text, the page break you specified may no longer reflect your wishes.

Use Repaginate again now to see the effect of Keep With Next ¶.

> Press Command-J to choose Repaginate.

Now, from the top, scroll through the document.

> Scroll to the top of the document with the scroll box, then scroll slowly through the document with the bottom scroll arrow.

Adding a Full-Width Letterhead

The next element to add to the style guide is the letterhead that spans the width of the first page. It is created in MacPaint. Adding a full-width MacPaint letterhead to a Word document is a little more complicated than adding a letterhead that's no wider than a window, because you have to cut the full-width letterhead from MacPaint in two pieces and paste it into Word in two columns. We'll discuss the concepts behind using Word's multiple-column formatting feature in Chapters 11, 12, and 13, but for now we'll simply describe the steps necessary to insert the letterhead.

The letterhead used in Figure 10-1 is shown full-size in Figure 10-2, though in two parts because it's wider than the pages of this book. If you want your letterhead to look exactly like ours, you can trace it by one of three methods: Hold the page of this book up to the screen and trace the outline of the letterhead with the appropriate MacPaint tool (you should be able to see the tool through the page), photocopy the page onto regular photocopy paper and hold the photocopy up to the screen while you trace, or photocopy the page onto acetate. Acetate is the easiest to work with, but is more expensive than regular photocopy paper.

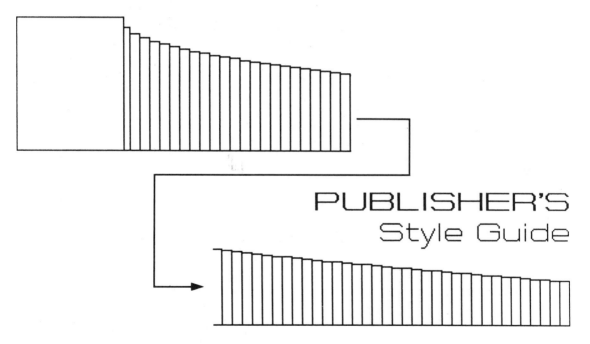

Figure 10-2. Full-size style-guide letterhead in two parts

Once you have the graphic for the letterhead, it is time to add the title. We used the Stuttgart font from Mac the Knife for the lettering. If you happen to have Mac the Knife, you might want to use the same font. Otherwise, you can simply trace the lettering, too.

> Eject your Word Working Master disk, insert your MacPaint disk, and restart the Mac.
>
> Create your letterhead in MacPaint.

After you create the letterhead, you need to cut it to the Scrapbook in two parts of identical size. Be especially careful that your top and bottom selection lines are on exactly the same two horizontal lines of pixels. Otherwise, the two halves of your letterhead won't line up vertically in Word. We designed the style-guide letterhead to make this task easier: The top of the rectangle on the left is on the same vertical line as the top of the word *Publishers*. So, you can position MacPaint's selection rectangle one pixel above the top of the left rectangle for the left half of the letterhead and one pixel above the top of the lettering for the right half. Make sure the selection rectangle is one pixel below the line that extends the width of the letterhead and one pixel past each end.

> Cut the letterhead (in exactly two halves) to the Scrapbook.

Now you can leave MacPaint, start Word, and copy the Scrapbook file to the Word disk.

> Quit MacPaint, drag the Scrapbook file icon to the data disk directory window, eject the MacPaint disk, insert your Word Working Master disk, and restart the Mac.
>
> Drag the Scrapbook icon from the data disk directory window to the Word disk directory window.

When you reopen the style-guide document, the next step in inserting the letterhead is to divide the page into two parts. The first part will be formatted with two columns, one for each half of the letterhead. The second part will remain formatted with one column for the text that you've already entered. You divide the page by pressing Command-Enter. The division mark is displayed as a double dotted line.

> Double-click on the style-guide document icon.

The insertion point comes up on the left side of the first line of text, which is where you want it.

Press Command-Enter to create a division mark.

Now you're ready to actually insert the first half of the letterhead.

Click the insertion point on the left end of the division mark.

Choose Scrapbook from the Apple menu, scroll until the first half of the letterhead appears in the Scrapbook window, press Command-C to choose Copy from the Edit menu, and click the Scrapbook close box.

Press Command-V to choose Paste from the Edit menu.

You'll want a little space between the letterhead and the first line of text, so add a blank line.

Press Return.

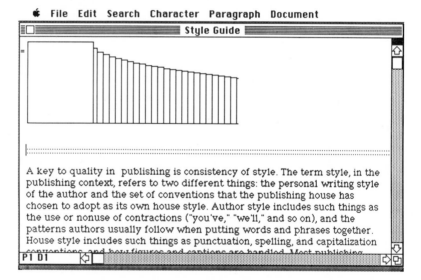

Now you need to tell Word that the first half of the letterhead is in the first of two columns, that there will be no space between the columns, and that the first half of the letterhead will be right-aligned within the column. (The second half of the letterhead, in the second column, will be left-aligned, so that the two halves merge.) You also need to widen the first column, since the first half of the letterhead won't fit in the default column width of a double-column format with no space between columns (3 inches).

Choose Division Layout… from the Document menu, type 2 in the Number of Columns text box, type 0 in the Column Spacing text box, and click OK.

Select the graphic by clicking anywhere on it.

Press Command-M to choose Formats… from the Paragraph menu.

Drag the right indent marker to the 3½-inch mark on the ruler.

Click Right and click OK.

This takes care of the first half of the graphic. Next you need to tell Word that you want the second division on the same page and not on the second page. You do that with the Division Layout… command from the Document menu.

Click anywhere under the division mark below the letterhead.

Choose Division Layout… from the Document menu, click Continuous in the Break box, and click OK.

The next step is to create a second column to hold the second half of the letterhead. We've already determined by trial and error where you should enter another division mark for the second column, so now all you need to do is follow our directions. But if you were creating the style guide on your own, at this point you'd need to print the first page to find that spot. Printing is really the only way to find out where you need to end one column and start the next, because Word displays your document on the screen as one long column, even if it's a multiple-column document. You see the arrangement of the columns side-by-side on the page only on a printout.

If you printed at this point, you'd find the paragraph that starts with *You will find that…* overlaying the right half of the first part of your text. So, you need to create a division mark for the second column just before that paragraph.

Click an insertion point on the left side of the line that starts with *You will find that….*

Press Command-Enter twice.

Click an insertion point on the left side of the bottom division mark.

Select Division Layout… from the Document menu, click Column in the Break box, and click OK.

Choose Scrapbook from the Apple menu, scroll until the second half of the letterhead appears in the Scrapbook window, press Command-C to choose Copy from the Edit menu, and click the Scrapbook close box.

Press Command-V to choose Paste from the Edit menu.

You widened the first column to accommodate the first half of the letterhead. Now you need to make room for the widened first column by moving the left indent of the second column ½ inch to the right. And since the second half of the letterhead is just as wide as the first, you also need to widen the second column to the right.

> Select the second half of the letterhead by clicking anywhere on it.
>
> Press Command-M to choose Formats... from the Paragraph menu.
>
> Drag the left and first-line indent markers to ½ inch on the ruler, drag the right indent marker to 4 inches, and click OK.

Widening the first and second columns to the right to accommodate both halves of the letterhead, as you've just done, would make the page look unbalanced to the right and put the right side of the letterhead too close to the edge of the paper if you printed the style guide as it now stands. Instead, you now need to shift the margins for the entire page back to the left a bit by using the Page Setup... command. By trying several margin settings, we found that shifting the page a quarter-inch to the left was enough to pull the letterhead away from the edge of the paper an adequate distance, while keeping the text roughly centered on the page.

> Choose Page Setup... from the File menu.
>
> Type *1* in the Left Margin text box, type *1.5* in the Right Margin text box, and click OK.

This finishes your letterhead. Now all you need to do is to tell Word to start the next paragraph on the next page and you'll be ready to add a running head.

> Click an insertion point on the left end of the first line of the second page.
>
> Choose Division Layout... from the Document menu, click Page in the Break box, and click OK.

Adding a Running Head

Running heads are frequently used in documents like the style guide to identify the document on all but the first page, where it is identified by the title. In Word, the running head can also include the page number. You type what you want to appear in the running head at the beginning of the second page.

Type the following:

Publisher's Style Guide

You can use one of the default entries of Standard Glossary to enter page numbers for you when you print. So, specify the position where you want the page number to appear (we picked 7 inches, or half an inch from the right margin) and type the word *page* there.

> Press Command-T to choose Tabs... from the Paragraph menu, type 7 in the Position text box, and press Enter (instead of clicking OK).
>
> Press Tab and type *page.*
>
> Press Command-Backspace to use the page-numbering entry in Standard Glossary and press Return.

The word *page* changes to *(page)* and remains on the screen, but is replaced by the page number when you print. Now tell Word that what you've just typed is a running head by choosing the Running Head... command. Also tell Word how far from the top of the page to print the running head with the Division Layout... command.

> Select the running head, choose Running Head... from the Document menu, click the First Page check box, and click OK.

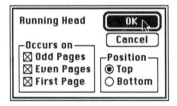

> Choose Division Layout... from the Document menu, type *0.55* in the From Top text box under Running Head Position, and click OK.

By clicking the First Page check box, you're telling Word you want the running head to appear at the top of the first page of this division. The other check boxes tell Word to put the running head at the top of all pages, both even-numbered and odd-numbered. The text of the running head remains at the top of the second page on the screen, but will be placed at the top of all the pages you specified when the document is printed.

Once everything is in place, it's a good idea to choose Repaginate one more time to check for possible adjustments made necessary by addition of the letterhead.

Press Command-J to choose Repaginate.

If everything looks as you want it, save the style guide, then print it.

Press Command-S to choose Save from the File menu.

Press Command-P to choose Print... from the File menu and press Enter (instead of clicking OK).

If you wanted to transmit the text for your style guide to a typesetter, once you had your printout, you could choose Save As... from the File menu, type a slightly different name in the Name of Current Document text box, and click the Text Only check box. Saving a document as text-only saves it in ASCII characters, which are readable by most other computers. Text Only also is the setting to select if you want to send a document over telephone lines, via a modem.

The letterhead in this chapter was your first experience with Word's multiple-column formatting. In Chapter 11, we show you how to set up a more elaborate multiple-column document: a newsletter.

11

A newsletter

Word's multiple-column formatting feature lends itself well to a newspaper or newsletter layout. And, in fact, that's the project for this chapter: a newsletter.

As we demonstrate how we created a newsletter called *The Investor,* we not only show you how to generate multiple-column pages, we also discuss how to insert illustrations created with other programs and how to prepare a three-column table.

If you want to follow along and prepare the newsletter exactly as we've done it, you'll need Microsoft Chart, UltraFonts (the independently produced font disk mentioned in Chapter 8), and MacPaint. If you're not fussy about duplicating this project exactly, you don't need all these extra products: You can approximate the illustrations with any graphics program. For best results, use an ImageWriter for printing. If you use any other kind of printer, you may not get the results described in this chapter. For instance, as we said in Chapter 5, if you use a fully formed character printer, you won't be able to print the graphics.

To set the scene for the newsletter project, let's say you're an investment counselor who mails a biweekly newsletter to clients. You write, lay out, and print a copy of the newsletter using Word, the Mac, and an ImageWriter. Then you take the ImageWriter printout as camera-ready copy to a print shop to have it reproduced by photo-offset printing. The front page of one issue, the page we'll demonstrate how to create in this chapter, is shown in Figure 11-1.

The Investor

Volume 2   Number 41   September 29

Too Good To Be True? It Probably Isn't True

We receive several prospectuses every week from our readers, wanting us to look at some spectacular investments. However, most of these cleverly distorted advertisements don't hold up under close scrutiny. Yet, despite warnings, there is never a shortage of investors willing to sink large portions of their portfolios into these once-in-a-lifetime opportunities.

When looking at a prospectus, assure yourself that the figures remain reasonably good under less than optimal conditions. Remember: There is a "once-in-a-lifetime" opportunity every day.

BUYING A HOUSE IS NO LONGER A QUICK-PROFIT INVESTMENT

The dramatic increase in the price of real estate during the inflation of the '70s has stalled in the '80s. Indications are that real-estate prices are now undergoing a long-term correction. Home-foreclosure rates continue to reach new highs, in spite of the economic recovery, testifying to the extreme excesses of the prior price run-up. For the first time in many years, current interest rates on savings are increasing more rapidly than the rise in home prices. Future home buyers reap the benefits of high interest as they save toward the purchase of a home.

	Rent	Buy
Cost of house	0	$125,000
Initial outflow	0	25,000
Interest savings	+208	0
Monthly payment	-750	-1067
Utilities	-50	-125
Property tax	0	-104
Tax savings	0	+322
Net outflow	-$592	-$974

Continued on Page 2

Stock Market Challenges Record Highs

The stock market has run into resistance each time it has approached its previous highs. The recent surge in the market included a record number of consecutive days in which advancing stocks outnumbered declining stocks. DOW theory criteria indicated a bull market, but the Federal Reserve Board didn't move to tighten the money supply. Therefore it seems most likely that this momentum will carry the market to new highs.

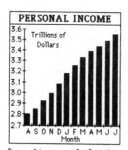

PERSONAL INCOME

Trillions of Dollars

3.6 3.5 3.4 3.3 3.2 3.1 3.0 2.9 2.8 2.7

A S O N D J F M A M J J
Month

Personal income up: See Page 4

Page 1

Figure 11-1. The Investor newsletter printed on an ImageWriter

Creating the Text

Before you begin typing, you may want to modify your Word disk by installing the border font we used to create the borders in the masthead. If you have UltraFonts, install the font called Borders on both your Word disk and your graphics program disk using Font Mover, as described in Chapter 8. Then you're ready to begin.

Insert your Word Working Master disk and a data disk.

Double-click on the Word disk icon to open the disk directory window, if it isn't open already, then double-click on the Word program icon to open a new document.

Type the following:

Too Good To Be True?[Return]

It Probably Isn't True[Return]

We receive several prospectuses every week from our readers, wanting us to look at some spectacular investments. However, most of these cleverly distorted advertisements don't hold up under close scrutiny. Yet, despite warnings, there is never a shortage of investors willing to sink large portions of their portfolios into these once-in-a-lifetime opportunities.[Return]

When looking at a prospectus, assure yourself that the figures remain reasonably good under less than optimal conditions. Remember: There is a "once-in-a-lifetime" opportunity every day.[Return]

BUYING A HOUSE IS NO LONGER[Return]

A QUICK-PROFIT INVESTMENT[Return]

The dramatic increase in the price of real estate during the inflation of the '70s has stalled in the '80s. Indications are that real-estate prices are now undergoing a long-term correction. Home-foreclosure rates continue to reach new highs, in spite of the economic recovery, testifying to the extreme excesses of the prior price run-up. For the first time in many years, current interest rates are increasing savings more rapidly than home prices are rising. Future home buyers reap the benefits of high interest as they save toward the purchase of a home.[Return]

[Tab]*Rent*[Tab]*Buy*[Return]

Cost of house[Tab]*0*[Tab]*$125,000*[Return]

Initial outflow[Tab]*0*[Tab]*25,000*[Return]

Interest savings[Tab]*+208*[Tab]*0*[Return]

Monthly payment[Tab]*−750*[Tab]*−1067*[Return]

Utilities[Tab]*−50*[Tab]*−125*[Return]

Property tax[Tab]*0*[Tab]*−104*[Return]

Tax savings[Tab]*0*[Tab]*+322*[Return]

Net outflow[Tab]*−$592*[Tab]*−$974*[Return]

Stock Market Challenges Record Highs[Return]

The stock market has run into resistance each time it has approached its previous highs. The recent surge in the market included a record number of consecutive days in which advancing stocks outnumbered declining stocks. DOW theory criteria indicated a bull market, but the Federal Reserve Board didn't move to tighten the money supply. Therefore it seems most likely that this momentum will carry the market to new highs.[Return]

When you're finished typing, save the document on your data disk as Newsletter Text.

Choose Save As… from the File menu, type *Newsletter Text* in the text box, click the Drive button, then click the Save button.

Creating the Illustrations

We created the masthead title, house illustration, and bull graphic for the newsletter with MacPaint, and we created the chart with Microsoft Chart. But, as we indicated at the start of the chapter, you can use any graphics program to create illustrations.

Eject your Word Working Master disk and insert the graphics program disk.

Create a masthead title and illustrations for your newsletter.

This book isn't about using graphics programs, so we won't give you detailed instructions for creating illustrations. But if you're curious about how we created the ones shown in Figure 11-2, we typed the masthead title in 72-point New York, cleaned it up with FatBits, and pulled the letters a little closer together so that the entire image fit in the MacPaint window. If you want your illustrations to look like the ones we created, you can trace the ones shown in Figure 11-2 using one of the methods described in Chapter 10. But don't worry too much about making your illustration the right size for the space in the newsletter. You can adjust the size by using the graphics selection box described in Chapter 3.

The Investor

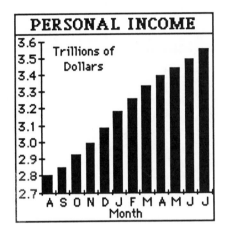

Figure 11-2. The masthead
title, chart, house, and bull
illustrations for *The Investor*

Once you've drawn your illustrations, select each graphic and store
it in the Scrapbook by using the Copy command. Then transfer the
Scrapbook file to your Word disk via your data disk.

Select each of the graphics one at a time and copy them into the
Scrapbook.

Quit the graphics program, then drag the icon of the Scrapbook file
from the graphics program disk directory window to the data disk
window.

Eject the graphics program disk and insert your Word Working
Master.

Drag the Scrapbook file icon from the data disk window to the Word
disk window.

Laying Out the Front Page

Before you start using Word's multiple-column formatting to create your newsletter on the screen, you need to plan the layout of the page on paper. Make some rough measurements of the illustrations and articles to find out what will fit on the page. Let's assume you're using a standard 8½- by 11-inch sheet of paper (Word's default page size). We've done the measuring for you, so you won't need to trim any of the illustrations or articles we show you in this chapter. But if you were laying out your own newsletter, you'd need to make a number of decisions about placement. Laying out a page is largely a matter of having an eye for balance. The following few tips might help.

Think of the page as a whole, with each article and illustration (including the masthead) as a simple geometric shape. When placing the blocks, balance the page visually, so that no one part of the page has more illustration or text with greater emphasis than any other. For example, notice how the house illustration in the investment newsletter is roughly in the middle of the page, the large graphic masthead is at the top, and the two small illustrations are toward the bottom.

When trying to achieve balance, don't give every element exactly the same size and visual weight. The page must have a sense of movement, as well as balance. Figure 11-3 shows how we diagramed the front page for *The Investor* on paper.

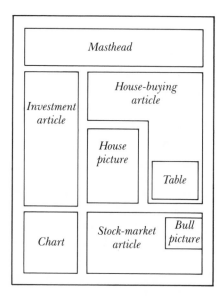

Figure 11-3. A layout of the front page of *The Investor*

Once you've laid out the page on paper, you can transfer the layout to the screen. To set up the layout shown in Figure 11-3 in Word, you need to format for three columns. The investment article and the chart will be in one column, the house-buying article, house illustration, and stock-market article will be in the second column, and the last part of the house-buying article and bull illustration will be in column three. First, set up a half-inch margin around the entire page.

Double-click on the Newsletter Text icon in the data disk window to open the newsletter document.

Choose the Page Setup... command from the File menu, type *0.5* in the Top, Bottom, Left, and Right Margins text boxes, and click OK.

ImageWriter (Standard or Wide)　　　　　　　　　[▷ OK]

Paper:　　◉ US Letter　　　　　○ A4 Letter
　　　　　○ US Legal　　　　　○ International Fanfold　　[Cancel]
　　　　　○ Computer Paper

Orientation:　◉ Tall　　○ Tall Adjusted　　○ Wide

Pagination:　◉ Normal pages ○ No breaks between pages

Reduction:　◉ None　　○ 50 percent

　　　　　　　　Margins:

Top:　[0.5"]　　Left: [0.5"]　　Gutter: [0"]

Bottom: [0.5"]　Right: [0.5"]

You'll be using the ruler periodically throughout the formatting of the newsletter, so you might as well display it on the screen now.

Choose the Show Ruler command from the Edit menu.

Now you need to tell Word you intend to use three columns. You do that with the Division Layout... command from the Document menu.

Choose Division Layout... from the Document menu, type *3* in the Number of Columns text box, click the Continuous button in the Break box, and click OK.

To create the masthead, you need to use Word's multiple-column formatting in a way that might not be immediately apparent: overlapping one column horizontally into another by adjusting the column margin. You can specify the margins for any column anywhere on the page. For instance, you can create the masthead in a single column extending the full width of the page, instead of in three parts in three columns. But you need to space down past the masthead in the second and third columns so that the text in those columns isn't printed across the masthead. You add the space by pressing Return several times at the start of the second and third columns. We have already determined how many times to press Return to add just the right amount of space for this project, but you'd normally need to figure that out for yourself.

Now stretch the first column across all three columns by adjusting the right margin on the ruler.

> Press Return.
>
> Click anywhere above the first line of text.
>
> Scroll right until you can see the 7½-inch mark on the ruler, then drag the right indent marker out to 7½ inches.

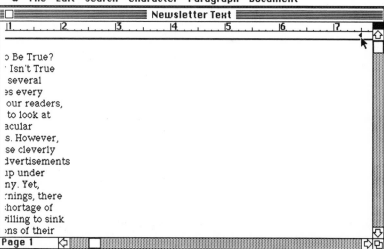

Next, add the double line that appears above the title. We used the Borders font from UltraFonts.

> Choose Formats... from the Character menu (Command-D).
>
> In the Character Formats dialog box, click Borders in the Font Name list box and 9 in the Font Size list box. Click OK.

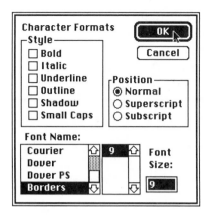

Press the S key 50 times, then press Return.

Now, insert the masthead title you created in the graphics program.

Choose Scrapbook from the Apple menu.

Make sure the masthead title is in the Scrapbook window, then choose Copy from the Edit menu.

Click the Scrapbook close box.

Choose Paste from the Edit menu to insert the masthead.

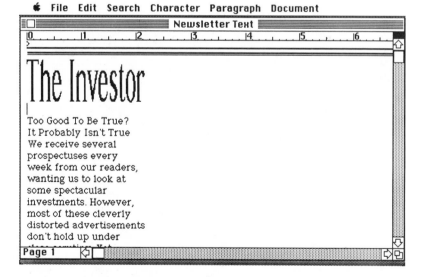

Don't worry that the title looks squashed. It's been compacted into a single narrow column. So, you can take care of that now. Set the margin for the full width of the page, center the title, and add the volume, number, and date box.

Select the masthead title by clicking anywhere on it.

Scroll to the right until you see the 7½-inch mark on the ruler, then drag the right indent marker to 7½ inches.

Choose Centered from the Paragraph menu.

Click anywhere beneath the masthead title and above the first line of text.

Choose Formats… from the Character menu, click Borders in the Font Name list box, and click OK.

Type *z*, 48 *x*'s, then *c*, and press Return.

Click tab markers at ⅛, 1, and 6⅜ inches on the ruler to position the volume, number, and date.

Type *v*.

Choose Formats… from the Character menu, click New York in the Font Name list box, and click OK.

Press Tab, type *Volume 2*, press Tab, type *Number 41*, press Tab, and type *September 29*.

Choose Tabs… from the Paragraph menu and type *7.34* in the Position text box. Click OK.

Choose Formats… from the Character menu, click Borders in the Font Name list box, and click OK.

Press Tab, type *b*, and press Return.

Type *n*, 48 *m*'s, and a comma. Press Return.

Since you'll be using the masthead in future editions of *The Investor,* save it in a glossary. Then, you'll just need to change the issue, volume, and date. We used the glossary name *mast,* but you can use any name.

Select all five lines of the Masthead.

Choose Copy from the Edit menu.

Choose Show Glossary... from the Edit menu, type *mast* in the Name in Glossary text box, choose Paste from the Edit menu, then click the close box on the glossary window.

This is a good time to save and print the newsletter to make sure the masthead will appear as you want it to. Since it's now more than just text, let's change the name to *Newsletter.*

Choose Save As... from the File menu.

Type *Newsletter* in the Save Current Document As text box, and click OK.

Choose Print... from the File menu, and click OK.

Check the printout to see that the masthead is aligned properly, but don't be concerned about the rest of the page: We'll get to it shortly. You are now ready to start formatting the text. First increase the font size on the first two lines to make them look more like a headline.

Select the first two lines—the headline that reads *Too Good To Be True? It Probably Isn't True.*

Choose Formats... from the Character menu, click 14 in the Font Size list box, and click OK.

Now let's justify the text of the first article and indent the first line of each paragraph.

Click on the left edge of the third line of text—the beginning of the article on investment opportunities.

Scroll to the end of the article, then hold down the Shift key and click on the right end of the last line of the article to select the entire article.

Choose Formats... from the Paragraph menu, type *0.25* in the First Line text box, click the Justified button, and click OK.

If you scroll down through the text, you'll notice a lot of distracting space in the line that reads *cleverly distorted.* To correct this, you need to adjust the point at which the line breaks. You do that by hyphenating the first word in the next line to bring a little more text up to the offending line.

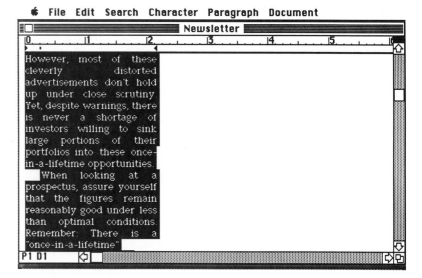

Scroll down to the line that reads *advertisements don't hold.*

Click between the *r* and the *t* in *advertisements* and type a hyphen.

Word rebreaks the loose line and brings *adver-* up to fill in some of the white space. Now do the same for the line that reads *once-in-a-lifetime* by hyphenating *opportunity* in the line below it.

Scroll to the end of the article.

Click an insertion point between the *r* and *t* of *opportunity* in the last line and type a hyphen.

There, you have your first article formatted and in place. But you still have some space at the bottom of the first column. In laying out your page, you may find that your articles and illustrations do not always fit exactly on one page. For instance, let's say that in laying out the front page of your newsletter, you are disappointed to find that you don't have room for an in-depth article on the continuing growth in personal income. But you have this small amount of space at the bottom of the first column. So you decide to use what's known in the newspaper trade as a "teaser"—a brief synopsis of something the reader will find on an inside page. You already have the chart you are going to use with the article, so you decide to use it on the front page instead. Paste it in from the Scrapbook now and add a line telling the reader where to find the story.

> Choose Scrapbook from the Apple menu, scroll until the chart is in the Scrapbook window, choose Copy from the Edit menu, and click the Scrapbook close box.
>
> Scroll to the beginning of the house-buying article and click the insertion point on the left side of the first line of the headline *BUYING A HOUSE IS NO LONGER.*
>
> Press Return, then choose Paste from the Edit menu.
>
> Press Return and click anywhere in the blank line beneath the chart.
>
> Choose Formats... from the Character menu, click 9 in the Font Size list box, and click OK.
>
> Type the caption *Personal income up: See Page 4.*

You are now at the bottom of the first column and ready to set up the second column. As mentioned earlier, the second column will contain the first part of the text for the house-buying article, the house illustration, and the text for the stock-market article. First, you need to tell Word to start a new column.

> Click on the left end of the first line of the headline *BUYING A HOUSE IS NO LONGER.*
>
> Choose Division Layout... from the Document menu, click the Column button in the Break box, and click OK.

Now, as we mentioned earlier in this chapter, you need to make adjustments to accommodate the masthead in the widened first column. By adding some vertical space, you will prevent the top of the second column from being printed across the masthead.

> Press Return eight times.

Now change the right indent to widen the text to two columns.

> Scroll to the bottom of the document, then hold down the Shift key and click anywhere to the right of the last line to highlight the rest of the document.
>
> Drag the right indent marker to the 4⅞-inch mark on the ruler.

Again, you need to make the headline for the house-buying article look more like a headline by increasing its size.

> Scroll to the top of the house-buying article.
>
> Select both lines of the headline.

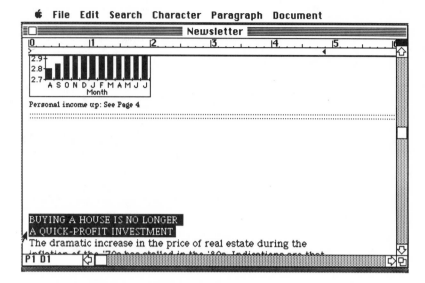

> Choose Formats… from the Character menu, click 18 in the Font
> Size list box, and click OK.

Like the investment article, the house-buying article should have
first-line indents and should be justified.

> Double-click in the selection bar to the left of the house-buying
> article to select the entire paragraph.
>
> Choose Formats… from the Paragraph menu, type *0.25* in the First
> Line text box, click the Justified button, and click OK.

Now you need to determine where to divide the text of the article so
that the text and the table wrap around the house illustration but don't
extend below the bottom of the illustration. This is normally a trial-
and-error operation, but we've already gone through the trials and
made the errors for you. Since you don't want to cut the paragraph
marker while making adjustments—the paragraph marker holds the
formatting—this process will be a lot easier if you can see the paragraph markers.

> Choose Show ¶ from the Edit menu.
>
> Click an insertion point at the left end of the line that starts with
> *than the rise in home prices.*
>
> Hold down the Shift key and click between the final period of the
> paragraph and the paragraph marker.
>
> Choose Cut from the Edit menu.

Scroll to the bottom of the document and click an insertion point at the left end of the final division mark.

Choose Paste from the Edit menu and press Return.

Scroll back up the document until the full table is in the window.

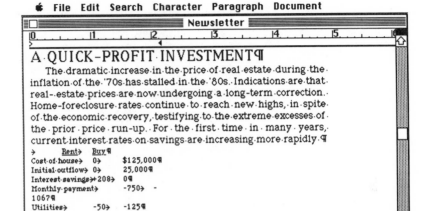

Notice that the final line in your shortened paragraph is not justified. Word does not justify the final line in a paragraph—and you wouldn't want it to. If your final line contained only a couple of short words, justifying might add too much unsightly white space between those few words. The last line in the paragraph is only a few spaces short of being a full line, so we fudged a bit and inserted an extra space between three evenly spaced pairs of words.

Add a space before *interest, savings,* and *rapidly.*

Now let's move the table to the end of the document.

Select the entire table (including the ending paragraph mark) and choose Cut from the Edit menu.

Scroll to the bottom of the document, click the insertion point at the left end of the division mark, and choose Paste from the Edit menu.

Scroll back to the start of the stock market article and click on the left end of the heading *Stock Market Challenges Record Highs* and press Return.

Here's where you insert the house illustration.

Choose Scrapbook from the Apple menu.

Scroll until the house illustration is in the Scrapbook window, choose Copy from the Edit menu, and click the Scrapbook close box.

Choose Paste from the Edit menu and press Return.

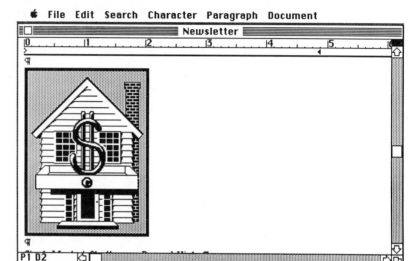

That is all you need to do to the house-buying article for right now. You now need to format the final article, starting with the headline.

Select the headline for the stock-market article.

Choose Formats... from the Character menu, click 18 in the Font Size list box, click Underline in the Style box, and click OK.

Scroll down to the beginning of the stock-market article, click an insertion point on the left end of the first line of the article, and press Return.

Double-click in the selection bar anywhere on the left side of the first paragraph of the article.

Adjust the right indent so that you have enough room to insert the graphic of the bull.

Drag the right indent marker in the ruler to 3¼ inches.

The space for the bull is four lines high and the last part of the article wraps around underneath the graphic, so you need to make an adjustment to the text to make a smooth break.

Click between the *n* and the *s* of the word *consecutive* in the fifth line, type a hyphen, and press Return.

Choose Formats... from the Paragraph menu, type *0* in the First Line Indent box, and click OK.

Now widen the bottom half of the stock-market article to the full two-column width and add some space to allow for a page number at the bottom of the page.

Double-click in the selection bar anywhere on the left side of the final eight lines of the stock-market article.

Drag the right indent marker to 4⅞ inches.

Click on the right end of the final line in the paragraph and press Return twice.

Click a tab marker at ¾ inch on the ruler.

Choose Bold from the Character menu.

Press Tab, then type *Page page* and press Command-Backspace to use the Standard Glossary automatic page-numbering feature.

That brings us to the bottom of the second column. The third and final column consists of only three elements: the last part of the house-buying article, the renting versus buying table, and the graphic of the bull. First you need to tell Word to start a new column.

Click on the left end of the line *than the rise in home* and press Command-Enter.

Now, make room for the masthead and the first part of the house-buying article, just as you did at the start of the second column.

Press Return 18 times.

Next, format the table for three columns aligned on where the decimal point would be if the figures included cents.

Select the entire table.

Drag the right indent marker to 2¼ inches on the ruler.

Choose Formats... from the Character menu, click 9 in the Font Size list box, and click OK.

Choose Tabs... from the Paragraph menu, click the Decimal button in the Alignment box, click at 1⁹⁄₁₆ inches on the ruler, click at 2 inches on the ruler, then click OK.

Notice that you didn't need to select each tab column to set the tabs for the table. You can just choose the Tabs... command and set a new tab mark for each stop. To complete the formatting of the table, underline the column headings.

> Click in the selection bar to the left of the line that contains the table headings *Rent* and *Buy*.
>
> Choose Underline from the Character menu.

Let's assume your layout can't accommodate the full house-buying article and you need to put the rest of the article on an inside page. You can add a little extra space at the point where the portion of the article that fits on the front page ends and type a line that tells the reader where to find the rest of the story.

> Click on the right end of the final line of the table and press Return twice.
>
> Choose Centered from the Paragraph menu.
>
> Type *Continued on Page 2*.

All that remains is to insert the bull illustration.

> Click on the left end of the final division mark and press Return four times.
>
> Choose Scrapbook from the Apple menu, scroll until the bull appears in the Scrapbook window, choose Copy from the Edit menu, and click the Scrapbook close box.
>
> Choose Paste from the Edit menu.
>
> Select the bull graphic by clicking anywhere on it, then choose Right from the Paragraph menu.

You might want to print one more test copy to check the vertical spacing. If lines of text or text and graphics appear too close together, you can increase or decrease the point size of a blank line above the problem area. Just select the paragraph mark for the blank line and then choose a larger or smaller font size by using Formats... from the Character menu. When you're satisfied with the result, print the number of copies you need.

> Choose Print... from the File menu, type the number of copies you need in the Copies text box, and click OK.

There, you're done with a highly professional, efficiently executed, state-of-the-art newsletter.

In the next chapter, we take multiple-column formatting another step by printing a business form on the LaserWriter.

12 A business form

Newsletters and reports aren't the only types of document that can benefit from Word's advanced formatting features. You can also create your own specially designed business forms using Word's column and tab formatting, as you'll see from the project in this chapter.

Creating your own business forms rather than buying preprinted forms from an office-supply store gives you forms that are customized to your own needs, not someone else's idea of what your needs might be. What's more, as your needs change, so can your forms, and you won't be saddled with a stockroom full of forms you can't use.

An attractive form with the name of your business across the top can also enhance your firm's image and serve as the starting point for a computerized information system. You can transfer the information from your business forms to a database management program, such as Microsoft File, then use the information in any number of ways, including as a mailing list, as you saw in Chapter 9.

For the project in this chapter, let's suppose you have a real-estate firm and you need an information form that your agents can take with them when they visit properties for sale. You could print these forms on a dot-matrix or fully formed character printer, but, since they will be seen, and perhaps used, by clients and other real-estate firms, you decide to print them on a LaserWriter for the highest quality. The form is shown in its finished version in Figure 12-1.

Eventually, the information from these forms will be used to create advertisements, statistical studies, and an on-line listing service. For instance, your agents will use the form to gather information about the homes, and may even include photographs that will later be digitized for storage in your computer (we used a digitizer in the project

Smith & Thomas Realty, Inc.

12674 Mountain View Road,   Denver, Colorado 84963

Home Information Form

Name of owner_____Phone (Bus.)_____(Res.)_____
Address_____
City_____State_____Zip_____

Price_____ Lot size_____X_____ Garage_____
No. of rooms_____ Age_____ Fireplace_____
Bedrooms_____ Square feet_____ Pool_____
Bathrooms_____ No. of stories_____ Spa_____

Condition_____ Dishwasher_____ Patio_____
Roof_____ Disposal_____ Porch_____
Siding_____ Refrigerator_____ Insulation_____
Style/type_____ Oven/range_____ Solar_____

Electric 100 amp____200 amp____ Heating_____ A/C_____
Utility costs: Gas_____ Electricity_____ Water_____
Sewer_____ Cable TV_____ Taxes_____

Schools: Elementary_____ Junior high_____ High_____
Public transportation_____ Fire_____ Hospital_____

Dimensions of rooms (feet and inches)

Carpets Drapes

					Financing Information
___	___	Living room:	___X___		Balance of 1st_____
___	___	Kitchen:	___X___		Name of lender_____
___	___	Family room:	___X___		Percentage rate_____Assumable_____
___	___	Bedroom 1:	___X___		Monthly payments_____
___	___	Bedroom 2:	___X___		Number of years remaining on loan_____
___	___	Bedroom 3	___X___		Balance of 2nd_____
___	___	Bedroom 4:	___X___		Name of lender_____
___	___	Bedroom 5:	___X___		Percentage rate_____Assumable_____
___	___	Bathroom 1:	___X___		Monthly payment_____
___	___	Bathroom 2:	___X___		Number of years remaining on loan_____
___	___	Bathroom 3:	___X___		Balance of 3rd_____
___	___	Dining room:	___X___		Name of lender_____
___	___	Extra room:	___X___		Percentage rate_____Assumable_____
___	___	Utility room:	___X___		Monthly payments_____
					Number of years remaining on loan_____

Remarks:_____
_____
_____
_____
_____

Figure 12-1. A property listing form

in Chapter 13). The information will be entered into your database management program to form the basis for a listing service. Since Word and File are completely compatible and File can store graphics, such as digitized photos, File is a good choice for the database program. The information stored in your Macintosh could then be used in a print-merge operation to produce a listing of only those homes a prospective buyer is interested in viewing: A customer interested in a three-bedroom house with a fireplace and pool for under $150,000 could get a listing of homes with only those specifications.

Planning the Form

Since you're looking for specific information in specific categories, it's a good idea to organize the form so that similar kinds of information are grouped together in descending order of importance, as shown in the diagram of the form in Figure 12-2. For instance, below the firm's letterhead and the title of the form, it's logical to have information about the location and owner of the property. Next, you want the information that tells prospective buyers what they are getting and for what price. Then, you want space for financing information and, since not even your customized form can cover all the specifics, space for comments about special features and conditions.

You can use tabs to separate items in the section for features of the property, since all of that information will appear on a series of evenly spaced lines. But the two sections below are discrete sections, each

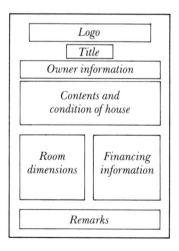

Figure 12-2. A basic layout for the home information form

with its own line-spacing requirements. Tabs won't work for separating them, so you need to put them in two columns that you can format independently.

Now that you know what you want on the form, we'll show you how to create it.

Creating the Form

Part of the form is in two columns and part in one column. It's difficult to switch back and forth between single- and multiple-column formats in Word, but you can format the entire form for two columns, then simply overlap one column into the other to create a single column where necessary. To start, you need to choose a two-column format for the entire form with the Division Layout... command from the Document menu.

> Insert a data disk and your Word Working Master disk on which the LaserWriter is installed, double-click on the Word Working Master disk icon if the Word disk window isn't already open, and then double-click on the Word program icon to open a new document.
>
> Choose the Division Layout... command from the Document menu.
>
> Type 2 in the Number of Columns text box.
>
> Type 0 in the Column Spacing text box.
>
> Click the Column button in the Break box.
>
> Click the OK button.

Setting the column spacing to zero removes the space between columns, making it possible for text to go from one column to the other without a gap. We'll use a column break to make the printer start the second column when it gets to the bottom of the first.

Now, set the page margins at ½ inch with the Page Setup... command from the File menu.

> Choose the Page Setup... command from the File menu.
>
> Type 0.5 in each of the four Margins text boxes (Top, Bottom, Left, and Right), and click OK.

The two-column format isn't actually used until later in the form, so you need to adjust the format to create a single column for the top part. You do that with the ruler.

> Click an insertion point to the left of the division marker (the pair of dotted lines).
>
> Choose the Show Ruler command from the Edit menu or press Command-R to display the ruler.

As you may remember from Chapter 3, the small black triangle at 3¾ inches on the ruler is the right indent marker, marking the right side of the first column. But you want the right indent at 7½ inches for the first part of the form so that it will be treated as though it were formatted as single-column. You need to reposition the marker where you want the right side of your text to be.

> Use the right horizontal scroll arrow to scroll right on the ruler, bringing the portion of the ruler between 7 and 8 inches into view.
>
> Drag the right indent triangle to the 7½-inch mark on the ruler.

You've finished with the ruler for now, but you can leave the ruler visible on the screen, since you'll use it again later.

Creating a Letterhead

You can create a simple, yet attractive letterhead for the form in Word by using some of the font styles available from the Character menu. You don't even have to change fonts. For example, the letterhead shown in Figure 12-1 is in the default font, New York, enhanced by choosing the Outline, Underline, and Superscript commands from the Character menu and by increasing the point size of the first letter of each word. Since you are now an advanced Word user, we'll show you how to choose these commands with the keyboard, instead of the mouse. First, center the text you're going to type with Command-Shift-C and type the name of the firm. Then, increase the point size of the first letter of each word to 36 points using Command-Shift-> and choose Outline with Command-Shift-D.

> Press Command-Shift-C.
>
> Type the following:
>
> *Smith & Thomas Realty, Inc.*[Return]
>
> Select the *S* of *Smith* and press Command-Shift-D.
>
> With the *S* still selected, press Command-Shift-> four times.

If you want to check and make sure the *S* is 36-point now, you can choose the Character Formats... command by pressing Command-D and looking at the Font Size text box. You can copy this new character formatting (outline style and 36-point size) to the first letters of the other words in the letterhead by using Option-Command and click, as you learned in Chapter 4.

> Select the ampersand, press Option-Command, then click on the S of *Smith*.
>
> Repeat the same procedure for the *T* of *Thomas, R* of *Realty,* and *I* of *Inc.*

Now go ahead and format the other characters of the letterhead, one word at a time. Choose Underline with Command-Shift-U and Superscript with Command-Shift-=.

> Select *mith* and press Command-Shift-D to choose Outline, Command-Shift-U to choose Underline, and Command-Shift-= to choose Superscript, then press Command-Shift-> twice to increase the font size to 18 points.
>
> Individually select the remainders of each of the other words in the letterhead (including punctuation), then hold down Option-Command and click on *mith.*

Next, type the address below the company name and add some extra space between the letterhead and the point where you'll type the name of the form. We picked 12-point Times as the font for the address, but you could choose another font.

> Click on the left side of the division marker and press Return.
>
> Press Command-D to choose the Formats... command from the Character menu.
>
> Click on Times in the Font Names list box and click OK.
>
> Type the following:
>
> *12674 Mountain View Road, Denver, Colorado 84963*[Return] [Return][Return]

Now that you have created an attractive letterhead, why not save it in a glossary for use on letters and other forms? Use the procedure for creating a glossary that you learned in Chapter 4.

> Select the letterhead.
>
> Press Command-C to choose the Copy command from the Edit menu.
>
> Choose the Show Glossary... command from the Edit menu.
>
> Type a glossary name, such as *ST,* in the Name in Glossary text box, then press Command-V to choose Paste from the Edit menu.
>
> Click the close box to save the glossary.

The next time you want to use the letterhead, all you need to do is select where you want the letterhead to appear, type *ST* or whatever other glossary name you chose, then press Command-Backspace.

Adding a Title and the Owner Information

For the title of the form, we picked 14-point Helvetica in boldface and underlined.

> Press Command-D to choose the Formats... command from the Character menu.
>
> Click Helvetica in the Font Name list box, click 14 in the Font Size list box, click both Bold and Underline in the Style box, and click OK.
>
> Type the following:
>
> *Home Information Form*[Return][Return][Return]

In addition to increasing or decreasing the font size of characters in your text, you can also increase or decrease the size of line spaces (the places where you pressed the Return key). To adjust the spacing between the title of the form and the point where you'll create the owner information categories, select the blank lines and decrease their size.

> Select the two blank lines after the title.
>
> Press Command-Shift-< to decrease the font size from 14 points to 12 points.

The rest of the form is left aligned, or flush left, so now you need to change the paragraph alignment selection from centered to left aligned. While you're making this adjustment, you might as well return the text to 14-point Helvetica plain. You can choose the Plain command from the Character menu with the keyboard by pressing Command-Shift-Spacebar.

> Choose the Left command from the Paragraph menu.
>
> Press Command-Shift-> to increase the font size from 12 to 14 points.
>
> Press Command-Shift-Spacebar to remove all font style options.

Much of this form or any form is fill-in blanks. To align these blanks in neat columns, you want to use tabs, similar to the tabs you enter on a typewriter. There are several ways of creating the lines for the blanks. You could use the underscore character on the keyboard, but this could take a long time and result in lines with a slightly ragged appearance. You could also type spaces, then choose underlining from the

Character menu. But this approach has the same drawbacks as using underscores. Instead, you can use Word's tab character feature and let Word create smooth, even blanks for you. A tab character, called a leader, is a character that can be repeated as many times as is necessary to fill the area between tab fields. As you can see in the Tabs dialog box displayed when you choose the Tabs... command from the Paragraph menu, Word offers you several kinds of tab leaders: blank space, a dotted line, a dashed line, and a solid underline. Blank space is the default choice. But the solid underline will work well for the home information form.

Press Command-T to choose the Tabs... command from the Paragraph menu.

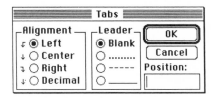

Click the solid underline button in the Leader list box.

Click tab arrows at 4, 6⅟₁₆, and 7½ inches on the ruler, then click OK.

Through experimentation, we found 4 and 6⅟₁₆ inches to be good tab stops for the home information form, since they allow enough room for the text needed, plus adequate space for a blank, in each tab column. The last tab stop is needed so that the last tab column has underlines, too. Go ahead and type the first field name and press Tab.

Type the following:

Name of owner[Tab]

You are rewarded with a nice, solid underline from the end of the word *owner* to the place where you'll type the next field name. Finish the first line now.

Type the following:

Phone (Bus.)[Tab]*(Res.)*[Tab][Return]

The words *(Bus.)* and *(Res.)* need to be in a smaller point size, so go back now and change them.

Select *(Bus.),* choose Formats... from the Character menu, click 10 in the Font Size list box, and click OK.

Repeat the same procedure for *(Res.).*

The second line of the owner information section has only one field name, Address. But you still need to press Tab three times so the line will be the same length as the others in this section. The third line is similar to the first, with three field names.

Type the following:

Address[Tab][Tab][Tab][Return]

City[Tab]*State*[Tab]*Zip*[Tab][Return][Return]

Pressing Return twice after the third line creates a little extra space between the owner information section and the section for the condition and description of the property.

Creating the Condition and Description Section

The fields in the condition and description section aren't the same as those in the owner section, so you need to adjust the tabs. After experimenting with different tab column widths, we found that tabs at 2⅜, 4¾, and 7½ inches create adequate space for each field in each column. Change the first two tab stops by dragging the tab arrows to their new positions on the ruler. But you don't want the underline leader to run into the following field name, so add narrow columns with blank leaders at 2½ and 4⅞ inches, to add space between the three columns of information.

On the ruler, drag the leftmost tab arrow from 4 to 2⅜ inches and the middle tab arrow from 6¹⁄₁₆ to 4¾ inches.

Click new tab stops at 2½ and 4⅞ inches. (There's no need to specify blank leaders, because that's the default option.)

With the new tabs in place, you can type the first line of this new section. Remember, though, that you need to press Tab twice between each field name because of the narrow blank columns.

Type the following:

Price[Tab][Tab]*Lot size*[Tab][Tab]*Garage*[Tab][Tab][Return]

To add the capital *X* in the second field, you need to add a new tab stop with underline leader at 4⅛ inches on the ruler.

> Click an insertion point immediately after *Lot size.*
>
> Press Command-T to choose the Tabs... command from the Paragraph menu.
>
> Click a new tab stop at 4⅛ inches on the ruler.
>
> Click the solid underline button in the Leader list box, then click OK.
>
> Press Tab and type *X.*
>
> Click an insertion point at the beginning of the second line.

Now you need to delete the tab stop at 4⅛ inches so that you don't have to type an extra tab on the rest of the lines.

> Select the tab arrow at 4⅛ inches and drag it down into the text area to delete it.

Type the rest of the section, adding one extra blank line each after *Spa, Solar, Taxes,* and *Hospital.*

> Type the following:
>
> *No. of rooms*[Tab][Tab]*Age*[Tab][Tab]*Fireplace*[Tab][Return]
>
> *Bedrooms*[Tab][Tab]*Square feet*[Tab][Tab]*Pool*[Tab][Return]
>
> *Bathrooms*[Tab][Tab]*No. of stories*[Tab][Tab]*Spa*[Tab] [Return][Return]
>
> *Condition*[Tab][Tab]*Dishwasher*[Tab][Tab]*Patio*[Tab][Return]
>
> *Roof*[Tab][Tab]*Disposal*[Tab][Tab]*Porch*[Tab][Return]
>
> *Siding*[Tab][Tab]*Refrigerator*[Tab][Tab]*Insulation*[Tab][Return]
>
> *Style/type*[Tab][Tab]*Oven/range*[Tab][Tab]*Solar*[Tab] [Return][Return]
>
> *Electric: 100 amp*[Tab][Tab]*Heating*[Tab][Tab]*A/C*[Tab][Return]
>
> *Utility costs: Gas*[Tab][Tab]*Electricity*[Tab][Tab]*Water*[Tab][Return]
>
> *Sewer*[Tab][Tab]*Cable TV*[Tab][Tab]*Taxes*[Tab][Return][Return]
>
> *Schools: Elementary*[Tab][Tab]*Junior high*[Tab][Tab]*High*[Tab] [Return]
>
> *Public transportation*[Tab][Tab]*Fire*[Tab][Tab]*Hospital*[Tab] [Return][Return]

To add the *200 amp* field name beside *Electric,* use the same procedure you used in adding the *X* in the Lot size field.

> Click an insertion point immediately after *100 amp.*
>
> Press Command-T to choose the Tabs... command from the Paragraph menu.
>
> Click a new tab stop at 1⁹⁄₁₆ inches on the ruler.
>
> Click the solid underline button in the Leader list box, then click OK.
>
> Press Tab and type *200 amp.*

You can group subdivisions of the same categories of fields by their font sizes.

> Select *100 amp,* choose Formats... from the Character menu, click 10 in the Font Size list box, and click OK.
>
> Use the same procedure for *200 amp, Gas, Electricity, Water, Sewer, Cable TV, Elementary, Junior high,* and *High.*

Creating the Room-Dimensions Section

With the room-dimensions section, the form becomes a two-column format for which the two-column Division Layout was selected at the start of the project. Since you've already selected a two-column layout, there's little more you need to do now for the room-dimensions section. But we'll demonstrate a different technique for creating the underlined blanks.

First, enter the name of the section in 12-point underlined type, followed by a small amount of space. Set tabs for the subheadings *Carpets* and *Drapes* (and the columns under them), then type the subheading names in a smaller point size.

> Click on the left side of the division mark.
>
> Type the following:
>
> *Dimensions of rooms (feet and inches)*[Return][Return]
>
> Select the section title you just typed and press Command-Shift-U to choose Underline from the Character menu.
>
> Drag the existing tab arrows at 2⅜, 2½, 4¾, and 4⅞ inches down into the text area to delete them.

By experimenting, we found 7-point to be the right size for both the blank line space and the subheading, and ⅜, ¹³⁄₁₆, and 2 inches to be the correct tabs for the blank columns that will separate the information fields.

Click tab arrows at ⅜, ¹³⁄₁₆, and 2 inches on the ruler.

Type the following:

Carpets[Tab]*Drapes*[Return]

Select both the blank line after the section title and the line *Carpets Drapes.*

Choose Formats... from the Character menu and type 7 in the Font size text box.

Change the font size back to 12 points.

Now it's time to enter the room descriptions and add keyboard underscores (Shift-hyphen) for the fill-in blanks. Unfortunately, there's only one way to create an underscored *X* in this section: manually, with the keyboard.

Click an insertion point to the left of the division mark.

Type the following:

[Shift-hyphen][Shift-hyphen][Shift-hyphen][Tab][Shift-hyphen] [Shift-hyphen][Shift-hyphen][Tab]*Living room:*[Tab]

Choose Underline from the Character menu and type 16 spaces followed by *X* followed by 16 more spaces. Then press Return.

Choose Plain text from the Character menu.

Use the same procedure to enter the following:

Kitchen:

Family room:

Bedroom 1:

Bedroom 2:

Bedroom 3:

Bedroom 4:

Bedroom 5:

Bathroom 1:

Bathroom 2:

Bathroom 3:

Dining room:

Extra room:

Utility room:

Creating the Remarks Section

You add the remarks section that goes at the bottom of the form next. Since there are no tab columns, you can remove all tab arrows except the one at 7½ inches.

Press Return.

Remove all tab arrows from the ruler (except the one at 7½ inches) by dragging them down into the text area.

Now all you have to do is type the name of the section, then press Tab and Return five times to complete the section.

Type the following:

Remarks:[Tab][Return][Tab][Return][Tab][Return][Tab][Return] [Tab][Return]

Creating the Financing Information Section

The financing information section is the only part of the form that is printed in the second column. To start, add a page-break mark and add some blank lines to place the financing information text approximately where you want it on the page. Don't worry if it doesn't come out exactly right the first time you print it; you can always go back and adjust the line spacing by increasing or decreasing the font size of blank lines.

Press Command-Enter at the end of the remarks section to enter a column break.

Press Command-D to choose the Formats... command from the Character menu, click 14 in the Font size list box, then click OK.

There is only one column in most of the lines in this section. So, set up a tab stop at 3¾ inches and use the solid underline leader again.

Press Command-T to choose the Tabs... command from the Paragraph menu.

Click a tab arrow at 3¾ inches, click the solid underline button in the Leaders list box, then click OK.

Press Return 29 times to move the insertion point from the top of the page to where you want the financing section to appear.

Type the following:

Balance of 1st[Tab][Return]

Name of lender[Tab][Return]

Percentage rate[Tab][Return]

Monthly payments[Tab][Return]

Number of years remaining on loan[Tab][Return]

Balance of 2nd[Tab][Return]

Name of lender[Tab][Return]

Percentage rate[Tab][Return]

Monthly payments[Tab][Return]

Number of years remaining on loan[Tab][Return]
Balance of 3rd[Tab][Return]
Name of lender[Tab][Return]
Percentage rate[Tab][Return]
Monthly payments[Tab][Return]
Number of years remaining on loan[Tab][Return]

To insert the Assumable blank on the Percentage rate lines, use the same procedure you used for the Lot size and 200 amp blanks.

Click an insertion point immediately after the first *Percentage rate*.

Press Command-T to choose the Tabs… command from the Paragraph menu.

Click a new tab stop at 2¼ inches on the ruler.

Click the solid underline button in the Leader list box, then click OK.

Press Tab and type *Assumable.*

Use the same procedure to insert *Assumable* after each of the other two occurrences of *Percentage rate.*

The *st, nd,* and *rd* of *1st, 2nd,* and *3rd* would look better in superscript. But simply choosing Superscript for them would add a slight amount of vertical space between lines. To get around this problem, you can reduce their font sizes slightly, in addition to making them superscript.

Select the *st* of *1st.*

Press Command-Shift-< twice to reduce the font size to 9 points.

Press Command-Shift-= to choose Superscript from the Character menu.

Do the same thing to *nd* and *rd.*

Now you're ready to print. Your first few printouts will test the placement of the second column, so expect to make minor adjustments of vertical spacing by increasing or decreasing the font size of blank lines. Not all fonts of the same point size are exactly the same height, so you might try changing the font of the blank line to get even finer adjustment. Unfortunately, there is no easy way to adjust vertical spacing; it's largely a matter of trial and error.

Once you fine-tune your form, however, you'll have a document you can use again and again. Then you can turn to the final project of this book, a brochure for a resort community.

13 A brochure

The sample project in this chapter—a three-panel brochure that mixes graphics and text—demonstrates the professional look you can give your documents using Word's advanced formatting features and a top-of-the-line printer.

As we describe it in this chapter, the brochure project uses Word, a LaserWriter, Microsoft Chart, MacPaint, MacDraw, a video camera, and Koala's MacVision digitizer, a device that turns video pictures into images that can be stored by the Mac. Using Word with these hardware and software products enables you to do more with it, but you don't need them to use many of the formatting features described in this chapter. You'll get a lot out of this chapter whether or not you have the additional products mentioned.

As in previous chapters, we won't take the time here to fully describe how to use Chart, MacPaint, MacDraw, and the LaserWriter. If you're interested in these products, you can find out how to use them elsewhere. But we will describe those uses of these products that relate directly to Word.

For our sample project, let's suppose you have a small business in Idyllwild, a picturesque mountain resort village in Southern California. As a member of the Idyllwild Visitors Bureau, you have agreed to develop a brochure that can be passed out to tourists and mailed in response to requests for information. By pooling resources, you and other members of the visitors bureau come up with a Macintosh, a LaserWriter printer, Word, MacPaint, MacDraw, Chart, MacVision, and a video camera. You spend an evening designing the brochure shown in Figure 13-1, which features multiple-column formatting, scaled graphics, a chart, digitized photos, printing on both sides of the sheet, and the LaserWriter's Landscape paper orientation.

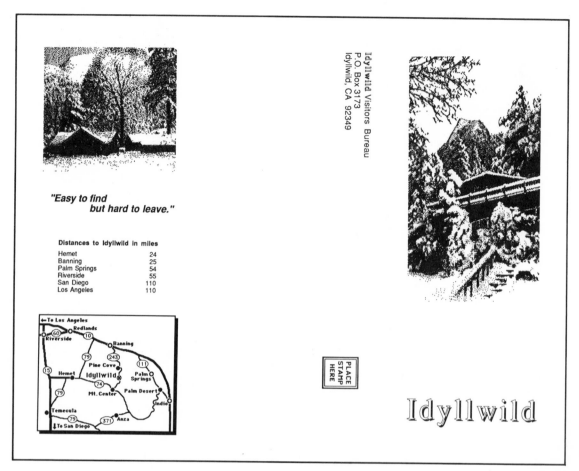

**"Easy to find
but hard to leave."**

Distances to Idyllwild in miles

Hemet	24
Banning	25
Palm Springs	54
Riverside	55
San Diego	110
Los Angeles	110

Idyllwild Visitors Bureau
P.O. Box 3173
Idyllwild, CA 92349

PLACE STAMP HERE

Idyllwild

continued

Figure 13-1. The completed
Idyllwild visitors brochure
(outside)

With a project this complex, you obviously need to start with a little advance planning. First, you need to design the brochure. Then, you need to find a few photographs that emphasize Idyllwild's woodsy surroundings and that are appropriate for digitizing. Next, you need to research and write the text (knowing you'll likely need to edit it to fit the layout later). To show how visitors can get to Idyllwild, you decide to draw a map in MacPaint. And, as a way of illustrating the mild climate Idyllwild is famous for, you want to create a temperature chart in Chart. Finally, you will use Word's powerful formatting features to transfer your design onto the screen and then to paper.

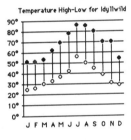

In a woodsy mountain valley just 2 1/2 hours from Los Angeles or San Diego, tucked in the towering peaks of the San Jacinto range, lies the rustic village of Idyllwild. Attracted by the natural beauty and pleasant pace of life, visitors can find artistic and intellectual nourishment in this unique retreat, remote from the hustle and bustle of the city.

Wilderness Activities

Nearly 275 miles of marked trails lead hikers, backpackers, and horseback riders into the high country and several wilderness campgrounds. Camping, fishing, and boating are features of local lakes. Tahquitz and Suicide Rocks are international favorites for rock climbers. Special areas have been prepared for winter cross-country skiing, snowshoeing, and sledding.

Climate

In this mile-high hideaway, the seasons change from snowy winter to verdant spring to balmy summer to bracing fall. In winter, average low temperatures are below freezing, while in summer, average highs are in the 80s.

Temperature High-Low for Idyllwild

90°
80°
70°
60°
50°
40°
30°
20°
10°
0°
    J F M A M J J A S O N D

Natural Setting

Traveling the Palms to Pines Highway from Palm Desert gives you a fascinating view of changing life zones, from desert floor, chaparral, grassland, and mountain meadows, to wooded mountain slopes. At Idyllwild Village, you find a delightful blend of oak, pine, fir, and the beautiful incense cedar.

You can drive to several points of interest in the area. From Inspiration Point, you see a panoramic view of the mountains and of San Jacinto Valley. One of the world's tallest arched masonry dams, Hemet Dam, built from 1891 to 1895, has been called, "the great engineering wonder of the nineteenth century." Tahquitz Rock is a sheer-walled, granite monolith that towers over the area.

An interesting way to visit "the Hill," as Idyllwild is known by local residents, is to take the Palm Springs Aerial Tramway from Palm Springs to the Mountain Station at Long Valley and hike the 8 miles by trail to the Village.

The Idyllwild County Park Visitor Center has a natural history museum, with environmental and interpretive programs, and a naturalist on duty. Books are available on natural history and native plants. The park has 200 acres of hiking trails, a campground, and picnic areas. Here and at nearby Indian Relic Park, you'll also find ancient pictographs and mortar holes that suggest the early Cahuilla Indians gathered and ground acorns and pine nuts in the valley.

Wildlife and Plants

There are no dangerous animals in the area. Gray squirrels and raccoons abound.

There are coyotes, deer, nuthatches, hummingbirds and flickers, and an occasional bald eagle. Five varieties of birds are found in the San Jacintos in numbers larger than anywhere else in North America: mountain quail, spotted owl, Lawrence's goldfinch, Williamson's sapsucker, and white-headed woodpecker.

Native plants and wildflowers decorate the surrounding area. Idyllwild was once called Strawberry Valley because of wild strawberries that grew along the riverbanks. You'll also find an assortment of wild lilacs, purple-flower Ajuga, manzanita, native lupine, honeysuckle, holly, daisies, and snowberries.

Culture

Nestled in the woods at the edge of town, ISOMATA, the Idyllwild School of Music and the Arts, provides harmonious surroundings for visual and performing arts. The school presents gallery exhibits, concerts, theater productions, dance performances, seminars, and summer workshops.

Several antique shops carry fine selections, and the many art galleries feature the work of local artists. There is a movie theatre and a very active summer softball league. The fifteen local restaurants offer an assortment of menus that vary from down-home to gourmet.

Holiday festivities include: Memorial Day Western Days and American Legion celebration; Spring Festival and pancake breakfast; July 4th parade, street games, and entertainment; Labor Day yard sales; and Thanksgiving Harvest Festival of handmade arts and crafts.

Figure 13-1 (inside)

Designing the Brochure

There are practical considerations to designing any page layout. For instance, with the Idyllwild brochure, the budget available and the way you expect the brochure to be used are two prime considerations. You don't want an expensive multi-page booklet; you want something that can simply be stapled, stamped, and mailed. Using a three-column format and a Landscape page orientation will allow you to fold an 8½- by 11-inch sheet of paper twice to make a convenient-size mailer with three columns inside and three outside, as shown in Figure 13-2.

Figure 13-2. The Idyllwild brochure, folded twice to mailer size

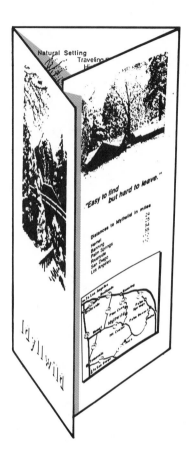

You pride yourself on having an eye for design, so you take the time to lay out the inside of the brochure with the text artistically contoured around the illustrations. To accomplish this effect, you'll set up the page for six columns instead of three. The three additional columns, which will alternate with the columns containing text, will each contain one illustration. Then, one at a time, you'll specify the beginning and end of each line that wraps around the illustrations, overlapping the text and illustration columns where necessary.

For the outside of the brochure, you plan a cover illustration in one column, a place for an address label, stamp, and return address in the middle column, and another illustration, some text, and a map in the third column.

Having designed the brochure, you map out the steps needed to create it. First, you'll create all of the illustrations. Then, you'll create the text and insert the illustrations for the inside of the brochure. Next, you'll create the illustrations and text for the outside. Finally, you'll print the brochure. Each brochure will need three printing passes: one pass to print the inside on one side of each sheet, a second to print most of the outside on the reverse side of each sheet, and a third to print the return address.

Preparing the Illustrations

As mentioned earlier, we created all the illustrations for the Idyllwild brochure by using a video camera, a digitizer, MacPaint, MacDraw, and Chart. If you don't have these items, you can approximate the illustrations using any graphics program. But it's important that your graphics are fairly close to the size shown in Figure 13-3 so they fit properly. (Illustrations for the outside are slightly larger than they'll appear because the outside will be reduced during printing.) You can trace the illustrations in Figure 13-3 using one of the two methods described in Chapter 10.

We used Koala's MacVision digitizer and software with a video camera and video recorder to put the images of the pine bough, raccoon, squirrel, and two snow scenes on disk. But there are many other digitizers on the market, including Magic by New Image Technology, Inc., Micro-Imager from Servidyne Systems, Inc., and ThunderScan from Thunderware, Inc. Most digitizers work in pretty much the same way. An optic device scans an object or photograph, reading it as if it were a series of white or black pixels. The scanned, or digitized, image is then stored as a file on disk. With MacVision, as with most digitizers for the Mac, you can create a MacPaint file.

Contouring the text around the left side of a graphic, as shown in Figure 13-1, is possible only if the graphic is inserted from MacDraw. If you try to use a MacPaint graphic, you'll find that the lines of text you are trying to overlap are cut off in a straight vertical line when you print the document. Here's why:

Programs for the Mac can use either of two modes to paste graphics into the Clipboard: OR or COPY. You can think of the OR mode as being "transparent" and the COPY mode as being "opaque." MacPaint uses the opaque mode for those selections copied or cut to the Clipboard using the lasso or rectangle tools. Word uses its own selection rectangle to retrieve graphics from the Clipboard (which you can see when you select the graphic by clicking on it, as we demonstrated in

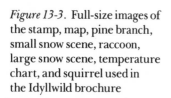

Figure 13-3. Full-size images of
the stamp, map, pine branch,
small snow scene, raccoon,
large snow scene, temperature
chart, and squirrel used in
the Idyllwild brochure

continued

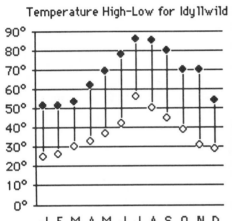

Temperature High-Low for Idyllwild

Figure 13-3 (continued)

Chapter 3). The edge of Word's graphic selection rectangle is the cut-off line you see on the printout. Word tells the Mac to construct an image of the printed page in memory a column at a time, moving from the left side of the page image to the right. When two columns overlap, if the Mac creates a column of text, then creates a graphic in the next column in part of the space occupied by the first column, a graphic copied from your graphics program in opaque mode will obscure the text in the first column. However, if the Mac creates the graphic in the first column and text in the next column, the graphic will be visible through the text, since text in Word can be thought of as always being in the transparent mode.

To correct this problem of graphics cutting off text, you need to paste the illustrations of the pine bough, raccoon, and squirrel from the scrapbook into MacDraw and then put them back in the Scrapbook before you paste them into Word. MacDraw places items in both the Clipboard and Scrapbook in transparent mode.

You also need to paste into MacDraw the chart you create in Chart, but for a different reason. When you copy a chart to the Clipboard from Chart, the size of the selection rectangle Word uses to retrieve it is the size of the Chart window, and not the size of the chart. Like Mac-Paint, Chart copies illustrations in opaque mode, meaning that extraneous white space around the chart could obscure text. Passing the chart through MacDraw so that it is pasted into Word in transparent mode corrects this problem.

Now let's get on with preparing the illustrations.

> Insert MacPaint or your graphics program disk in the internal drive, your data disk in the external drive, and start the Mac.
>
> Create your illustrations.
>
> One at a time, use Cut and Paste or Copy and Paste to transfer your illustrations into the Scrapbook.

Two of the graphics will need some additional manipulation. The large snow scene for the outside front cover is too large to copy in one piece. You'll need to copy it in two sections, if you want to recreate the brochure exactly as it's shown in this chapter. The best way to do this is to use what printers call a register mark, a small mark placed on the master copy just outside the area being reproduced that aids in aligning placement of images on the page. In MacPaint, register marks placed about an eighth of an inch from either side of the image of the snow scene, roughly midway between the top and bottom, can help you locate MacPaint's selection box so that you don't cut or copy the same row of pixels in both parts or skip a row of pixels while you are cutting or copying.

The second illustration that requires manipulating is the stamp graphic, which you should create in a normal orientation, then rotate 90 degrees to the right before copying it to the Scrapbook.

Quit the graphics program and copy the Scrapbook file from the graphics program disk to your data disk.

Eject your graphics program disk.

If you have Chart and you want to follow the project as closely as possible, you next need to create the temperature chart. If you don't have Chart, you can approximate the chart in any graphics program, but the steps may be slightly different.

Insert your Chart disk in the internal drive and restart the Mac.

Copy the Scrapbook file from your data disk to the Chart disk.

Double-click on the Chart icon.

For the brochure, you need to create a chart on the screen the size you want it to appear in the final brochure because, as we mentioned, Word uses the full screen as the graphic image.

Create your chart with Chart's default size settings.

After you've created the chart, you can adjust the dimensions.

Choose Select Chart from the Chart menu.

Drag the little black size boxes around until you have the chart the size you want it.

Now copy the chart to the Clipboard and then to the Scrapbook. When you copy the chart to the Clipboard from Chart, you are given the choice of copying it as it appears on the screen or copying it as it would appear on the printer. Select the option that copies it as it appears on the screen.

Choose Copy Chart... from the Edit menu.

Click the As Shown on Screen button in the Copy Chart to Clipboard dialog box and click OK.

Choose Scrapbook from the Apple menu, choose Paste from the Edit menu, and click the Scrapbook close box.

Quit the Chart program.

Copy the Scrapbook file to your data disk.

Eject the Chart disk.

Now, as explained earlier, you need to transfer the pine branch, the raccoon, and the squirrel illustrations through MacDraw so that you can contour text around them. Recall that you also need to transfer the temperature chart through MacDraw.

Insert your MacDraw disk in the internal drive and restart the Mac.

Copy the Scrapbook file from your data disk to the MacDraw disk.

Double-click on the MacDraw icon.

Choose Scrapbook from the Apple menu.

Scroll until the pine branch is visible in the Scrapbook window, choose Cut from the Edit menu, and click the Scrapbook close box.

Choose Paste from the Edit menu.

Click anywhere outside the graphic to deselect it, choose Select All from the Edit menu, and choose Cut from the Edit menu.

Choose Scrapbook from the Apple menu and choose Paste from the Edit menu.

Repeat this same procedure for the raccoon, squirrel, and chart illustrations.

When you have returned all of your graphics to the Scrapbook, you can quit MacDraw and open Word.

Click the Scrapbook close box.

Choose Quit from the File menu.

Copy the Scrapbook file back to your data disk.

Eject the MacDraw disk and insert your Word Working Master in the internal drive.

Restart the Mac.

Copy the Scrapbook file from your data disk to the Word Working Master disk.

Double-click on the Word icon to open Word with a new document window.

Creating the Inside of the Brochure

You'll be setting up the inside of the brochure in one file and the outside in another file. Because the inside is much more detailed, let's start with it.

First, you need to set up the margins and orientation for the entire page; we found ½-inch margins to work well for the brochure. You'll be making several test printings of the brochure at various stages. To make these test printings go more quickly, it's a good idea to turn off the LaserWriter's smoothing option, since smoothing takes a lot of time. You can turn on the smoothing option again just before the final printing.

> Choose Page Setup... from the File menu, type *0.5* in the Top, Bottom, Left, and Right text boxes, click the Landscape button beside Orientation, make sure there is no X in the Smoothing? check box, and click OK.

It's a good idea to type all of the text in 10-point Helvetica with justified margins so you get an idea how much of the text space you've filled at any point. You can reformat specific portions of the text, such as headings, for different font sizes and margins later.

> Choose Formats... from the Character menu, click Helvetica in the Font Name list box, click 10 in the Font Size list box, and click OK.
>
> Choose Justified from the Paragraph menu.
>
> Type in the following text:
>
> *In a woodsy mountain valley just 2½ hours from Los Angeles or San Diego, tucked in the towering peaks of the San Jacinto range, lies the rustic village of Idyllwild. Attracted by the natural beauty and pleasant pace of life, visitors can find artistic and intellectual nourishment in this unique retreat, remote from the hustle and bustle of the city.*[Return][Return]
>
> *Wilderness Activities*[Return]
>
> *Nearly 275 miles of marked trails lead hikers, backpackers, and horse-back riders into the high country and several wilderness campgrounds. Camping, fishing, and boating are features of local lakes. Tahquitz and Suicide Rocks are international favorites for rock climbers. Special areas have been prepared for winter cross-country skiing, snowshoeing, and sledding.*[Return][Return]
>
> *Climate*[Return]
>
> *In this mile-high hideaway, the seasons change from snowy winter to verdant spring to balmy summer to bracing fall. In winter, average low temperatures are below freezing, while in summer, average highs are in the 80s.*[Return][Return]
>
> *Natural Setting*[Return]
>
> *Traveling the Palms to Pines Highway from Palm Desert gives you a fascinating view of changing life zones, from desert floor, chaparral, grassland, and mountain meadows, to wooded mountain slopes. At Idyllwild Village, you find a delightful blend of oak, pine, fir, and the beautiful incense cedar.*[Return][Return]

You can drive to several points of interest in the area. From Inspiration Point, you see a panoramic view of the mountains and of San Jacinto Valley. One of the world's tallest arched masonry dams, Hemet Dam, built from 1891 to 1895, has been called "the great engineering wonder of the nineteenth century." Tahquitz Rock is a sheer-walled, granite monolith that towers over the area. [Return] [Return]

An interesting way to visit "the Hill," as Idyllwild is known by local residents, is to take the Palm Springs Aerial Tramway from Palm Springs to the Mountain Station at Long Valley and hike the 8 miles by trail to the Village. [Return][Return]

The Idyllwild County Park Visitor Center has a natural history museum, with environmental and interpretive programs, and a naturalist on duty. Books are available on natural history and native plants. The park has 200 acres of hiking trails, a campground, and picnic areas. Here and at nearby Indian Relic Park, you'll also find ancient pictographs and mortar holes that suggest the early Cahuilla Indians gathered and ground acorns and pine nuts in the valley. [Return][Return]

Wildlife and Plants[Return]

There are no dangerous animals in the area. Gray squirrels and raccoons abound. There are coyotes, deer, nuthatches, hummingbirds, and flickers, and an occasional bald eagle. Five varieties of birds are found in the San Jacintos in numbers larger than anywhere else in North America: mountain quail, spotted owl, Lawrence's goldfinch, Williamson's sapsucker, and white-headed woodpecker.[Return][Return]

Native plants and wildflowers decorate the surrounding area. Idyllwild was once called Strawberry Valley because of wild strawberries that grew along the riverbanks. You'll also find an assortment of wild lilacs, purple-flower Ajuga, manzanita, native lupine, honeysuckle, holly, daisies, and snowberries.[Return] [Return]

Culture[Return]

Nestled in the woods at the edge of town, ISOMATA, the Idyllwild School of Music and the Arts, provides harmonious surroundings for visual and performing arts. The school presents gallery exhibits, concerts, theater productions, dance performances, seminars, and summer workshops. [Return][Return]

Several antique shops carry fine selections, and the many art galleries feature the work of local artists. There is a movie theater and a very active summer softball league. The fifteen local restaurants offer an assortment of menus that vary from down-home to gourmet.[Return][Return]

Holiday festivities include: Memorial Day Western Days and American Legion celebration; Spring Festival and pancake breakfast; July 4th parade, street games, and entertainment; Labor Day yard sales; and Thanksgiving Harvest Festival of handmade arts and crafts.

Before you go to all the work of pasting in the graphics and wrapping the text around them, it's a good idea to print the document and proofread it. Nothing is more frustrating than spending half an hour readjusting a paragraph and then discovering you've made a spelling error that changes everything (this is the voice of experience).

Choose Save As... from the File menu, type *Brochure Text* in the Save Current Document As text box, and click Save.

Choose Print... from the File menu.

When you're confident that your document is error-free, you can begin formatting the text. The first thing you'll want to do is set up the page for six columns to accommodate the design.

Select Division Layout... from the Document menu, type *6* in the Number of Columns text box, type *0* in the Column Spacing text box, click Continuous in the Break box, and click OK.

Word arranges all of your text in one long, skinny column. Widen the text that will appear in the first column to the width it will be in the final printout. Later, you'll shift the second and third columns of text (actually, the third and fifth Word columns) to the right to get a wide enough space between the columns.

Choose Show Ruler from the Edit menu.

Hold down the Command key and click anywhere in the selection bar to select the entire document.

Drag the right indent marker out to 2⅝ inches and the first-line indent marker to ¼ inch.

Before you get fancy and wrap the text around the graphics, you should take care of the simple formatting for the text columns. At this point, you know that the first paragraph of text will wrap around the pine-branch graphic on its right. So, you want this paragraph to be left aligned, instead of justified. You might as well make that change now, since the extra spaces that Word adds to the lines to justify them might be confusing when you're trying to decide where to break the lines to wrap them around the graphic.

Click anywhere in the first paragraph and choose Left from the Paragraph menu.

Now format the headings for the first column.

Click in the selection bar next to the heading *Wilderness Activities*.

Drag the first-line indent marker back to 0 on the ruler.

> Choose Bold from the Character menu.
>
> Click in the selection bar next to the heading *Climate.*
>
> Drag the first-line indent marker back to 0.
>
> Choose Bold from the Character menu.

There is a lot of white space on the first line of the climate paragraph, so hyphenate *seasons* to eliminate some of it.

> Click between the *a* and *s* in the word *seasons* in the second line of the climate paragraph and type a hyphen.

There, that looks better. Now you can paste in the chart that helps make the point about the temperature ranges being ideal.

> Click an insertion point on the left end of the heading *Natural Setting.*
>
> Press Return to put a little more space between the text and the graphic.
>
> Choose Scrapbook from the Apple menu.
>
> Scroll until the chart is in the Scrapbook window.
>
> Choose Copy from the Edit menu and click the Scrapbook close box.
>
> Choose Paste from the Edit menu.

Notice that Word automatically sets the margins on the graphic back to the narrow six-column format.

> Select the chart by clicking anywhere on it.
>
> Drag the right indent marker to 2⅝ inches on the ruler.

The first column is finished except for wrapping the text around the pine branch. So that's what you need to do next. In order to see where to break the lines of text, you need to have the pine branch in place.

> Click an insertion point on the left end of the heading *Natural Setting.*
>
> Press Command-Enter to create a new division for the second column.
>
> Choose Division Layout... from the Document menu, click Column in the Break box, and click OK.
>
> Choose Scrapbook from the Apple menu, scroll until the pine branch is inside the Scrapbook window, choose Copy from the Edit menu, and click the Scrapbook close box.
>
> Choose Paste from the Edit menu.

Now you need to widen the second column to accommodate this wide graphic. The column must be wider than the 2⅝-inch width of the first column, because the graphic is so wide. It doesn't matter how much wider you make the column, as long as it's wide enough for the entire graphic to fit comfortably.

> Select the pine branch graphic.
>
> Drag the right indent marker out to 3 inches.

As long as you have the graphic in place and you need to wrap the first column of text around it, you might as well wrap the text in the third column at the same time. Go ahead and do the basic formatting to the third and fourth columns, then make your first attempt at wrapping text around a graphic.

> Click an insertion point on the left end of the heading *Natural Setting*.
>
> Press Command-Enter to create a new division for the third column.

Now select all of the text for the third column and shift all of the indents to the right by ⅜ inch to create a little more space between columns. Normally, figuring out where a column ends is a trial and error process. But we've gone to the effort of finding the proper location for you. If you're using an illustration that doesn't look like the one we're using, you may need to break the lines at different places, so the column may end at a different place.

The line ending with the sentence *Gray squirrels and raccoons abound* is the end of column three. So start by selecting the text that will be in the third column.

> Scroll until the line ending with *Gray squirrels and raccoons abound* comes into view, then hold down the Shift key and click to the right of this line to select the text for the third column.
>
> Drag the left indent marker to ⅜ inch, the first-line indent marker to ⅝ inch, and the right indent marker to 3 inches.

The first paragraph in the third column will wrap around the right side of the pine branch, so you need to unjustify and right align it.

> Click anywhere in the paragraph beginning *Traveling the Palms to Pines* and choose Right from the Paragraph menu.

Now format the headings for column three.

> Click in the selection bar to the left of the heading *Natural Setting* and choose Bold from the Character menu.
>
> Drag the first-line indent marker to ⅜ inch.

> Click in the selection bar to the left of the heading *Wildlife and Plants* and choose Bold from the Character menu.
>
> Drag the first-line indent marker to ⅜ inch.

Now add some space to separate the third and fifth columns.

> Click on the left side of the line that starts with *There are coyotes.*
>
> Press Command-Enter twice to create a new division for the fourth and fifth columns.
>
> Scroll to the end of the document, hold down the Shift key, and click anywhere to the right of the last line.
>
> Drag the left indent marker to ¾ inch, the first-line indent marker to 1 inch, and the right indent marker to 3⅜ inches.

Since the first paragraph of the fifth column is actually a continuation of the last paragraph in column three, you don't want the first line indented. Also, you'll be wrapping it around the squirrel, so you might as well unjustify it now.

> Scroll back to the start of the fifth column and click anywhere in the first paragraph.
>
> Drag the first-line indent marker to ¾ inch.
>
> Choose Left from the Paragraph menu.
>
> Click in the selection bar to the left of the heading *Culture* and choose Bold from the Character menu.
>
> Drag the first-line indent marker back to ¾ inch.

At this point, it's a good idea to save and print the document to help you judge how many lines of vertical space the graphic occupies and to get a feel for where you'll need to break the lines to wrap the text. The upper left corner of your printout should look like the printout in Figure 13-4.

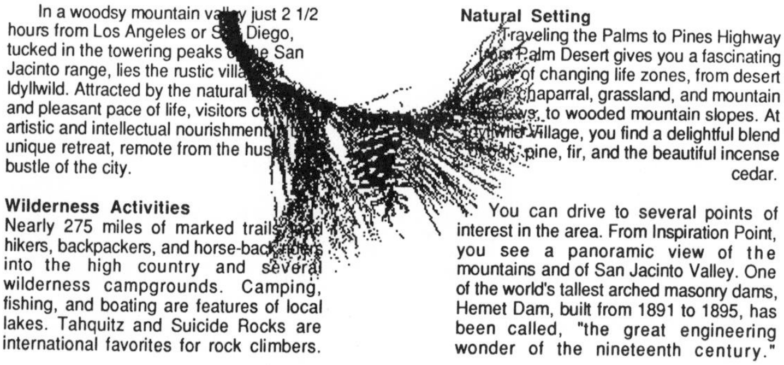

Figure 13-4. The upper left corner of printout of the inside of the brochure

In a woodsy mountain valley just 2 1/2 hours from Los Angeles or San Diego, tucked in the towering peaks of the San Jacinto range, lies the rustic village of Idyllwild. Attracted by the natural and pleasant pace of life, visitors of artistic and intellectual nourishment, unique retreat, remote from the hustle and bustle of the city.

Wilderness Activities
Nearly 275 miles of marked trails lead hikers, backpackers, and horse-backers into the high country and several wilderness campgrounds. Camping, fishing, and boating are features of local lakes. Tahquitz and Suicide Rocks are international favorites for rock climbers.

Natural Setting
Traveling the Palms to Pines Highway from Palm Desert gives you a fascinating view of changing life zones, from desert to chaparral, grassland, and mountain views, to wooded mountain slopes. At Pinewood Village, you find a delightful blend of pine, fir, and the beautiful incense cedar.

You can drive to several points of interest in the area. From Inspiration Point, you see a panoramic view of the mountains and of San Jacinto Valley. One of the world's tallest arched masonry dams, Hemet Dam, built from 1891 to 1895, has been called, "the great engineering wonder of the nineteenth century."

Choose Save As... from the File menu, type *Brochure Inside* in the
Save Current Document As text box, and click Save.

Choose Print... from the File menu.

Now you can start measuring lines. A short (about 6-inch) transparent ruler will help in measuring the length of the lines of text on the screen. The first break is easy to judge, since the end of the branch is covering the word *valley*. You need to break the first line after the word *mountain*.

Scroll to the beginning of the document.

Click an insertion point between the space following *mountain*
and the *v* in *valley* and press Return.

Notice this makes a new paragraph starting with *valley* and Word indents the first line of this paragraph ¼ inch. You don't require this indent, because the second line isn't really a new paragraph.

Drag the first-line indent marker back to 0.

Next, measure where the branch intersects with the second line of text on the printout. According to our calculations, this occurs at approximately 1¾ inches. Looking at the screen, you see that 1¾ inches falls on the *o* of *Los* in the second line of text. So, you need to begin the new line with *Los Angeles*.

Click an insertion point between the space following *from* and the *L*
in *Los* and press Return.

This gives you a general idea of the process of wrapping lines of text around a graphic. Using this as a guide, go ahead and break the rest of the lines as shown in Figure 13-5. If you want to make minor adjustments to some of the lines to bring them closer to the illustration, add an extra space or two between words by using the spacebar or you can apply a different character format to the spaces between words.

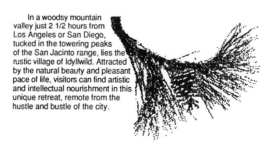

In a woodsy mountain valley just 2 1/2 hours from Los Angeles or San Diego, tucked in the towering peaks of the San Jacinto range, lies the rustic village of Idyllwild. Attracted by the natural beauty and pleasant pace of life, visitors can find artistic and intellectual nourishment in this unique retreat, remote from the hustle and bustle of the city.

Figure 13-5. The first paragraph wrapped around the pine branch

Notice in the first printout in Figure 13-4 that the pine branch extends into the first three lines of the second paragraph, but, after wrapping the first paragraph, the graphic only overlays one line of the second paragraph on the screen. Break that line now so it will wrap around the pine branch.

Click an insertion point between the space following *marked* and the *t* in *trails* and press Return.

Drag the first-line indent marker back to 0.

The first column is finished. Now you need to wrap the first paragraph of the third column around the right side of the pine branch. Wrapping to the left involves the same principles of measuring and rebreaking lines as wrapping to the right. On the printout, measure from the right margin of the text back to the visible edge of the graphic. Then, on the screen, measure the same amount from the left edge of the same line of text to find out where to break that line. It is actually much easier than it sounds. For example, the point at which the graphic intersects the first line of text to the left is approximately 2 inches from the right margin. Measuring from the left edge of the *T* in *Traveling*, 2 inches falls on the *h* in the middle of *Highway*. So, you need to move *Highway* down to the next line. After you've seen the effect of breaking the first line at a new point, you can see where you need to break the second line. In this way, you can continue rebreaking lines, one at a time.

Click an insertion point between the space following *Pines* and the *H* in *Highway* and press Return.

Continue to break the lines as shown in Figure 13-6. When you get to the break in *grassland,* click an insertion point between the *s* and the *l,* type a hyphen, and press Return.

Natural Setting
Traveling the Palms to Pines
Highway from Palm Desert
gives you a fascinating view
of changing life zones, from
desert floor, chaparral, grassland, and mountain meadows,
to wooded mountain slopes.
At Idyllwild Village, you find a
delightful blend of oak, pine, fir,
and the beautiful incense cedar.

Figure 13-6. The first paragraph of the third column wrapped around the right side of the pine branch

All you have to do to finish the inside of the brochure is insert the raccoon and squirrel illustrations, then wrap the text around them.

Scroll to the double division markers between the text for the third and fifth columns.

Click on the left edge of the bottom division mark and press Return 39 times to place the raccoon at the bottom of column four.

We arrived at 39 as the number of times to press Return by printing the brochure, then counting the total number of lines in the text column to the left.

Choose Scrapbook from the Apple menu, scroll until the raccoon is inside the Scrapbook window, choose Copy from the Edit menu, and click the Scrapbook close box.

Choose Paste from the Edit menu.

Select the raccoon graphic by clicking anywhere on it and drag the right indent marker to 2½ inches, which is just wide enough for the raccoon to fit.

Choose Right from the Paragraph menu.

Scroll up until the last two paragraphs of the third column are in view and rebreak them as shown in Figure 13-7.

Scroll to the division marker at the end of the document.

Click on the left edge of the division marker and press Command-Enter to create a division for the sixth and final column.

Choose Scrapbook from the Apple menu, scroll until the squirrel is in the Scrapbook window, choose Copy from the Edit menu, and click the Scrapbook close box.

Choose Paste from the Edit menu.

Figure 13-7. The last two paragraphs of the third column wrapped around the raccoon

The Idyllwild County Park Visitor Center has a natural history museum, with environmental and interpretive programs, and a naturalist on duty. Books are available on natural history and native plants. The park has 200 acres of hiking trails, a campground, and picnic areas. Here and at nearby Indian Relic Park, you'll also find ancient pictographs and mortar holes that suggest the early Cahuilla Indians gathered and ground acorns and pine nuts in the valley.

Wildlife and Plants
There are no dangerous animals in the area. Gray squirrels and raccoons abound.

Figure 13-8. The first paragraph of the fifth column wrapped around the squirrel

There are coyotes, deer, nuthatches, hummingbirds and flickers, and an occasional bald eagle. Five varieties of birds are found in the San Jacintos in numbers larger than anywhere else in North America: mountain quail, spotted owl, Lawrence's goldfinch, Williamson's sapsucker, and white-headed woodpecker.

> Select the squirrel graphic by clicking anywhere on it and drag the right indent marker to 2 inches.
>
> Choose Right from the Paragraph menu.
>
> Scroll up until the first paragraph of the fifth column is in view and rebreak it as shown in Figure 13-8.

The inside of the brochure is complete. Save it and then print a copy to make sure it looks the way you want it to look.

> Choose Save from the File menu.
>
> Choose Print... from the File menu.

If the printout of the inside of the brochure looks acceptable, you can move on to the outside of the brochure.

Creating the Outside of the Brochure

Compared to the text-wrapping and line-breaking entailed in creating the inside of the brochure, the outside of the brochure is easy. It's done in three columns, largely without margin adjustments. The only new wrinkle is that you'll create the page slightly larger than you plan to print it, then you'll reduce it to 76 percent when you print it. Reducing makes for a sharper image on the LaserWriter.

The outside of the brochure will be stored in a new file, so close the document for the inside of the brochure and open a new document.

> Choose Close from the File menu.
>
> Choose New from the File menu.

You want to reduce the entire page when you print, so you might as well tell Word right now that's what you want. Also, set up the page for three columns.

> Choose Page Setup... from the File menu, type *76* in the Reduction text box, make sure all of the margins are set to 0.5 inch, and click OK.
>
> Choose Division Layout... from the Document menu, type *3* in the Number of Columns text box and *0* in the Column Spacing text box, and click OK.

The first column, which will be the leftmost panel of the outside of the brochure, contains the smaller of the two snow scenes, a slogan, a distance table, and a map. So, to start, insert the small snow scene.

> Choose Scrapbook from the Apple menu, scroll until the small snow scene is in the Scrapbook window, choose Copy from the Edit menu, and click the Scrapbook close box.
>
> Choose Paste from the Edit menu.

Add a little space and then type the scintillating slogan *"Easy to find but hard to leave"* on two lines. You can return later to format this slogan and the rest of the text you'll type for the outside of the brochure.

> Press Return twice.
>
> Choose Formats... from the Character menu, click Helvetica in the Font Name list box, click both Bold and Italic in the Style box, click 18 in the Font Size list box, and click OK.
>
> Choose Show Ruler from the Edit menu and click a first line indent at ⅜ inch.
>
> Type the following:
>
> *"Easy to find*[Return]
>
> Drag the first-line indent to 1⁷⁄₁₆ inches and type the following:
>
> *but hard to leave."*[Return]

Next, add some more line spacing and type the distance table, with the second tab column right-aligned.

> Press Return twice.
>
> Choose Tabs... from the Paragraph menu, drag the first-line indent marker to ⅝ inch on the ruler, click the Right button in the Alignment box, type *3.25* in the Position text box, and click OK.
>
> Choose Formats... from the Character menu, click 12 in the Font Size list box, and click OK.
>
> Choose Italic from the Character menu to deselect italics.
>
> Type the following:
>
> *Distances to Idyllwild in miles*[Return][Return]

Choose Plain text from the Character menu.

Type the following:

Hemet [Tab] *24*[Return]

Banning [Tab] *25*[Return]

Palm Springs [Tab] *54*[Return]

Riverside [Tab] *55*[Return]

San Diego [Tab] *110*[Return]

Los Angeles [Tab] *110*[Return]

Now, insert the map and start the second column.

Press Return three times.

Choose Scrapbook from the Apple menu, scroll until the map is in the Scrapbook window, choose Copy from the Edit menu, and click the Scrapbook close box.

Choose Paste from the Edit menu.

Press Command-Enter to enter a division mark for the second column.

The only thing in the second column is the stamp graphic, which you need to insert at the very bottom right corner. As we mentioned earlier in this chapter, the return address will be added from a separate file during the third printing pass.

Press Return 37 times.

Choose Scrapbook from the Apple menu, scroll until the stamp is in the Scrapbook window, choose Copy from the Edit menu, and click the Scrapbook close box.

Drag the right indent marker to 4¼ inches.

Choose Paste from the Edit menu.

Click anywhere in the graphic to select it, then choose Right from the Paragraph menu.

Now you're ready to start the third column, which contains the large snow scene that you copied from MacPaint in two sections and the word *Idyllwild*. You'll need to change the left indent so that the large illustration is centered.

Press Command-Enter to insert a division break.

Press Return.

Drag the left indent marker to ⅞ inch on the ruler.

Choose Scrapbook from the Apple menu, scroll until the top half of the large snow scene is in the Scrapbook window, choose Copy from the Edit menu, and click the Scrapbook close box.

Choose Paste from the Edit menu.

Choose Scrapbook from the Apple menu, scroll until the bottom half of the large snow scene is in the Scrapbook window, choose Copy from the Edit menu, and click the Scrapbook close box.

Choose Paste from the Edit menu.

Press Return 10 times.

Choose Formats... from the Character menu, click Times in the Font Name list box, type *54* in the Font Size text box, click Shadow in the Style box, and click OK.

Type *Idyllwild.*

Save this document as *Brochure Outside* and print a copy to check spacing and alignment.

Creating the Return Address

As we said, the return address is a separate file that's printed on a separate pass. You could simply create it as a MacPaint graphic rotated 90 degrees to the right, as you did with the stamp graphic. But to use Word and the LaserWriter's more attractive fonts, you need to print it in a separate pass, as a separate file. So, open a new document, type the text, and save it as *Return Address.*

Choose Close, then New from the File menu.

Choose Page Setup... from the File menu, click the Portrait button, type *76* in the reduction text box, type *4* in the Top margin text box, type *.5* in the Left margin text box, and click OK.

Type the following:

Idyllwild Visitors Bureau[Return]

P.O. Box 3173[Return]

Idyllwild, CA 92349[Return]

Select the word *Idyllwild* in the first line and choose Outline from the Character menu.

Choose Save As... from the File menu, type *Return Address* in the Save Current Document As text box, then click Save.

You might want to print a copy of the return address to assure yourself that it's placed correctly on the page. When you're satisfied, your brochure is all ready for printing.

Printing the Brochure

Just as you made test printings when setting up the inside and outside pages, it's a good idea to test print one copy of the whole brochure to make sure you know which way to insert the paper on the second and third passes. Printing 50 or 100 copies and then discovering that you inserted the paper the wrong way can be time-consuming and costly.

First, open the file containing the inside of the brochure and check the settings in the Page Setup dialog box.

> Choose Close, then Open... from the File menu. Double-click Brochure Inside in the list box.
>
> Choose Page Setup... from the File menu, click the Smoothing? button, and click OK.
>
> Choose Print... from the File menu and click OK.

When the paper comes out of the printer, put it back in the paper tray with the printing up and the text oriented toward you as you stand in front of the printer. Then print the outside of the brochure.

> Choose Close, then Open... from the File menu. Double-click Brochure Outside in the list box.
>
> Choose Print... from the File menu and click OK.

When the second printing pass is finished, return the paper to the paper tray with the inside of the brochure facing up and the text upside down. Then print the return address.

> Choose Close, then Open... from the File menu. Double-click Return Address in the list box.
>
> Choose Print... from the File menu and click OK.

When you're confident of the paper insertion, you can print the number of copies you need, with several copies per pass.

This brochure should be enough to convince you that Word is the most advanced word-processing program available for the Macintosh. We've attempted to demonstrate Word's advantages in practical ways, but Word offers even more than we've been able to address in this book. There's no need for you to stop just because the book does. You're an advanced word processor now, so it's up to you where you go from here. Good luck!

Index

David Kater & Richard Kater

Printer technology expert David Kater received his Bachelor of Arts degree in Mathematics from the University of California at Los Angeles and completed his Master of Arts at San Diego State University. At the beginning of his career, David taught courses in mathematics, BASIC, and Fortran. In 1980, he went to work for CompuSoft founder David Lien, writing manuals for Epson printers. David was later hired by Epson America to write manuals for their FX and RX series of printers. He has authored several books, including *Getting the Most Out of Your Epson Printer, Macintosh Graphics and Sound, TRS-80 Graphics For The Model I And Model III,* and *TRS-80 Word Processing With Super-SCRIPTSIT.* He has contributed articles on printer technology to *BYTE* and *Popular Computing* magazines. In addition to writing, David Kater operates a successful consulting and publishing firm, EduKATER, based in San Diego, California.

Richard Kater graduated from the University of California at Los Angeles with a Bachelor of Arts degree in Business and English. After spending 30 years in the aerospace industry, Dick has recently turned his attention toward writing, and has contributed significantly to Edu-KATER's books. He is also the co-author of *Using Epson Printers.* Dick Kater lives in Los Angeles, California.

The manuscript for this book was word processed using
Microsoft Word on the Apple Macintosh and submitted to
Microsoft Press in electronic form. Text files were processed
and formatted using Microsoft Word on an IBM PC.

Cover design by Tim Girvin. Cover airbrushed by Stephen
Peringer. Interior text design by Steve Renick.

Text composition in Baskerville and Helvetica Light. Typesetting
by Microsoft Press, using the CCI system and the Mergenthaler
Linotron 202 digital phototypesetter.

Cover art separated by Color Masters, Phoenix, Arizona. Printed
on 12 pt. Carolina by Philips Offset Company, Inc., Mamaroneck,
New York. Text stock, 60 lb. Glatfelter Offset, supplied by
Unisource Corporation. Book printed and bound by Fairfield
Graphics, Fairfield, Pennsylvania.

Other titles from Microsoft Press

THE APPLE ENVIRONMENT

THE APPLE MACINTOSH BOOK   *Cary Lu*
   ISBN 0-914845-00-4 $18.95

PRESENTATION GRAPHICS ON THE APPLE MACINTOSH   *Steve Lambert*
How to Use Microsoft Chart to Create Dazzling Graphics for Professional and Corporate Applications
   ISBN 0-914845-11-X $18.95

MACWORK MACPLAY   *Lon Poole*
Creative Ideas for Fun and Profit on Your Apple Macintosh
   ISBN 0-914845-22-5 $18.95

THE ENDLESS APPLE   *Charles Rubin*
How to Maintain State-of-the-Art Performance on Your Apple II and IIe
   ISBN 0-914845-27-6 $15.95

MICROSOFT MULTIPLAN: OF MICE AND MENUS   *The Waite Group, Bill Bono, and Ken Kalkis*
Models for Managing Your Business with the Apple Macintosh
   ISBN 0-914845-33-0 $16.95

INSIDE MACPAINT   *Jeffrey S. Young*   *Introduction by Bill Atkinson, creator of MacPaint*
Sailing Through the Sea of FatBits on a Single-Pixel Raft
   ISBN 0-914845-31-4 $18.95

APPLEWORKS   *Charles Rubin*
Boosting Your Business with Integrated Software
   ISBN 0-914845-47-0 $16.95

GENERAL

SILICON VALLEY GUIDE TO FINANCIAL SUCCESS IN SOFTWARE   *Daniel Remer, Paul Remer,*
and Robert Dunaway
   ISBN 0-914845-09-8 $19.95

ONLINE   *Steve Lambert*
A Guide to America's Leading Information Services
   ISBN 0-914845-35-7 $19.95

LEARNING COMMODORE 64 LOGO TOGETHER   *Kenneth P. Goldberg*
An Activity Book for Creative Parents, Teachers, and Kids
   ISBN 0-914845-24-1 $14.95

OUT OF THE INNER CIRCLE   *"The Cracker" (Bill Landreth)*
A Hacker's Guide to Computer Security
   ISBN 0-914845-36-5 $9.95 softcover   ISBN 0-914845-45-4 $19.95 hardcover

A MUCH, MUCH BETTER WORLD   *Eldon Dedini*
   ISBN 0-914845-50-0 $6.95

Available wherever fine books are sold, or write:

Marketing Department • Microsoft Press • 10700 Northup Way • Box 97200 • Bellevue, WA 98009